PRAISE FOR AMANDA PROWSE

'Amanda Prowse is the queen of family drama'

Daily Mail

'A deeply emotional, unputdownable read'

Red

'Heartbreaking and heartwarming in equal measure'

The Lady

'Amanda Prowse is the queen of heartbreak fiction'

Mail Online

'Captivating, heartbreaking and superbly written'

Closer

'Uplifting and positive but you may still need a box of tissues'

Cosmopolitan

'You'll fall in love with this'

Cosmopolitan

'Powerful and emotional drama that packs a real punch'

Heat

'Warmly accessible but subtle . . . moving and inspiring'

Daily Mail

'Magical'

Now

Women Like Us

ALSO BY AMANDA PROWSE

Novels

Poppy Day
What Have I Done?
Clover's Child
A Little Love
Will You Remember Me?
Christmas for One
A Mother's Story
Perfect Daughter
The Second Chance Café
Three and a Half Heartbeats
Another Love
My Husband's Wife
I Won't Be Home for Christmas
The Food of Love
The Idea of You
The Art of Hiding
Anna
Theo
How to Fall in Love Again (Kitty's Story)
The Coordinates of Loss
The Girl in the Corner
The Things I Know
The Light in the Hallway
The Day She Came Back
An Ordinary Life

Waiting to Begin
To Love and Be Loved

Novellas

The Game
Something Quite Beautiful
A Christmas Wish
Ten Pound Ticket
Imogen's Baby
Miss Potterton's Birthday Tea
Mr Portobello's Morning Paper
I Wish . . .

Memoir

The Boy Between: A Mother and Son's Journey From a World Gone Grey
(with Josiah Hartley)

Children's Book

The Smile That Went a Mile (with Paul Ward Smith)

Women Like Us

A Memoir

AMANDA PROWSE

Little
a

Published by Little A, New York

www.apub.com

Amazon, the Amazon logo, and Little A are trademarks of Amazon.com, Inc.,
or its affiliates.

ISBN-13: 9781542038812
ISBN-10: 1542038812

Cover design by James Jones

All photos in the book and on the cover are from the author's personal
collection

Printed in the United States of America

Women Like Us *is dedicated to all the women who have gone before. The women who have paved the way, earned their stripes, and lived the lives that await us. Women who we love and admire and women we will one day, if we are very, very lucky, become. All the mums, all the nans, all the great-grans, all the sisters, all the aunties and great-aunts, all the neighbours, teachers, friends and cousins, all those who looked us in the eye and said, 'Never forget how wonderful you are!'*

I guess the first question to ask is, what kind of woman am I? Well, you know those women who saunter into a room, immaculately coiffed and primped from head to toe? Those women who seem to have it all together? Raven-haired beauties who can pull off red lipstick? The women who teeter pertly on killer heels and in skinny jeans? The women who flick their hair with a sexy smile, as they stride in confidently to talk self-assuredly to whoever looks to be of most interest, and, with a manicured hand, grab a glass of bubbles from a passing tray as they go?

Well, if you look behind her, you'll see me.

I'm the woman wearing a floaty top to cover her ample bottom, who is worried her back fat might be bulging visibly from beneath her bra strap, who is clutching her oversized handbag, not only as a prop, but so that her reading book, Fox's Glacier Mints and box of super-absorbent panty liners don't roll out in public. I'm quite likely to have a false eyelash that has slid off and stuck to my cheek. I'm the woman who clings to the wall, kind of wanting to join in, smiling a lot, hoping someone talks to her, but not someone too clever so she feels stupid. The woman who asks if she can have Diet Coke instead of champagne, as she prefers the taste, and does it all with one eye on the clock so she can work out how quickly she can go home, ping off that damned bra, shove on her PJs and climb into bed to watch *MasterChef* on catch-up.

Yep, that's me.

I am a wife, mum, daughter, sister, auntie, cousin, niece and friend.

I'm a writer.

I'm a Londoner, who now lives on a farm in the middle of bloody nowhere and who owns a wax jacket, proper wellies and two stinky dogs.

I only clean the house when I'm expecting visitors.

I swear in the car. A lot.

I'm a bit boring.

Most often I am to be found with my head in a book or staring into a cupboard wondering what I can rustle up for supper.

I have the sense of humour of a twelve-year-old (apparently) and a good day is one where I have laughed until tears have rolled or I've needed to pee. My body, it seems, insists on leaking from one end or the other if something is *that* funny.

I make award-worthy Yorkshire puddings. From scratch.

I can't tell the time on a 24-hour clock.

I don't particularly like ice cream (I know!).

I love driving on the motorway (while swearing).

I grow epic spider plants.

I will love Duran Duran until the day I die.

I wake up at a little before 6 a.m. every single day.

I'm not and never have been a night owl.

And my favourite cheese is any variety with a hole in it.

My blood type is Americano with an extra shot.

Oh, and I've sold millions of books all over the world.

For most of my years on the planet, I've felt like I didn't quite fit, like I'm not quite good enough. It's as if my gut contains a leaky bucket and any success or moment of joy might top it up briefly but pretty quickly my inner voice of self-sabotage pulls the plug and I feel all confidence drain away. I've spent a large chunk of my life feeling a little uncomfortable in my skin, a little less than . . . as if all the good stuff like success, happiness, sexiness and self-esteem were the right of other people but not me. And this was how I lived, taking my place at the back of the queue and wondering how to navigate a world in which my hopes, dreams and desires always felt a little out of reach. I spent hours trying to figure out how I could get to be one of those women who seemed to have it all, waving furiously, trying to be seen, but it felt like my feet were encased in concrete while everyone around me dashed ahead. It was exhausting.

Talking about my weight, my size, my aged face and my lack of confidence is something I have avoided for . . . forever. But the fact is, for years self-revulsion and intense self-scrutiny have dominated my every waking thought. I've let opportunities slip through my fingers, denied myself experiences based solely over concern at what I might wear and what I might look like from behind (yes really!) and these worries have greatly affected my life and my relationships. It makes me immeasurably sad to write and acknowledge this. But it's my truth. I believe personal growth starts with honesty and that honesty has never been more needed in a time when everyone is publicly living their 'very best life', seeking out the 'hygge' in the everyday while idling their time on social media, comparing their sometimes harassed or less than perfect existence to another person's highlights.

I realised that I'm very good at *giving* advice:
'Don't care so much about what others think!'
'Why does your size matter?'
'Life begins when you let it!'
'Wrinkles show character – they're beautiful.'

And I started to feel like a fraud, dispensing these pearls of wisdom to my readers, friends and family before hurrying home to snaffle giant bags of crisps and cry in the bath. I needed to figure out how to walk the walk and not just talk the talk. For my own authenticity and self-respect, I needed to try to plug some of the holes in my leaky bucket with action and a change of mindset instead of doughnuts.

They say that in order to know where you're going, you need to know where you've come from, and I certainly believe this, knowing that every step I've taken, every second I've lived, and every experience, good and bad, has led to this very moment.

This is my story . . .

Chapter One

'PART SNAIL'

What are little boys made of?
Snips and snails
And puppy-dogs' tails
That's what little boys are made of.

What are little girls made of?
Sugar and spice
And all things nice
That's what little girls are made of.

I made my grand entrance a little over half a century ago in the East End Maternity Hospital, formerly the Mothers' Lying-In Home, on the Commercial Road, Stepney, London – the same hospital where my nan and great-nan had also been born. Never one for convention, I arrived hand and arm first, followed by my head and shoulders, much to the detriment of my mother's nether regions and to the challenge of the midwife who insisted she 'KEEP PUSHING!' I know. I'm clenching and wincing too. My poor mum, fresh out of her teens and without access to the wealth of material that the internet provides, thought it must be 'normal'. It still amazes and perplexes me that she went on to have three more babies who, she admits, were by comparison a cinch to deliver – no shit, Annie!

My nan, apparently, on hearing of my rather unorthodox entrance, offered this sage sentiment: 'Maybe she's going to be a diver. Maybe we should get her a bloody swimming pool!'

Very funny, considering they had only recently acquired an inside loo.

Eschewing that diving career, I made my debut as a ballerina – you may laugh. I was five years old and have a picture, all of us little girls of a similar age, lined up on a stage.

1973: My nan's back garden in East Ham. A rather clumsy curtsey! When I see my face in this picture I want to dive in and cuddle my younger self and tell her it will all be okay, you'll never have to wear a dress that shows your knickers or curtsey ever again . . .

I am sturdier than the rest and not fat but certainly solidly built, not petite or diminutive like my contemporaries.

Mine was a busy and physically active childhood, careering around the playground, playing stringers, lava and other games that involved a lot of running and jumping, and then when I got home, I would play in the street, usually stick in the mud, space hopper racing or trying not to smash out my newly hatched front teeth with the handle of the pogo stick. The only time I would sit very still was when my 'clicky hips' made me feel uncomfortable and it felt easier to remain immobile.

I complained of the various aches and pains that were put down to collateral damage done during my rather unorthodox birth. Too young to fully explain just how I was in discomfort, I understood the rather loose explanation that my hips were clicky and accepted the offered remedy of some sweets, a cuddle and a few kind words of reassurance.

My ballet debut was, however, a defining moment for me. My lack of coordination meant while everyone adopted one pose, I did quite another before clomping around the stage elephant-style. I heard the titters of the assembled crowd and it bothered me, already looking around at the other tiny girls and comparing my heavy-handed self to them. No one was laughing at them. It didn't feel good.

My family are all pretty much tall and slim. My dad and brothers stand around the six-foot two mark and my beautiful mum, a former Mary Quant model, no less, is a slender five foot eight. I am five feet four inches and was always, in comparison to everyone else, a bit of a munchkin.

Throughout my life my family have ribbed me about my height and my general lack of grace. It's funny I guess, and I know the comments are made good-naturedly, wrapped in love, but I also know that the belief stuck. It was the start of the erosion of confidence in my physical self. The idea formed in my head that I was big, clumsy, a bit of a wrecking ball, and my lack of refinement went hand in hand with the image of myself as oversized and awkward.

This was my family, large, loving and with tongues laced with acerbic humour.

Anyone who had so much as a toe in the 1970s would have heard the nursery rhyme at the beginning of this chapter from the mouths of parents and grandparents, seen it printed in our bedtime storybooks or even, as was the case for me, on a poster in the library corner of our school classroom. It was nearly always accompanied by the picture of a little girl in a vaguely Victorian guise, wearing tones of pink, satin slippers, often a fancy bonnet tied in a large ribbon under her dainty chin. And a boy in raggedy clothing, grazed knees, obligatory smudge of dirt on the nose and with his unsavoury wares tumbling from his torn pockets.

I liked the poem. I could remember it. And being a girl, who along with my two younger brothers made up our family of five, it felt quite nice to be elevated in this way. Who wanted to be snails when you could be sugar? But of course, it wasn't elevating me. It was pigeonholing me, it was cornering me, and it confused me, painting a standard that I had no hope of attaining. What if I wasn't petite, sugar-coated and into pink ribbons? What if I was actually a big-framed, chunkier than average chick who was happier in wellington boots than satin slippers and wanted to grab the world by its balls and give it a good old shake? What if I feared I was part snail?

I have never been dainty. My clumsiness was and is legendary. I'm that person who falls up steps, trips on wires and clears tables with the swish of an arm. On an average day I will tumble over my feet, smack my head on any number of cupboards and doors, hit myself in the face with my laptop, snap the plant I'm watering, break a glass, spill coffee on my lap, watch helplessly as supper slips off tilted plates onto the kitchen floor, and I wear samples of the food I've eaten on my clothes, sporting an edible Jackson Pollock each night as I climb up the wooden hill to Bedfordshire. And, believe me, I try hard not to!

I can still recall adults wincing when as a child I had to carry a full glass and the way they held their breath in anticipation if I ferried food from the kitchen to the dinner table, as if everyone was fully expecting me to drop it, which I often did. No shit! In fact, anything of a delicate nature – Airfix-model building, jigsaws, cake decorating – excluded me because it was inevitable that I would cack it up, to use a technical term. I know beyond a shadow of a doubt that my family adore me, but I do remember being called a 'little fairy elephant', and this resonated, as I was indeed ungainly, awkward and heavy-handed, and I had an odd walk, which I knew was connected to my clicky hips.

As I grew a bit older it was a confusing time. Not yet in double figures and without the first clue about sex, relationships or the mechanics of life, I was absolutely confident that I wanted to grow up and get married (to David Cassidy). Mistress of my own kitchen, I would never, ever cook vegetables – yuck! And I'd definitely scrap my seven o'clock bedtime and clop up the stairs whenever I wanted. But even while only a little girl, I was ridiculously uncertain that I was even eligible for marriage; I wasn't very good at the whole 'ladylike' thing. And apparently ladylike was, according to my nan, what would be most attractive to a man when looking for a suitor.

Just read that back – when is this book set, the early 1800s? Am I about to go full *Bridgerton*? Well, not quite, but it was often mentioned that I would have a *lovely* life if I could find a *lovely* husband and, yes, I could be whatever I wanted to be . . . as long as I had a husband by my side.

I can see that this view was firmly rooted in the Victorian upbringing of the women I loved: my great-nan was born in the

1880s – in a time where a life without a husband would not have been an easy one, nor one she could contemplate, as if any husband was better than none. These women were also, understandably, unable to conceive of such a shift in our society, where a girl had options other than to marry and make a home. Because making a home and feeding the family was their mission in life and a husband was the means to achieving this. It was at their knee that I learned the basics of being a grown-up, lessons that would enrich, hinder and confuse me for a lifetime.

My strongest early childhood memories feature food. Gathering in the tiny back room of my great-nan's house, the only room with a fire in it and therefore the only room where we all congregated, as coal was heaped onto the hearth, brought in from the coal hole by the back door in a black scuttle. The rest of the draughty Victorian terraced house was like an icebox. Pushed against the wall would be a square table, set with an immaculate starched white linen tablecloth that was stiff to the touch. If I lifted my nose, I could just about see levelly over it, quite taken by the display and the smells.

Hordes of us crowded around to admire the array of grub, lovingly prepared by three generations of women for whom money was scarce. My family lived in a world of privation and strict routine, where the women wore wraparound floral pinnies to save their frocks while laying out elaborate buffet teas on a Sunday afternoon. Sausage rolls, cheese straws, pickles, egg mayonnaise sandwiches, my grandad's home-grown tomatoes cut in half and sprinkled with salt, bowls of crisps, a bottle of salad cream to go on the limp lettuce and sliced radish that constituted 'the salad' and a beer glass full of celery for some reason. And always, always taking pride of place, centre stage on the table, one of my nan's fabulous glossy, cherry-studded fruit cakes, which we all admired and the praise for which she revelled in, bless her.

There might have not been much cash knocking around, but these displays were fit for a king, and we were grateful. To eat what we wanted from square floral china side plates held aloft or on our laps made us, we knew, very, very lucky. It was a world of make do and mend, of taking it in turns and letting the grown-ups sit on the chairs while we kids nestled on the floor with our legs crossed, the skirts of our party dresses pulled down over our bruised knees. There was always room for more people. No one was ever turned away without a cup of tea and a slice of cake; we'd simply all heed the call to 'budge up' and make space.

And in the middle of that family unit, with full tums, a constant trickle of laughter and even the odd sing-song, I knew warm and unconditional love. It was in these rooms and with these people that I learned what really mattered in life – being with people who loved you and whom you loved in return . . . and feeding them!

Sunday table display at my great-nan's in the early 1970s. Obligatory glass of celery, home-grown tomatoes and ashtray perched on the old telly!

Aged seven, my horizons were small and my memories of them vivid. I might have been born within gobbing distance of the River Thames and the City, but it was not the fashionable suburb it is now. A current trip to E1 will find you surrounded by smart-suited banking types or beard-wearing, soy-latte-drinking hipsters. When I chose the esteemed postcode, however, in which to make my grand entrance, there certainly wasn't a bewildering choice of bijoux, shoebox-sized million-pound apartments, sushi restaurants and farmers' markets on a Sunday – no siree, it was nothing like that. Sushi? Our fish was cooked in beef dripping, clagged in batter and served wrapped up next to flabby chips. Accommodation was rented and ropey and the whole place was . . . in the words of my mum whom I asked to describe it circa 1968, 'a bit of a shithole really, you know, grubby, dodgy'. Nice.

My whole world consisted of a few streets: Lonsdale Avenue, East Ham. Sherrard and Rosedale Roads, Forest Gate. Roedean Avenue, Enfield, and Charlotte Gardens, Collier Row. Spread over east and north London and the outer suburbs of Romford, these were the streets where my parents, grandparents, aunties and uncles lived. All the houses were different in design and location but shared some startling similarities. First, none had an east wing, extensive grounds or a bell-and-pulley system with which to summon staff. Some were flat-fronted council houses; others rented Victorian terraces with bathrooms tacked on the back, where tales of war and the scent of loss and mothballs lingered. Houses where tea was served in cups and saucers with a crazed glaze, and which had felt the touch of my great-grandparents' and great-great-grandparents' hands.

In this modern world, where space comes at a premium and we fill every corner of our homes, it feels odd to write that in these small houses, there was often a rarely entered 'front room'. This room had a small sofa and two chairs, positioned squarely around a rug atop the polished wooden floor and crocheted or embroidered antimacassars draped uniformly over the backs of the seats. There was a varnished coffee table with a doily on it and on which sat an empty pressed glass fruit bowl, which my great-nan had purchased just after the war from Woolworths. This very fruit bowl now lives on my windowsill, a precious thing. More precious because she paid for it weekly, putting pennies away in a life that was tough, dictated by hard physical graft. An often brutal, sometimes ugly life made beautiful, no doubt, by the saving for and the acquisition of a pressed glass fruit bowl. I never did see any fruit in it. I'm guessing because most of the fruit consumed in her house came in a tin and swam in heavy syrup before being doused in evaporated milk.

I can picture the way the milk and syrup would marble in a glorious pattern in the bowl before mixing entirely, meaning your pud ended up in a sweet, thick cream of the palest apricot hue. Pictures on the wall were Vernon Ward floral prints or mass-produced oil paintings, thickly and crudely spread with a palette knife, which I found utterly terrifying, depicting clowns, big-eyed, doll-like children in rags or crinoline ladies. They were cheaply framed and hung with pride. I now collect these very pictures, no doubt trying to recreate the walls where love and laughter echoed.

I remember greasy playing cards being slapped down onto polished surfaces by men in hair oil, the women in curlers and most with a soggy rolled-up cigarette hanging from their lip. A working-class world of manual labour and loving like giants, where every family in the neighbourhood and all the skeletons in their cupboards were known, and immediate neighbours blurred the line between friend and family. Every woman on the street was 'auntie' and knocking on wood for luck and chucking salt over your shoulder for good measure was the norm. A hard life, punctuated by births, deaths and marriages, where the men worked for other men. The women too had menial jobs.

My mum's great-aunt was a toilet attendant in the public lavatory at Upton Park station, in the days when such attendants sat in a little room, shielded from view by a net curtain and with plastic plants in brightly coloured pots. On the days she wasn't working, she wore a moth-eaten fur coat and orange lipstick. I am *passionately* anti-fur, but I weep to think of her in this symbol at the time of success and wealth. My great-nan worked as a cloakroom attendant in the function room of the Green Man pub in East Ham, giving out little paper tickets and hanging up coats and hats, as well as working there as a cook during the day, serving hot grub to the gangland characters who propped up the bar. My great-grandad, a sheet metal worker by day, looked after the 'men's' cloakroom, waving to my great-nan across the dusty hallway, tapping their toes in their cubbies, leaning through the hatch, while others swirled and twirled on the dance floor. My mum and dad had their wedding reception at this very pub, there in the back room.

St Mary Magdalene's Church, East Ham. My parents on their wedding day in 1967. Aged nineteen and twenty.

I paint this picture to show the foundation on which my future self would stand – to explain how I was raised, within walls built with muscle and held together with loyalty, inside a steel ring of protection. I knew I could take on the world and probably win because I was allowed to fail, and God forbid any force – human, vegetable or mineral – that crossed me because I had at least a dozen East End women with calloused hands, shot teeth and a good grip on a rolling pin at my back.

Even by the tender age of seven, it was at these family gatherings that I became further aware of what constituted 'un-ladylike' behaviour. It wasn't a definitive list and was added to on a semi-regular basis. I often received half-joking verbal admonishments from my grandparents and wider family that I knew were designed to set me on the path to being dainty and feminine – admonishments that only reinforced how I displayed the very opposite of these desired traits. It was about trying to help me understand that there were things I couldn't do because I was a girl.

I know, I know. I hear your wrath and feel your pain, but stay with me . . .

It was circa 1975, a time when the ceiling for women wasn't glass, it was concrete, when we were referred to (in my neck of the woods) as 'birds' or 'housewives' – the latter always reminding me of 'housecats', pretty things, who are domesticated and don't go outside to roam or shit – a time when, broadly speaking, men earned the lion's share of the money and women cooked the tea. My mum and nan would often say, 'Mandy, can you lay the table?' or 'Mandy, can you put the salt and pepper out?' or 'Mandy, can you go and tell everyone that tea is ready?' while my brothers lounged on the carpet in front of the TV or hared around the garden. It was as if I was expected to do these things, to help with the meal-times, because I was a girl. Not that I minded; I liked helping these women I so loved.

The things that were off limits to me because of my lack of penis were many. They included but were not limited to: wrestling in the front room – not very ladylike or NVLL, answering back, whistling, sniffing, shouting loudly in the street, swearing – *definitely* NVLL, and showing my bum in the garden, no matter how funny it might seem, because . . . You know the rest. And yet these habits were part of me, part of my make-up. I'm currently fifty-four and I still answer back, whistle, sniff, shout and swear. I have, however, managed to stop showing my bum to various family members in the garden and only wrestle in the front room when the occasion absolutely calls for it.

Our house, despite the strict routine of breakfast, school, supper, bath time, bed, was chaotic and noisy, bursting at the seams with laughter as my brothers and I tiptoed barefoot around the spilled contents of our upturned toy box. A house where the top-loader twin-tub danced around the small kitchen as it spun, while we willed the faded wooden laundry tongs to judder and fall from the corner of the rusting machine where they had been rested. And a good day was one where Mum made a tent using sheets draped over a table and my brothers and I ate our lunch in its confines.

It was, however, clear to me that my dad, like most of the men in my life, lived in two worlds: the world outside the front door, where everything unknown and exciting lurked, and our world at home, which was warm, predictable and small. I loved my mum, I *love* my mum – she is my whole heart, but even at that tender age, one thing I did know was that despite not being a boy, I wanted a job like my dad's and not a job like hers. Every morning he got to drive away to the Ford factory in Dagenham in his silver, gas-guzzling Cortina with its black vinyl roof, music playing and his jacket hanging on a little chrome hook over the rear side window. My mum cut people's hair in our kitchen for extra cash, in between running around after her slightly unruly children, building tents, doing laundry and making shepherd's pie. I wanted his freedom. It intrigued me. What *was* that life to be had outside our little terraced house in Collier Row, Romford?

My mum, nans, aunties and neighbours, however, had no such option and were more or less tethered to the kitchen, although not seemingly unhappily, as they caught up outside the school gates or at the shops. Making each other laugh and providing tea and sympathy while learning the intimate highs and lows of each other's lives, laughing about the drudgery that was the backdrop to their existence.

1973: East Ham, London. In my nan's back garden with my brothers Simon and Paul in front of the rickety table. It's the table on which my nan used to do her handwashing, using the plastic bowls on the floor. This is me, clutching a cake, taking a break from space-hopping and thank goodness I've had the vision to match my sandals with my ride . . .

Mum says it was the happiest time of her life, when we were small, and I believe her. I mostly picture her laughing, but I can also recall her staring out of the window sometimes with a faraway look in her eye and telling us tales of her life before she became our mum, of working 'up West', hanging around in Soho coffee shops and riding mopeds down to Southend on a bank holiday. And no wonder she liked to reminisce; if those were her years of great adventure and exploration when fresh out of her teens, she gave it all up to assist us with Lego, cookie making, putting the sprinkler on in the garden for us to run through when the weather was warm, helping us into our PJs before kissing us goodnight and turning out the light, our tums full of that shepherd's pie.

My years of exploration were all ahead and my biggest adventures were to be found inside the pages of books. It was when I hit eight that my love of reading began in earnest. The day I was given a library ticket was the day my life changed. I didn't know how to be dainty and feminine, and with seedlings of low self-esteem taking root, had already begun to feel the beginnings of claustrophobia, hemmed in by the boundaries set for me by society and class.

Ours was a house without books – apart from the Littlewoods catalogue and a Haynes car manual for said Cortina. My parents, young and working hard to support their three children, didn't have time to read at home. In fact, they barely sat down. My dad worked an extra job at night, shovelling tarmac for the great boom in motorway building: motorways that would see him travel up and down the country in his executive roles later in life.

The day I was given my first library card was momentous. I can picture my navy T-bar shoes treading the carpet tiles, as I headed to the librarian's desk where I was told about the Dewey decimal system and shown how the files worked to locate a particular book. There were hundreds of green cards in alphabetical order, sitting in small, but long wooden drawers containing the card index, which pulled out for miles, all with the number, title and author name typed neatly. I took in what I could, but it all felt rather complicated. The bookshelves were grey metal and quite utilitarian. It was about as far from the image I had in my head of a library, formed from those I had heard about in stories or seen in movies.

Those libraries, often in grand houses, were opulent and subtly lit, with leather-topped desks, wing-backed chairs, floor-to-ceiling glass-fronted wooden cabinets and air that was weighted, as if it was full of all the wisdom those glorious books contained. I used to imagine someone opening a leather volume and the echo of the words fluttering up to the ceiling where they would dance, swoop and settle in the rafters, falling on all the unsuspecting visitors in a fine mist of learning.

This was nothing like that. Not that the cold, grey racks bothered me per se. In my mind, books were books and all I wanted to do was walk among them, run my fingers over the spines until one called to me and, between you and me . . . I wanted to inhale the scent of them. Other book lovers will know the scent I mean. It is an intoxicating combination of dust, damp, worn leather, the bloom of paper mould, ageing cardboard, grease-thumbed pages and the particles emitted in deep sighs, exhaled at the beauty, surprise or comfort of the written word. Even remembering that smell makes me smile. All my worries and life doubts disappeared when I walked inside the rather uninspiring 1970s facade of the library, I instantly knew that it was my thing, my indulgence, my happy place and my utter, utter joy! The rows of book spines were lined up to form a kaleidoscope of colour, each with a story to reveal within. My heart still races and my pulse flutters when I step into a library or a bookshop or even when I see my TBR list waiting on my Kindle – there is nothing more thrilling than knowing I have a great read lined up. And the thought of not having anything to read – well, I can only imagine!

The librarian wore a dark green turtleneck sweater and smelled of violets. Her tone was clipped; her hands small and neat and she had kindness in her eyes. As nuts as it sounds, I got the feeling, and I *know* it sounds ridiculous, that she was a little proud of me, as if recognising a fellow bookworm. She told me that I could choose not one, but a whole heap of books to take home. I stared at her, thinking what's the catch? It felt like such a privilege to be trusted with these most precious things, BOOKS!

With a stack of them up to my chin, I walked home quickly, expecting, I think, to feel a tap on my shoulder and for someone to take them out of my hands. The moment I got home, I selected a title from my haul, settling on a book called *Mandy*, chosen for obvious reasons, and written by Julie Andrews. I curled into the corner of the sofa in our noisy, chaotic home, while my brothers danced on the rug to the *Why Don't You?* theme. And for me the room fell silent as I tuned out the real world. I couldn't hear the TV, the shouts, my mum's beloved Motown wafting from the radio, the traffic, the dog barks, the laughter or the whir of the twin-tub washing machine as it jolted around the kitchen. I was instantly hooked, fascinated, not only by the story of a young orphan who longed for a home of her own, but by the fact that someone had written this story.

Someone had written *all* of the stories!

Who were these people and how did they know how to do that? Was it a job? If it was, it was unlike any job I had ever heard of. How was it possible to write pages and pages of words that pulled someone in and held them captive until the final full stop? How did a writer know what order to put the words in and how to join them all up and make them so much more than the sum of their parts? How did someone I'd never met know what *I* was feeling? Because that was what these stories did: they made me *feel*. It was like reading about my own worries, joys, passions and dreams.

These stories expressed all the things I found hard to say when my parents were working hard, or across the dinner table where we laughed and joked. How could I have begun to express my worries that I was a big girl, not dainty, not petite, not made of sugar and spice, and burdened by these characteristics, how was I ever going to get picked by David Cassidy or anyone else for that matter? Who'd want a little fairy elephant? And how could I broach the topic that my bones hurt and that a sweetie, a cuddle and a reassuring word didn't always make me feel better? And how could I explain exactly what hurt when the answer was EVERYTHING! It all felt a little overwhelming, so it was easier to smile, go with the flow and say nothing.

But inside those library books, I became the characters. I laughed and cried with them. I lived the stories of *Anne of Green Gables* and *Carrie's War* and so many others. Losing myself entirely within the pages of books like *Black Beauty* by Anna Sewell and the 'Follyfoot' series by Monica Dickens – both of these feature horses and riding across Britain's green and pleasant lands. I suspect that was part of the appeal as I travelled to such places in my mind from the corner of the sofa. Putting myself on the back of those horses, I'd sometimes go off-piste. And before I fell asleep, I'd write my own branch of the adventure in my head – creating my own stories and building worlds that were fantastical and delightful in equal measure.

I might never have been abroad, but I had travelled further in my mind than anywhere I could point to on a map or head to on a package holiday. Complete stories, other adventures for the characters in the book I was reading, would pop into my head like a film being downloaded (although at the time such things were mere science fiction!) and this happened with such regularity that I devised a system to sort and store them in my brain – one I use to this day.

I pictured the battered green metal filing cabinets I had seen on a trip to my dad's workplace. They were slightly wonky and had tarnished brass handles and three deep drawers per cabinet. Creating a room in my mind, I filled it with these filing cabinets on a wooden floor, and I still keep track of my thoughts, ideas and stories in this way. I make no other physical note or plan and never have; everything I need is in these drawers. The story or thought placed at the front of the drawer is the most recent, but the drawers never run out of space. The cabinets are in alphabetical order, with all my stories in the drawers, but they're not always filed in the most obvious way: for example, my novel *To Love and Be Loved* is under C for cliff because this is the opening scene! My earliest childhood stories are probably still there if I look hard enough.

I also added a dictionary to my mental filing cabinets, figuring that as long as I was learning words for spelling tests, I might as well save them, so I didn't have to learn them again. Any word I learned, or which interested me went into it. I started to read the actual dictionary (I know, weird kid!) and if I spelled a word wrongly and had to look it up, I'd put a star by it to make sure I properly learnt it. I still have my dictionary full of stars, but don't look at it any more, partly because of spellcheck but also, and I don't want to brag, I rarely spell a word wrong. Once they are in my dictionary that's that, it's locked in and it's as if I've learned nearly all the words I need! My grammar, however, is another story altogether.

It's fair to say those early library books changed my life. None of the characters I chose to spend time with in stories cared if I was clumsy, solidly built or dainty or whether I had a penis or not. I loved them and I knew they loved me back for bringing them to life, for letting them move around freely inside my head. And as for reading: this unique form of escape – pictures visualised in *my* head that had come straight out of the author's head – I mean, WOWSERS! I thought and still think that it's the closest thing to magic.

It didn't matter where I was or what was going on around me, books were where I could feed my imagination and settle my whir of thoughts. I can only put a modern slant on it to say that 'I had found my kind!' I was a good reader, no, a *great* reader.

Every parents' evening discussion and school report gave my 'reading age' as way above my years, and this was important to me, as I felt very average at just about everything else. My reading ability made learning easy, and even if I didn't have many friends, I had my books! I took pride in my reading, putting energy and thought into it, wanting to excel at it. And I did.

That first time in a public library was life-changing. It was the greatest gift anyone could have given me, and even now I am so very thankful to libraries that opened up this world for kids like me.

1974. Me aged six with my little brother Simon. Wonky fringe and all . . . But compared to my brother's, it's not too bad. He had cut chunks out of his at the front and one side with the nail scissors!

Chapter Two

'THE RAIN IN SPAIN . . .'

As he hit his early twenties, my dad, a super-smart manufacturing engineer, saw his star rise in the workplace. With three little kids and a wife to support, he made his next career move. Having grown up in a world where there was more than a suggestion that it was easier, safer when it came to ambition, to operate within the boundaries set by previous generations – thus minimising the risk of disappointment in life, it took guts to challenge this. He announced he was giving up the security of the known and heading out into the *un*known, for no more than the chance of a lift in our living standard. My parents changed their lives and ours by running towards the horizon, grabbing handfuls of opportunity as they went, unafraid to meet new people, settle in a new postcode, embracing change and all its wonderful possibilities. As a small child, I can picture them discussing adverts for jobs that popped up in the papers and how likely my dad would be to get the position. While Dad was out working one of two jobs, Mum would write his application letters and trundle down to the postbox, sending off requests for interview. I know this chasing attitude, the quest for betterment, seeking financial stability while crucially satisfying his own high ambition, baffled my grandads, one a docker all his life, man and boy, and the other working in factories, part of a proud manufacturing history. They worked the same job for decades because loyalty and pride in length of service was what counted. And if they were lucky, after fifty or so odd years of toil, they might be presented with a carriage clock to sit on the mantelpiece, engraved on the back with their dates of employment that had passed in a blink.

Creatures of habit, my nan and grandad shopped on the same day every week and kept a strict routine that revolved around cups of tea and supper. There was a washing day, a cleaning day, bin day and visit the grandkids day. They even telephoned me, my mum and my auntie at the same time every evening. Everything they needed, their whole world, in fact, sat within a few streets of where they lay their head every night. And actually, age has taught me there is much to be said for that level of contentment.

My dad was offered a job with Rolls-Royce's small engine division where he would be working on the manufacture of helicopters in Leavesden. Now behind a desk, he was tasked with improving the manufacturing process. To make his commute possible (in his first company car: a roomy toffee brown metallic Ford Consul) the family, after much debate, was on the move.

It felt scary, aged eight, to leave the streets that were familiar and the house that was our home and the library where I was a regular. I certainly didn't want to leave my school. I liked my teacher, Miss West. She was nice to me. I remember my last day at Clockhouse Junior School and that sick feeling in my tum like I was heading out into open water where danger of the unknown lurked, but hadn't this been what I wanted? To live life outside that front door? This, I guess, was my first understanding that to stretch your wings and push your horizons came with consequences and required a little courage.

Mum collected me on the last day of term, as she did every day, and I wanted to cry: partly because I was scared, but also because I was aware that all the kids in my class would regroup after the holidays and someone else would sit in my chair. Miss West would peel the sticky label with my name on it from the grey plastic tray where my schoolbooks lived, and it would be as if I had never been there. I hated the whole idea of it. The fact that I was going through something so life-changing and yet for my classmates it would be like any other Monday, as they collected their little bottle of warm milk at break time and listened to the afternoon story as they lay their head on the triangle of their arms on the desktop. I figured none of them would give me a second thought, whereas I knew those early years would live clearly in my memory and they have. They, like every chapter in my life, have their own drawer in my filing cabinet.

It was the start of the summer holidays when we packed up and moved out. Even at that young age, I was aware of an elevation in our living circumstances, partly from the reaction of my nans and great-aunts when they came to visit. All were still within easy driving distance and came to the house weekly. Any disapproval at the decision to uproot the family and start over was quickly forgotten as they wandered the three-bed terraced house with their clip-top handbags resting on their arms, keeping their cardigans on to ward off any potential chill.

'Ooh, this is very nice!'
'Posh, innit?'
'You paid 'ow much?!'

We had moved into a smart new development in St Albans, Hertfordshire. My new bedroom was not vast, but a huge improvement on my last room, as I could get on and off the bed without having to leap from the doorway! The place was indeed 'very nice', with an abundance of trees, well-kept lawns and cars that were shiny and not jacked up on bricks. There was even a river running through it where a weeping willow kissed the banks and ducks and swans ambled across our gardens, shitting as they went.

I felt a little lonely, not having anyone to knock for and play with, and it was the first time I felt the power and reassurance of having siblings. The boys had always been either my playmates or an irritation, but as I was about to enter a new school with a couple of brothers in the two years below me, it felt like an enormous comfort to know that if I needed to, I could seek them out at break time. It made me feel a little less nervous, but only a little.

My mum was extra jolly on the first day of school, I now know in an effort to buoy us up, but I was petrified and felt tearful. I would've given anything to be back at Clockhouse Juniors with Miss West teaching the class. The kids at my new school, I noticed, spoke a little differently from me, without my strong cockney twang and what I now know is more of a classless, estuary accent. It made me a little self-conscious of how I spoke, and I tried to emulate them. I lived in St Albans until I was sixteen and organically lost much of my cockney inflection. I still speak with a neutral voice that makes it hard to place where I'm from. That is until I get angry, riled, excited or sloshed and I go full Pearly Queen.

My new school was fancy, flint-walled and neat with well-tended hanging baskets and a proud history. It adjoined a sturdy Norman church where we would spend (in my humble opinion) a disproportionate amount of time learning hymns by rote. My husband now jokes that this was when every other school kid was doing sums, hence my ability to belt out 'Oh Jesus I Have Promised', with vigour but not have the first clue about long division.

It was all very different from what I was used to. In this quiet, quaint suburb with a park and yet more ducks on the meandering river, there was not so much as a whiff of lorry diesel nor the shriek of wailing sirens. The whole place felt 'different', and that difference was money. For the first time I realised that money meant opportunity. This is why I am now so passionate about education for those without either; I'm personally aware of the great gulf between a good and bad education and the path it sets young children on.

The majority of the kids in my class had been abroad; some even had a spare bedroom! Can you *imagine*? A bedroom for just in case . . . What world was this I had stumbled into? One or two of the boys teased me about my voice, and I remember desperately wanting to be like them.

It was while I was still finding my feet – new to the school – that I, along with my classmates, was asked to write a poem that rhymed. Simple enough! I attacked the task with enthusiasm and was lucky enough to be assisted by a wonderful 'helper', I guess the modern equivalent would be a teaching assistant. Her name was Mollie Newell. Mrs Newell was large and magnificent and spoke like the Queen. She had a booming voice and a booming laugh. She wore bright beads and pale grey sweaters and was absolutely marvellous. I can only picture her laughing or smiling. She sat me down one day and patiently explained that my poem didn't quite work.

'Why?' I looked up at her, confident enough to ask because she was kind and fabulous.

'Because, darling, the task was to find rhymes.'

'But I have!' I pointed indignantly at the sheet of paper in her hand.

'Hmmm . . . Not really.' She smiled and we both stared at the words I had rhymed: 'school', 'wall', 'wool' and 'ball'.

I said them out loud, not quite understanding how Mrs Newell didn't get it.

'Skawl. Wawl. Wawl. Bawl.' It rhymed perfectly in my head and indeed had rhymed perfectly when I read it out loud. Mollie Newell laughed, the sound brimming with affection.

'Quite right.' She smiled. 'Quite right.'

She took away some of the shame I had felt, and she encouraged me to read more and to write more and I owe her so much. Now, not everyone can have a Mollie Newell, sadly, and not every teacher can *be* a Mollie Newell.

As if to prove the point, I also had a teacher called Mrs Blight (Dictionary definition: 'a thing that spoils or damages something' – how very appropriate). She looked a lot like how I imagined Aunt Spiker from Roald Dahl's *James and The Giant Peach*. She was tall, thin and bloodless, with thin pale lips and small teeth. Her nose was sharp, her eyes small and her voice warbling. She found my work terribly amusing. But I couldn't figure out what was so funny! What had I done wrong? It ladled self-doubt onto my belief that I was a great reader and a great writer; maybe I wasn't. This worry pierced my heart – reading and writing was what I loved and if I was only mediocre at it, what did that leave? Certainly not ballet!

One day, she asked us all to stand and tell the rest of the class what we would like to do for a job when we grew up. I mean, flippin' 'eck, we were only eight – I didn't know what I wanted to do until I was forty-two! At eight I was more concerned with reading another chapter before bedtime and what we might be having for tea. Anyhoo, most of the boys plumped for footballer and a couple went for taxi driver and one I seem to remember wanted to work for Cadbury's so he could eat all the chocolate – smart thinking. The girls went for doctor, actress and teacher and not necessarily in that order.

When it came to my turn, I took a deep breath and announced I wanted to write a book. I hadn't said it out loud in public before and it felt like a big deal, exposing and brave at the same time. By that stage I understood that writing books *could* be your job – talk about living the dream. Despite this understanding it didn't make it any easier when I expressed across the dinner table that I wanted to be a writer. The huffs and eye rolls of the older family members who had just as much of a hand in raising me as my parents, were not mocking, but certainly dismissive as if to say, 'That sounds like pie in the sky. Unrealistic and risky! That's an ambition that will only lead to disappointment and won't put food on the table!' And I got it, because my own views were similar, enough to paralyse me with fear for more years than I care to think about.

But on that day, standing in front of Mrs Blight, it took every bit of confidence I possessed to admit it. I looked her in the eye and announced, 'I want to write books. I want to write stories.'

With a slight shake of her head, she removed her glasses and laughed, drily onto the back of her palm with her gold-rimmed bifocals dangling from her fingertips. I can picture this moment so clearly and I suspect I always will. I pushed the toe of my shoe into the wooden floor trying to disappear. It's filed in my mind under 'S' for 'Shitty', as this was both a shitty thing to do and made me feel shitty too.

'I see, well, let's hope you have a plan B!'

She made a noise that was part tut and part chuckle and I sat down with cold rocks of disappointment and shame lining my stomach. Mortified, I stared at the scarred wooden desktop with the golf-ball-sized hole where a ceramic inkwell sat, a reminder of another era, focusing on anything other than the stares of my classmates who had witnessed my humiliation. My face felt hot and my legs wobbly. Of course, she was right, what was I thinking?

I was quiet when my mum collected me at home time and went to bed that night replaying the moment over and over in my mind, wishing I could go back and do things differently, only this time I'd go for nurse, hairdresser, plumber, footballer . . . anything other than embarrassing myself by admitting my desire to write.

That tone of dismissal stayed with me. To put it bluntly, she made me feel 'smawl'. It was the first time I began to let self-doubt creep in, the first time I was aware of that inner voice of negativity when it came to my ability. It never occurred to me to question her opinion. This lady, a very ladylike lady, who I doubt ever showed her bum in the garden, was laughing at me, as if I wasn't quite up to the mark, and it stuck. I figured she must be right, she knew stuff! She was after all a teacher, who spoke '*properly*', and I knew for a fact she had a spare bedroom.

It was the first brick in a wall I began to build in my mind, a wall behind which my behaviour was measured, reined in because of something I felt embarrassed about, a perceived inferiority. A wall with confidence and high self-esteem on the other side.

A wall I might have started to construct aged eight, but one that would be decades in the completion . . .

Me aged eight heading off to my new school with my brothers.

31

Chapter Three

'AN UGLY DUCKLING'

The impact of my teacher's words lessened a little with time and did not entirely strangle my ambition to write; in truth there was nothing else I wanted to do. But they certainly wrapped the thought in a slippery caul that I would struggle to grip and make real for the longest time. Having settled into our new school, new house and new life with the shitting ducks, I was nine when my mum had my third and final baby brother – he's now a plumber who stands well over six foot, but I still think of him as little Nicky. It was such a happy time with a new little baby to play with. Even though I felt clumsy and walked awkwardly because of my hip and discomfort issues, both of which made me feel a little self-conscious outside the house, everything inside it was lovely.

I don't remember giving the clothes I wore, my hairstyle or my face any thought at all. Which might explain why up until I started secondary school aged eleven, I looked like a slightly shorter version of Jim Carrey circa his *Dumb and Dumber* years. Why did no one tell me? My childhood was the opposite of vanity. I was more interested in books and living inside them than my outer casing. There was no emphasis on physical attributes, beauty or fashion and only a small mirror above the sink in the bathroom, which my brothers and I used to jostle in front of for position while we cleaned our teeth, eagerly trying to gob toothpaste foam onto each other's hands. Revolting yes, but we were young and unaware of how nasty gobbing one's tooth foam onto a sibling was. FYI we also took swigs from the same bottle of Panda Pops and licked the same lollies. Yuck. So yes, one small mirror, but there wasn't a full-length mirror anywhere in the house. Bath time was a quick in and out of the tub and my mum cut my nails, chose my clothes and trimmed my hair.

I don't think I was fully conscious of what I looked like, not really; my thoughts and apprehensions of being NVLL were based more on my lack of grace than how I physically looked. There were of course no computers or mobile phones or social media inform-ing me that this was what I should aspire to/dress like/emulate. Fashion and beauty were, I thought, for grown-ups.

My mum putting on her make-up, taking her time and doing so with precision was a fascination. Ingrained in my mind is the image of her with her long, dark, glossy hair blow-dried into Charlie's Angels style waves, as she artfully applied her lipstick, Shiny Conker by No7, which she wore for years, painting it on before she left the house to go out with my dad, while my nan and grandad babysat. Watching the ritual was intimate and interesting all at once, but it didn't occur to me that one day I would do something similar. Not only did I not know how, but also, she was a 'grown-up', and I was just a kid, and I couldn't imagine life any other way. I do remember thinking it seemed like an awful lot of effort to go to just to go out for the evening with my dad, who knew full well what she looked like without make-up, only to then come home and wipe it all off with cleanser – and I still think that now!

The seventies! Mum and Dad. Mum resplendent in her shiny conker!

I might not have been interested in clothes but did, however, like to be cosy and enjoyed that lovely feeling of pulling a warm Bri-Nylon nightie over my head before bedtime. My mum would warm it on the radiator, and it would feel like a soft hug against my skin, readying me for sleep. My very thick hair standing up on end and sparks, yes, actual sparks flew from my nightdress as I dived and skidded along the carpet on my tum, keeping up with the boys who similarly dived in front of the TV.

Looking back, I can see that my haircut was almost identical to that of my brothers, and when not in school uniform I wore the same as them: hand-knitted Aran jumpers lovingly and expertly knitted by my clever nan, jeans and wellington boots. Playing outside with the boys was how we cemented our relationship. I wasn't fast or agile like them, but I liked the pressure-free environment where it didn't matter a jot if my behaviour was boisterous. It was a way I broadened my horizon, happy to be out of the house with the boys and getting grubby. My brother Simon still makes me laugh like no one else. In our new back garden, slightly bigger than the one we had left, we'd go outside to play, ride bikes, dig up the garden, play with Bimbo, the vicious rabbit we'd got from the local vicar, and perform stunts.

Yes, you read that correctly, this was the age of Evel Knievel and Eddie Kidd, of daring Hollywood blockbusters involving car chases and special effects that blew our minds. And when I wasn't reading, stunts were a huge preoccupation. And before you conjure images of death-defying leaps, pyrotechnics and slo-mo falling from great heights into a stack of foam mattresses, let me set you straight. Our stunts primarily involved building a smallish ramp using a sheet of bloated plywood resting on a rock and any garden implement we could find, taking it in turns to go over it on the bike and jousting each other with a hoe and a rake. We would then finish with a fancy flourish, hold the pose and the crowd would go wild! And trust me, jousting with a hoe over a rickety ramp was no less dangerous than taking our chances on the rusting playground equipment in the park, which was sharp, brutal and anchored into concrete, guaranteeing a fall meant at least one broken bone. A modern-day health and safety nightmare, covered with a whole array of graffiti using words I'd never heard of. One I learned and, having arrived home after one such trip, announced to a table packed with family that I was just off upstairs for a 'piss'. I can picture my nan's face now. If we ever tripped or fell, rather than submit to the embarrassment and guaranteed subsequent ridicule, we would jump up with arms held out and shout 'Stunt!' as if it was intentional. We still do that now. We range in age from fifty-four to forty-three – and it still makes me laugh just as much as it ever did. With my brothers I was just one of the gang, no matter how NVLL, and I liked being that way.

It didn't occur to me to think about the clothes I wore or the fact that there was currency to be found in beauty. I didn't think it mattered and I had no concept of the importance society placed upon it.

I was ten when we were travelling home after school one day with Mum pushing my little brother Nicky in a blue-and-white striped buggy that was all the rage in the late seventies, the ones that used to tip up and fall sharply backwards when you put your shopping on the handles. My brothers and I walked alongside. A woman Mum knew stopped her for a chat. She said something like, 'Oh, I love your boys!' and smushed Paul's cheeks. She then looked at me and said, 'And there's still time for this ugly duckling to become a swan.'

I can close my eyes and tell you every detail about that moment: what we were wearing (school uniform), how we stood (clustered on the edge of the pavement), what she was wearing (astrakhan coat and knee-high leather boots), the weather (cooling, as dusk bit) and the light (lilac and fading). It clearly had an impact on me. Particularly as the woman who said this was vivacious, trendy, worked in fashion and clearly therefore must have known an ugly duckling when she saw one.

I was . . . gobsmacked. I wasn't upset by it, more shocked, but I can now see that it was another brick in the wall I had begun to build, another comment to snip at the tender shoots of self-confidence that might have started to bloom. It changed the way I looked at myself; more specifically it changed my self-awareness, and not in a good way. I mean, I *knew* I wasn't a swan, although could at times pass for a cygnet, but had no idea I was an ugly duckling!

Three of my favourite things in one picture: my pink bedroom, my little brothers and reading my Brownie annual!

Family holiday to Devon, 1978. I think this is when I learned you can hide a lot of your ugly duckling face behind big goggles, a tactic I still employ!

It was only years later as a teenager, when Mum and I were discussing the impact of throwaway comments, I confided in her that this was what I had heard. She told me I was beautiful, of course she did. But I didn't believe her. Her view was and is blinkered by her absolute devotion to her children – any artworks, stick people included, were framed and hung as if they were masterpieces. Any criticism was rebuffed and diluted with an opposing, positive view and this to me was just another example of that. It felt baseless, biased and rooted in love.

Aware of my lack of beauty, after this I started to doctor the way I smiled. Throughout my childhood I heard that if I was good, well behaved, I could have a sweet. If I did my homework, I could have a sweet, completed a chore, I could have a sweet, didn't fight with my brothers, I could have a sweet. And it might be a long car journey, but don't worry, you've guessed it . . . Popping boiled sugar into my mouth became as routine as drinking water. But sweeties were so much more than just foodstuff. They were reward for something well done, they were medicine. Sweets and sugar were how my family showed me 'love'. Every single one of my teeth was filled with a silver/grey amalgam filling by the time I reached twelve. I stopped feeling comfortable and developed a laugh and smile where I pressed my lips tightly together. I still do this, much to the irritation and bemusement of the numerous photographers who ask me to smile 'naturally' and despite the fact that my teeth at the front look fine. It was the start of an awareness of how I was lacking, something to feel ashamed and self-conscious about. Another brick in that wall I was crafting.

As the end of primary school dawned, despite Mrs Blight's words dancing in my thoughts, I began to think about how I might achieve my dream of writing. That concrete ceiling was low enough that even at the tender age of eleven, I could almost touch it. In most schools in the early seventies, toys were divided into girls' toys: dolls, dolls' prams, tea sets, mini household appliances, dress-up frocks and dolls' houses, and boy's toys: guns, plastic knives and general weaponry, toy cars, building blocks, mini hammers, tools and nuts and bolts. And subjects too: home economics, needlework, childcare and dance were for the girls. It will come as no surprise to hear that we were being groomed for motherhood and housekeeping, while the boys were being readied for a life on a building site, as a craftsman or to sit in an office, the route paved by studying woodwork, metalwork, technical drawing and orienteering. I guess the establishment figured these boys didn't need to know how to sew, cook or put a nappy on a baby because there was a whole generation of girls like me learning how to take care of those very things! Can you believe this was only forty or so years ago?

It was as unfair, sexist, limiting and ridiculous as it sounds. But, and how I hate to use this catch-all, excuse-all, insipid phrase, 'it was just how it was'. I began to feel the flickering flame of conflict in my gut, not knowing how I could avoid being rubber-stamped in this way – yes, I wanted to be like my mum and all the women I admired: wonderful, generous homemakers who made safe nests for us, but I also wanted to leave the house each day in a car like my dad. I wanted to know what that world was all about. I wanted it all!

I started secondary school in 1979, aged eleven. This period in my life, as it is for most of us, was to be formative in ways I couldn't possibly have imagined. If I had to look ahead, I thought I may get to know more about boys and that there might be the possibility of snogging when I hit my teens – and while keen to have a go, it was a thought that paralysed me with fear; how did you learn how to do *that*?

I was also desperate to get my ears pierced. My mum, who was less keen on the idea, told me it was illegal until I was eighteen and I believed her. A favourite hobby of mine was surreptitiously pointing out girls on the bus or Tube who sported enviable gold hoops in their lobes, in response to which my mum would bend low and whisper in my own shell-like, 'Hope the police don't catch them.'

I didn't confess that I wouldn't mind getting busted by the feds if it meant I had some bling nestling in my lobes.

Starting 'big school' was a huge event in our house: everyone discussed the leap from baby school and how it was my first step into the world of grown-ups. Most of my generation had watched the popular UK teatime show *Grange Hill*, set in a rowdy school, and much of my fear of this giant leap stemmed from the events that unfolded on screen: teenage pregnancy, drug addiction, playground fights, having your head flushed down the loo by bullies! Was it any wonder I was scared? The looming dread of it dulled any joy in the summer between primary and secondary education.

My nerves were largely down to the fact that I was the only person in my primary school to be sent to the sprawling comprehensive school across town. All my peers were either off to private (paid) school or else had siblings that they were following to all-girls' or all-boys' schools in the area. I was never going to private school; I mean, we might have seen an upturn in our fortunes, but come on! And as the oldest, *I* was the sibling who would have paved the way for any little sisters.

My parents kept telling me what a great time I was going to have and about all the new friends I was going to make. I guess I might have been celebrating never having to sit in a class run by the sneering judgemental Mrs Blight – but what was I about to walk into? I had read enough in books like the 'Malory Towers' series, to know that starting a new school could be equivalent to entering the lion's den. And it wasn't as if I could meet up with my brothers in the playground.

It was a situation where I felt marked, selected to be different. Although of course there was nothing personal in it. The local council allocated school places based on numbers, demographics and statistics, but that meant little when I was the only one from my primary school heading off without a friendship group and a gut full of nerves. My thoughts ranged from, *what is wrong with me? To what did I do wrong? Was it that poem that didn't rhyme?* It was another brick in the wall. Another reason to feel less than.

My new school uniform was functional, boxy and generously oversized to allow for growth and most crucially to ensure my parents didn't have to cough up for a new uniform before the year was out. Money wasn't as tight as it had been, but there was still not a lot spare for pricey blazers. On that first day, I remember the exhausting ritual of putting it all on and feeling the weight, physical and mental, of the full attire. I felt like a different person, and I didn't like it. Off I trotted in heavy wool blazer, itchy shirt, polyester kipper tie and fawn knee-high socks with a long pleated skirt. My shoes were brown and clumpy with a crimped front that were worn by many and openly mocked as 'pork pie shoes' by the cool kids because of said natty crimp. And as if I wasn't dorky enough, not that I was aware of my less than trendy status, I carried a massive leather briefcase that used to belong to my dad with my name slotted into a little holder with a plastic window on the back. I tucked good luck notes into it from my mum, dad and wider family members and set off with the promise to call them the moment I got home and tell them all the great things I had experienced.

But the truth was I didn't experience many great things on that day. I found the whole experience overwhelming. Much of the day I spent alone with my briefcase, despite being herded together with all the other newcomers for a tour of our new school which seemed vast. Most of the other kids in my year were with mates from their respective primary schools, with whom they snickered and shared a lunch table. I felt ostracised, alien and awkward and didn't much fancy going back the next day. Although when met with a barrage of excited questioning and expectant smiles of my family, I didn't feel able to say this out loud, not wanting to disappoint or worry them.

The only thing I really liked about my new school was the long commute: a winding walk to the bus stop, which gave me a chance to peep into people's houses as I passed, which was and still is one of my favourite hobbies. And a bus ride, where I would sit on the top deck of an old Routemaster breathing in second-hand cigarette smoke and rubbing the steam off the windows with my sleeve to stare at the world as we whizzed by.

Plus, my bus journey was a chance to read and a good way to tune out the deafening yells and screeches of older pupils who treated that bus like a mobile nightclub/pickup joint/smoking lounge and wrestling ring. I laugh now to think of myself squashed into a velour-covered seat, briefcase on lap, in a world of my own, while hormone-riddled teenage girls and testosterone-filled teenage boys created mayhem all around me. It kind of sums up my teenage years, among it but not part of it, an observer, happier with my nose in a book. Occasionally I'd roll my shoulders in response to a foot in my back or wince at the glancing blow of an elbow to the face and would often feel an object whistle over my head as it was hurled from one end of the bus to the other, a text book, a lit cigarette, numerous shoes/plimsolls, a handful of chips and one time a large courgette or small marrow – it was hard to tell as it was travelling at speed. The driver would watch over the top deck via a kind of square periscope mirror that was fixed in the corner above his seat and which the more daring traveller would peer down. When things got a little too rowdy, he would sometimes holler that he was going to come up the stairs and knock the living daylights out of the perpetrators or worse, chuck them off the bus. His threats were always idle and always, always entirely ignored.

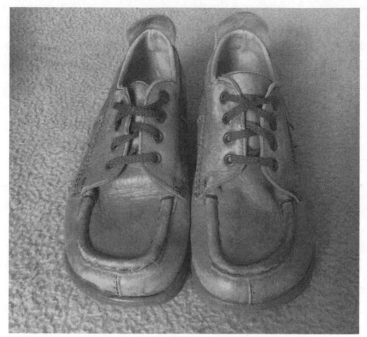

For those of you lucky enough not to have worn a pair and are ignorant of their delights – here are some pork pies!

To my shock and horror, I discovered on that first day of secondary school that only a small percentage of pupils were in the full uniform. The pressed and labelled regulation kit apparently marked me as 'posh', which was for me quite perplexing, as the last time I'd arrived at a new school I'd been labelled the very opposite.

It taught me that *how* you are labelled depends entirely on those doing the labelling. The school had sent a letter with a list of the uniform required. It had arrived during the summer holidays and in our house was stuck on the fridge door and treated like gospel with my mum ticking off each item as it was acquired – was I now to believe the whole ruddy, itchy, crappy ensemble was *optional*? These were the days before reasonably priced generic uniform was available in supermarkets, and I knew my parents had shelled out a pretty sum for the unflattering clobber purchased from a 'gentleman's outfitter', a throwback no doubt to the days when my shitty school was for boys only.

I clomped the halls with my hands lost inside the voluminous sleeves of my blazer, gripping my briefcase and far too preoccupied with surreptitiously glancing at the cool girls with pierced ears who wore over-the-knee socks, tight, short skirts and flat ballet-like pumps. They had badges of their idols pinned to their jerseys and carried canvas bags slung low on their hips with their band of choice inked onto them. This was the first time I had been up close to girls like these. Older girls, teenagers, QUEENS!

As I searched for a friendship group, it was beyond my wildest imaginings to think they might take me under their wing, show me the ropes (they didn't. This is not a movie!), but they did show me a world that was pretty and fashionable, and – like thumbing the pages of a glossy magazine that showcases all the things you can't afford – I liked to look at and admire them. For me, it wasn't so much about their beauty or the trappings of glitter and fashion, it was about their confidence, their assured walk, their air of worldliness.

It was at this tender age of eleven that I became aware of how the world seemed to be organised into the beautiful and blessed and the rest of us. It was a time of awakening and the first time I understood that popularity seemed to hinge on beauty. This ran contrary to how I had been brought up: 'it's what's on the inside that counts' slipped regularly from my mum's mouth. Easy for her to say when she was pretty and had modelled – literally paid because of her outer casing! I began to question whether this was *actually* true, having only recently discovered other foul lies my parents had peddled me.

If you swallowed chewing gum, it did not wrap around your heart, and you did not die.

Eating crusts from a slice of bread would not make my hair curlier – thank God!

Swallowing apple pips would not make a tree grow in my stomach with branches that would poke out of my ears.

We didn't actually have the world's oldest goldfish – the truth being that every time one died, my mum flushed it down the loo and went off to buy a lookalike. No wonder Norris McWhirter never answered my letter.

And this is my favourite Mum lie by far: she told me that there was a blue plaque outside the hospital in Stepney where I was born, saying, 'Mandy was born here'. Every time we drove past, I would crane my neck from the back seat to see it and then sulk when I couldn't. She would sigh and say, 'You were looking in the wrong place! I saw it!' Dad too would nod that he'd seen it, clearly! This went on for years and years. The ruse, however, came to a head when I was on a primary school trip and as we tootled along Commercial Road, I sat up, pointed and shouted, beyond excited, 'Ooh! This is where I was born and there's a sign on the wall that says, "Mandy was born here"!' It was only the laughter of the older kids, the smirk of the teacher and the sinking feeling in my chest that helped me finally get the joke. I reprimanded my mum over this very thing only recently and she told me that I was without doubt the most important baby ever born there, to her at least.

I mean, what next? Was I about to find out that you *could* legally get your ears pierced before the age of eighteen without being hauled into the clink? Surely not.

I can still see those fabulous older girls at big school now. I remember their names and as I sat on the grass leaning on my briefcase reading, I watched them walking, nay *gliding* en masse across the playing field in a cloud of 'Charlie' by Revlon, with school skirts adapted into minis. (I would never have been allowed to do this. Plus, my skirt was so long to make it short I'd have ended up with a hefty tyre around my waist!) They sported crimped Toyah-worthy hair and enough kohl around their eyes to rival Siouxsie. They were aloof, not too smart and not too sporty. They smoked, had black-painted fingernails and carried fanzines and rolled copies of the *NME*. They clearly knew stuff, stuff I was not going to learn in lessons, and I wondered how I could learn that stuff too. On the odd occasion when one of them would nod in my direction, it would make my day.

I was lonely and any acknowledgement was welcome.

Coming out of the toilet cubicle one afternoon to wash my hands, I stood next to one of this crowd and she looked at me in the mirror and said, 'All right.' I blushed crimson and overthought how to reply, feeling the pressure to get it right, to hide my inner (and outer) dorkiness. By the time I'd unstuck my tongue from the dry roof of my mouth and settled on 'all right' by way of reply, she'd long gone. The slam of the graffiti-covered bathroom door echoed around me, as if the room itself laughed at the missed opportunity.

Oh, those brilliant, amazing girls! Who sashayed and swayed (probably down to the very tight, very short skirts that restricted movement) and the clutch of drooling boys wearing their ties back to front with the fat bit tucked in and the thin bit on display, doing all they could to be on trend and stand out, following in their wake. I would have given anything, *anything* to be one of them. Just for a day. Just to know what it felt like. Seeing them was like being given a glimpse into a different world and it was a world of teenage fashion, sex and trendsetting. I was fascinated.

But I very much doubted that scrawling on my case and paint-ing my bitten fingernails would have made me any more 'with it'. Not when I was wearing those bloody pork pies and my hair was in a blunt-cut wiry bob with a wonky fringe. I'd never questioned my clothes, my haircut, my style or lack of and yet here I was, comparing myself to the coolest clique. It was a comparison that left me wanting in every sense and the first time I think I became fully conscious of all I was lacking physically. And more crucially without the first clue how to fix it.

◆ ◆ ◆

Around this time and with my long commute, I began to notice an increase in discomfort around my hips and back. Small aches and twinges which, having been there rumbling away in the background my whole life, I thought were 'normal', became sharper, the discomfort lingering for longer.

Never having compared notes with anyone on how they felt when they woke up each morning or had to climb stairs or run, I was in the dark as to whether my experience was unusual; at points in my hips and back, it felt alternately like the slow turning of a screw inside me, the point of which went deeper, or as if something inside me was twisted, waiting to 'unclick', and I felt it more keenly with movement. I hadn't really mentioned it often, as doctors' visits were usually to confirm that I did, like the rest of my school year, have chickenpox, strep throat and all the other commonplace nasties that meant a day or two off school under the duvet with a hot-water bottle for company and a sticky bottle of Lucozade on the sideboard. The orange plastic wrapper around the bottle made a delightful twisting noise as the cap was removed. I was reliably informed by the school nurse and my wider family that it was 'normal' to have growing pains and that I was possibly tired. Both probably true.

These aches and pains didn't really stop me doing anything. Oh no, what stopped me doing things was an absurd rule that said without a penis, certain subjects were off limits to me. ME! The chunky girl who had done stunts in the garden, one of the boys!

My parents caused an almighty stink at school because I wanted to take Woodwork, Metalwork *and* Home Economics. They wrote letters and had meetings and it was agreed I could do a little of each, the irony being I never mastered any of them and should have picked one and stuck to it.

Having been granted a place in the class, I felt so adrift among the sea of boys who mocked my efforts and waited for me to fail that I wished I'd never suggested it in the first place. It was yet another environment where I didn't quite fit. At the end of the lesson, I'd gaze longingly at the gaggle of girls leaving the Home Ec room with their freshly iced cupcakes in Tupperware containers, wishing I were one of them. I still can't make a bloody cupcake.

The UK had a female prime minister in the form of Margaret Thatcher. There were laws in place to protect women in the workplace in terms of pay, opportunity and education, and indeed my own burgeoning buds of feminism made me question why things were off limits to me based on my gender, yet I *still* very much felt as if marriage was expected of a working-class girl like me. This was largely because my nan and great-aunts would constantly talk about my future wedding and the day itself, which I can now see was a throwback to their own youths when their wedding day was the one day they would dress up, feel special and be the centre of attention, as well as, of course, providing them with the status necessary to leave home, enjoy the freedom of adulthood and have sex! And while I wasn't averse to the idea of marriage entirely, I knew there was more to life than traipsing up the aisle and saying I do. At least I bloody hoped there was – I wanted to be a writer! Despite Mrs Blight's comments, I held this dream in my mind, envisaging it, throwing it out into the universe, and feeling such joy at the thought of it. My flights of fancy helped quiet the background chatter from society, teachers, the media, even the music piped into my ears in lifts and while browsing the ladies' department with my nan and mum for all things frilly, which was peppered with lyrics suggesting, if not confirming, that my role in life was to be 'pretty' and 'subservient'. Songs like Burt Bacharach's 'Wives and Lovers' and even The Rolling Stones' 'Under My Thumb'.

But what if I didn't want to be the kind of girl who only spoke when she was spoken to? Who never combed her hair or fixed her make-up because she couldn't figure out why it mattered? Did that mean David Cassidy, or anyone like him, wasn't going to marry a girl like me? And if so what on earth could I do about it? Did I *have* to get married? What would happen to me if I didn't? Was it possible to live in a house on your own? I mean, who'd take the bins out, cut the grass and know how to use all those tools that I hadn't been given access to? What if, God forbid, I needed to wire a plug, tackle a tax return or mow a lawn? It was an era where despite giant leaps in terms of equality and the rise of the women's liberation movement, we were still being conditioned to become wives and homemakers, and the fact that I was an ugly duckling meant I was already worried no one would pick me. It felt easier not to mention the subject, worried, I think, that I would have my unsuitability for a life of domestic bliss confirmed. In fairness, I had by this stage given up on David Cassidy. Not least of all because he was nearly twenty years older than me, not so much of an issue in later life, but a bit tricky when you're eleven. Plus, he lived in New York, which I had of course never visited and didn't want to visit. No way! Not if *King Kong* and *The Towering Inferno* were the norm. I was a whole lot safer in our cul-de-sac. Plus, I thought I'd prefer to marry Simon le Bon and imagined him singing 'Planet Earth' just for me.

It wasn't all bad though. My parents, I think, are still in proud possession of the fish slice I created on a lathe and talk with pride of the cassette rack, dovetail joints and all, I presented to them during my brief time as a woodworker. These practical subjects were a neat diversion in my rather predictable crappy curriculum. I excelled at English and bumbled along in the middle of the road in every other subject. One teacher, Mr Green, was a beacon of encouragement and brilliance to whom I owe a huge debt. He was another Mollie Newell and I loved him. He wore oversized tweed jackets with patches on the elbows and carried a battered briefcase a bit like mine. He always smiled with his eyes closed when I handed in my homework, as if he knew it was going to be good. I was on a roll, and after a few months of plodding around on my own, I finally made friends.

Mine was not a tight band of best mates but rather a varied group of individuals, stragglers if you will, who were yet to find their people and whom I could chat to over lunch or meet up with outside of school for a Wimpy. Essentially, at my school the girls were divided into two groups: one small select band whose outstanding results meant they were bound for Oxbridge and academic success, and the majority of us who were being taught primarily how to make pineapple upside-down cake and how to pin a terry nappy on a dolly without simultaneously giving it a naval piercing. For me, these classes were redundant for two reasons: first, the advent of the disposable nappy in a world where plastic consumption was yet to be confirmed as a life-altering, ocean-clogging, fish-strangling, planet-destroying fact and second, I hate pineapple.

Joking is easy, but being in the not-so-smart, not-so-sporty, not-so-popular club helped cement the thoughts that I was just not enough. By the very nature of my placing on a particular table or in a particular set, I was being judged and my averageness cloaked me in inadequacy. I was frustrated at school, knowing in my head that I was smarter than I was able to express in exams and not knowing how I could convince the world that this was the case.

Lying in bed at night, I would feel the tingle of frustration at all the things I thought I might be capable of, like writing and travelling, yet knowing it was highly unlikely that I would achieve them. I wanted to be a writer who could weave tales of magic and I wanted to see my books in a library, but how? It felt easier to keep this dream to myself and to quietly pop my stories into my filing cabinets, rather than invite any Blightesque condescension that would only have confirmed my deepest fear: that for a girl like me, it just wasn't possible.

It made me quieter, a little less certain about responding to questions posed in class; it suppressed my desire to *ask* questions for fear of ridicule.

If I arrived home with less sparkle than I had set off with that morning or more aches and pains than I was comfortable with, a bar of chocolate or a double helping of pudding would take the edge off, fill a gap. My parents and both sets of grandparents were the last generations, I think, who encouraged us to clear our heavily laden plates and then as a reward – we got to have pudding. Oh my God, double whammy! You had to eat every single calorie on an already groaning plate and as a reward – you got more food!

And we are not talking about the slightly healthier puddings of today, which might constitute yoghurt or a piece of fruit; we are talking about the school-dinner puds of the 1970s, which my great-nan with her pub-cooking skills excelled at. Syrup or treacle steamed suet pudding with more treacle or syrup poured over the top. Chocolate sponges with a thick gooey chocolate middle that was molten lava in your mouth. Wide wedges of apple pie in a cinnamon-spiced syrup with a flaky or puff pastry topping that had browned sugar sitting in little clusters on the outer edge. Lemon meringue pies with a Mont Blanc of towering white meringue that was pulled from the oven in the nick of time to ensure the peaks had golden-brown summits and the zesty lemony curd filling, warm, sweet and sharp as it nestled on your tongue. Trifle! Trifle meant celebration, and part of the ritual was watching my mum or nan dig the tarnished 'trifle spoon' into the layers of cream sprinkled with hundreds and thousands, fruit, sponge and jelly. And if we were really lucky, that big old spoon would make a fart noise as it travelled back to the top of the pud, which sent my brothers and me into apoplectic fits of laughter, naturally. And it still would. I told you I had the sense of humour of a twelve-year-old.

As if the sugar and fat content of these various marvellous confections weren't enough to get your arteries wailing in protest, each pud was topped off with either custard, ice cream or cream, or in some instances a combination of two and in the case of apple pie – all three. These delicious 'afters', as we called them, eaten with such joy, were served with ribbons of double cream that formed little lakes into which you could dip your pudding-laden spoon or pools of melting ice cream that ran down your chin as you let the sugared pastry or sponge flood your system with happiness . . .

There is no question in my mind that these tender years as I nudged twelve were when the seeds for eating for comfort, eating out of routine not hunger, and seeing food as a reward or how to show love were sown.

Now – and this is important – please don't get the idea that I am blaming my parents and grandparents for my future overeating. I am not. Not at all. They might have misguidedly conditioned me, treating me to cavities and a better than average shot at diabetes throughout my formative years, but they did so with a potent mixture of ignorance and love. My brothers and cousins were all similarly treated and none of them are overweight. And when in recent years I've been knocking back rounds of toast and butter like it was going out of fashion and drinking tins of fizz instead of water, my overindulgent relatives were nowhere to be seen.

I wasn't overweight. My overeating was countered by miles of walking to and from school and routine exercise both in and out of school: bike riding, playing outside, running from my brothers, who were most likely lobbing something at me as this was one of their favourite pastimes. Still is – at family occasions I often have to dodge an incoming cushion!

But as puberty hit, I like most experienced a sea change in how I began to view myself. I started to be hyper-aware not only of the clothes I wore and my dorky haircut and shoes, but more fundamentally of how I was constructed – my big wrists, wide hips, thick thighs and a sticky-out bum. And I took the first steps down the dark and dismal road of body comparison, looking at the long-limbed, lithe, lovely girls who swayed as they danced like delicate tall trees while I clumped and tripped around the school hall in my pork pies – more of a sturdy oak. That spotty-chinned, hormone-laden twilight betwixt child and adulthood is a tricky enough time for most of us to navigate, and for me it was certainly when feelings of low self-esteem began to take a firmer hold, branching out and growing stronger like that apple tree I worried might grow in my gut, until it gripped me in a stranglehold.

Increased self-scrutiny and introspection became my preoccupation, as my body leapfrogged, or as in my case stuttered, towards becoming a woman. Practising how to hold my stomach in when walking, angling my face so I looked slimmer, wishing for narrower hips and hiding my smile became the norm.

Along with this wave of doubt, I felt my dreams of becoming a writer swirl down the plughole with the toothpaste foam. I was still no closer to figuring out *how* was I going to get to write stories when it felt success and the arts was the preserve of the lithe-limbed girls whose parents knew people . . . I just wasn't pretty enough or privileged enough. Maybe Mrs Blight was right. I needed to think of plan B.

On the mental health scale, I was nowhere near depression, but was certainly a little low, thoughtful and preoccupied as I navigated the beginnings of puberty, prompting questions from my mum:

'What's up, Dolly?' she'd ask.

'Nothing.'

'You sure?'

'Yep.'

'You can tell me anything.'

'I know, Mum.'

And I did know this, but whether I *wanted* to tell her anything was another matter. First, I wanted to keep negativity from her – she had a lot to cope with, keeping all the plates of home spinning, juggling four kids ranging in age from me approaching teenage and little Nicky who was a toddler, as well as holding down a part-time job in a shoe shop on the High Street, while my dad worked all the hours God sent to keep us fed, clothed, safe and happy in our little bubble. They were busy and doing their best and I was aware enough of the strain of their everyday lives not to bring an element of worry to it. And second, I didn't know how to phrase all that ailed me. Were my worries petty? Insignificant? Legitimate?

I'm not clever enough. I'm not pretty enough. I don't know how to make people understand that I am capable of more. I can be a writer, I'm sure of it, but I don't think anyone will take me seriously, I don't think I'll ever get the chance . . . And my back hurts, Mum, sometimes more than hurts, when I get in and out of the bath, I feel a sharp pain that makes me cry.

When I'd spoken before to the school nurse at check-ups and occasionally to my parents about my aches and growing pains, my descriptions were vague and non-specific, and I could see by my parents' expressions that they were at a loss for what to suggest. I figured there was little to be done; I just had to wait for the growing pains to be over.

This low hum of melancholy and trying to fathom my internal anxiety was tricky for me. Where did I fit? What kind of teenager or woman was I going to be? The women who popped up on my childhood TV screen were either sexy or comical – think Daisy Duke in *The Dukes of Hazard* or the comical, hapless Olive from *On the Buses*. I certainly wasn't Daisy Duke material so did that make me Olive? Wasn't there a happy middle ground for girls like me who were neither? Or girls like me who thought they might be a bit Daisy one day and then a whole lot of Olive the next?

New pyjamas always were and always will be a cause for celebration. This picture is quite poignant for me as it was just before my whole world came crashing down . . .

And then came a real kick in the tits for me. Actually, tits is probably a bit high, aim lower, in fact just below my bikini line and you are getting close.

Chapter Four

'PLAN B'

One of the things I most admired in the cool girls at school was how they walked, that knowing, hip-swaying shimmy that was as smooth as it was alluring. My efforts to imitate it, however, made me look more like a lopsided penguin than siren. The pork pie shoes had long gone, thank the lord! But it was a whole lot harder to get rid of my clomping gait. The fact that no one in my family seemed overly fussed by it meant that even though I embarrassingly suffered with a bad back in my tender years, thinking of it as an 'old person' thing, and I found sitting on a floor almost impossible, I got by. Partaking in 'Physical Education' as and when I could, I managed by going slowly and resting often, much to the annoyance of the PE staff who would shake their heads and ask why I just wasn't *trying* . . . I was trying, even if it didn't look like it.

My physical awkwardness and discomfort seemed to reach a peak as I hit thirteen. It was 1981, when the country was going nuts for the fairy-tale love affair between 'Charles & Di'. Their engagement sent a quiver of joy through many adolescent girls: '*See, it's not just a Disney dream! Princes really do fall in love with shy girls, and they will live happily ever after . . .'* It gave me hope. I too was awkward: could I bag a prince?

It's a year that sticks in my memory for the above, but also for something far more personal. For those of you who have never experienced a brain-splitting, stomach-clenching, breath-taking hit of pain – lucky you and I hope it is forever so. And for those of you who have, I'm sure you will understand when I say it changes you. Or at least it changed me.

I remember the first time. The first day. I was nearly thirteen and had returned to my primary school along with my mum to see my little brother Paul in a play. It was early afternoon, a warm day and there were rows of low benches for the audience to sit on. The kind that often line the edge of a school gym.

My mum sat down. I sidled into the row and went to sit next to her and that's when my whole world was turned upside down. Bending low, I felt something give, and the next thing I knew I was lying on the floor. I had distinctly felt something snap, break, and my entire body shook as it tried to come to terms with the all-encompassing sharp stab of pain that lanced my back, pelvis and hips, but also travelled down my legs and up under my ribs, around my gut.

My world was reduced to the white-hot searing bolt that scared me into silence and made it almost impossible for me to take a breath. Praying, willing it to stop, I concentrated on the pain and kept my eyes closed, as if I could transport myself away because it was too much, more than I knew I could handle, or at least that's what I thought. I couldn't move and could barely speak for fear of even the tiniest movement. Taking small, quick breaths, apparently, I murmured, whimpered, but I don't remember doing it. My skin was covered in a hot sweat, and I thought I might die. I didn't know how a body survived hurting that much. My limbs shook. I wanted

57

to coil up into a little ball as if this might help, but I couldn't because even the smallest movement was agony.

It was shocking and I didn't know what to do. It felt as if it went on forever. I vaguely remember Mum yelping in alarm then crying, then the scrape of the benches being pushed aside and the faces of adults looming over me. Then the sound of an ambulance siren . . . but mostly I remember the constant pulse of pain. And it was this sensation I concentrated on, the rhythm of it, trying to ride it, control it, and not the fact that I was lying on the ground or that 4A were waiting in the wings jostling their song sheets.

Sucking on great lungfuls of gas and air, I felt each movement, each jolt of the trolley on which I'd been strapped, each bump on the path, which was agony-inducing. I arrived at the district hospital for X-rays and examinations, where a team of doctors quickly confirmed that my pelvis was broken, or more accurately, crumbled, at the front.

If you think of the pelvic ring with the sacroiliac joints at the back and the symphysis pubis at the front, mine had a whacking great gap in the front – a lot like being in the full throes of labour. It was as I bent down low to sit that it finally did what it had been threatening to do for some time and gave way.

The surgeon explained to my parents (Dad had rushed to the hospital from work, the boys were with neighbours) that I had a congenital defect which, I have no doubt, was not aided by my rather traumatic birth. My parents sat either side of the hospital bed, shaking their heads in disbelief and distress, each gripping my hand as if they could will me better. If finger squeezing, telling me it was all going to be okay and crying was the solution, I would have somersaulted off that bed and down the hill all the way home.

Sadly, and obviously, the solution was rather more invasive: surgery. I was ambivalent towards the suggestion, not afraid as I might have imagined, largely because I just wanted the pain to go away and would have agreed to anything, but also because I was completely unaware of what an operation would entail or the aftermath. It was, I was told, unusual to see such an 'injury' in a person so young and many of the intervention solutions which were common practice were designed to suit an older, frailer person, whose injury had occurred after a fall and for whom, one supposes rather arrogantly, limitation of movement might not be quite so impairing. They were definitely not designed to suit a young girl about to embark on teenage life. One consultant had seen something similar in skiers. Nowadays, I am sure medical advancements are such that my treatment might be less brutal and more effective, but this was 1981 – the days when a knee injury or ACL rupture could end the career of a footballer rather than see them restored to the pitch in a matter of weeks or months.

I can't talk about this episode in my life without mentioning one significant consequence and something that has affected me my whole life. I've never shared this publicly, the simple fact that the numerous surgeries, which were invasive and on the face of it quite barbarous, all started with a scalpel being taken to the area just below my bikini line on my mons pubis (I'll wait while you Google that) and the end result is that this part of me is a little, well . . . butchered, for want of a better word.

My bikini area, I knew, was supposed to be beautiful, groomed, attractive and desirable; one quick glance beneath the bandages and I knew it was anything but. I woke up after the first operation, aged thirteen, feeling quite bereft that my body, especially such an intimate part of my body, bore this puckered, ugly, centimetre-wide scar that looked like a zipper. It had a dozen or so large metal staples along it and looked Frankensteinian at best. When the staples were removed, I was left with a bumpy, uneven track that had no sensation at all, like any other thick rind of scar. It felt and feels otherworldly, not part of me. I felt sick, literally sick, the first time

I saw it; there was metal in my skin. IN MY SKIN! The irony is not lost on me that there was a whole lot more metal and gruesome shenanigans going on under the skin, but this was visible, tangible and so very ugly. I felt horrified at the prospect of anyone else seeing it. *I* didn't want to see it. Sweet Jesus, I was already worried about no one wanting to pick me and now this?

Sadly, I didn't feel I could mention it to anyone. Was I being silly? It was after all only a vagina, but in a house where we couldn't even say the word, how was I to begin and even if I had found the confidence, what in the world could anyone do about it? I knew I was still only at the beginning of my surgeries, that much had been made clear. The surgeon had explained that rebuilding a crumbly, unstable pelvis felt a lot like trial and error and so the situation was likely to get worse before it got better. By concentrating on writing stories in my head, without the confidence to commit them to paper, I managed to allay my worries about this, calmly concentrating on the words I spun rather than what lay ahead. It was how I coped.

I was far from comfortable mentioning my scarring to anyone and no one mentioned it to me. No one. Not ever. It was just something I had to figure out. It's odd to me now as an adult that no one thought to talk to my young self about the fact that the front of her bikini area was going to be altered/disfigured, but they didn't. My scar bothered me, embarrassed me, of course it did. But I was at least reassured by the fact that it was hidden inside my pants and I would never ever want to show it to anyone. Ever. Until I *did* want to show it to someone . . . and I felt mortified, ashamed. A little freakish.

A further seven or so surgeries, all with a similar entry point of just above or just below the original scar, meant that the front of my lady bits, far from being alluring, smooth or even sexy, looked like someone had carved out a noughts and crosses grid in such a sensitive place. It further changed my relationship with my body. I hated to look at this part of me in the mirror and while I was grateful for the medical interventions that helped me walk more normally, as I got older, not liking my sexual area and not wanting others to see it was a big, big deal.

Being that kid in the school year who was in and out of hospital marked me as different, and my peers were either kind and protective or else avoided me, as if they were entirely unable to relate to my life. After each operation, I'd return nervously to school, but it felt like no time at all until I was back in hospital, meaning that each time I headed back into the classroom felt like starting over, catching up. The friendships I'd formed became flaky and my oldest friend, loneliness, came a visitin'. I took solace in reading, but you knew that, right?

My young teens should have been the time of my life, but instead, I spent months and months lying flat in various hospital beds in plaster or with an external metal frame screwed to my bones and sticking out of my nether regions or having metal plates affixed to my pelvis or carbon-fibre ties looped inside me and any other number of weird and wonderful operations that surgeons performed with skill and no doubt fingers crossed, as much of it was experimental. The whole drawn out experience was restricting, inconvenient and isolating. I've thought long and hard how to cover the medical interventions that eventually saw me (almost) restored and to be honest it could be a whole book – so instead I will try to summarise here:

Ten operations in five hospitals.

Several consultants up and down the country, from York to Bristol, who all tried different things to stabilise my pelvis and help me lead a 'normal' life.

Physiotherapy, hydrotherapy, crutches, hobbling, crying . . .

And then being sent home to recover.

This was my life aged between thirteen and eighteen.

How best can I describe those years? I think I will draw on my own mother's vernacular so beautifully expressed.

'It was shit really.'

And it was. Totally shit.

If you've ever been caught in the breakers, where one wave knocks you to the ocean floor and you scrabble to your feet and take a breath before the next one comes along and pulls you back under and each time it happens it gets harder and harder to stand up because you are tired and breathless and afraid . . . that was my life. Every surgery was the last I would need, YEEEEEHAAAAA! I'd go home with a sore body and a partially restored spirit to a bed made up in the corner of the dining room, so I didn't have to tackle the stairs. I'd return to school with the aid of crutches and navigate school life the best I could. I knew I was getting better each time when I was able to climb the stairs slowly, steadily, and Mum would help me bathe . . . until something happened and my pain would again increase, movement became stilted and it became obvious it *wasn't* the last surgery, and further intervention would be needed.

The incidents that saw me head back to the operating table were many – here are a few of my favourites: after sitting awkwardly on a beanbag, tripping over on grass, bending backwards to pick up my pencil case, falling down a step and on one occasion sneezing – yes really! And I would feel the whole thing collapse again, taking a moment to compose myself, breathing through the pain and trying to hold back the dark tide of disappointment that I thought might drown me, before tearfully and guiltily calling for my parents to get me to the hospital.

Why guiltily? I watched them struggle to keep the wheels turning when I was ill. It meant a constant round of babysitters for the boys, tiring bus trips and long walks for my mum, who visited me every single day, sometimes twice, and Dad would come to the hospital straight from work. Mum wasn't able to work when I was home recovering, and she looked after me during the day. The worry, the emotional toll of having a kid you couldn't fix . . . it was hard, and I knew it.

I felt terrible, seeing their tired faces paint on a smile as they sat for hours by the side of my bed. Relatives joined the visiting pool and provided a wonderful lift to my long, long days. My grandad would try and make me laugh, my nan would tell me about *her* trips to hospital and I remember my Uncle Tony, a tough nut to put it mildly, crying rather a lot at the sight of me – I didn't know what to do or say. He then accidentally pulled the red emergency cord instead of the light switch!

School friends would sometimes pop in, but the exchange was awkward. I felt embarrassed, prostrate in my hospital gown with a bag of wee on a stand attached to my catheter on full view, vulnerable and exposed while they stood around the bed in lip gloss, glancing at the clock. It was hard to join in. I had little to say as my days were not only all the same but were also incredibly dull. To hear of their excursions to Brent Cross to go shopping and their gossip only heightened my alienation, my difference. All I wanted was not to be dealing with something like this at all, to be back at home fighting for space on the crowded sofa while we watched Saturday night telly, to be with my small group of friends, to be invited to a party, to be drinking Babycham and trying to figure out who I was and practising with that make-up I'd had so very little interest in.

But I was stuck, immobile, in a great deal of discomfort and properly fed up at the fact that while my peers were schlepping off to the school disco to snog boys called Darren and Dean, I was lying flat and being fed goodies by an endless stream of visiting family who wanted to make me feel a little bit better. My mates were waiting on dates and trips to the park; I was waiting for another painkiller, X-ray or visit from my mum and dad.

If I had felt removed and inferior to the cool clique of girls in the years above, with no hope of looking and living like them, I now felt this way about the girls I was friends with. I got left behind. And this wasn't their fault. We were thirteen. It was hard in the days before mobile phones and the internet to catch up with someone who was cloistered away in a hospital bed for much of the time, and they were young, quite rightly grabbing life and running with it. Realistically, who wants to sit in a stinky ward while the clock ticks and a cloak of awkwardness muffles every topic of conversation?

My brothers would be hauled in to visit me wearing expressions of bewilderment. They too didn't know what to say, whether to muck about, make me laugh, and we were far too young for small talk. I hated how the family, *my* family, got to leave as a little group, waving from the corridor, while I lay immobile, blinded by the overhead strip light and listening to the squeak of the nurse's shoes on the shiny linoleum. In my mind, these trips in and out of hospital have merged together in my thoughts and it feels like I was there for years, staring at the ceiling . . .

I cried a lot at night. I cried because the dull thud of pain that started in my pelvis and radiated out along my hips and down my back was at times unbearable and I cried because I wanted to be at home. The pillows were covered in plastic that sat beneath the pillowslip and I remember how it crackled, the feel of it wet on my face where the tears soaked through the cotton and pooled on the surface. Everything felt unfair. It was as if the whole world was having a party to which I wasn't invited or running a race while I was in the stands, watching.

I would have been desperately lonely were it not for books. Schoolbooks allowed me to do assignments remotely, and then there was my beloved fiction. There was a whole world waiting to take me away from the discomfort and the reality of my situation. In terms of reading material, my tastes had changed a little and aged fourteen, I devoured the book that would, in ways I could never imagine, change my life. That book was *The Thorn Birds* by Colleen McCullough.

Even writing the title has brought a smile to my face. How I envy anyone who hasn't read it, knowing all that is waiting for you and the joy you will find inside the pages! Set predominantly in Australia, it is the epic tale of the Cleary family. Spanning lifetimes, it has the lot: unrequited love, lust, Machiavellian intervention, tragedy, sweet joy and redemption. I loved it then. I love it now. I will love it always. If ever I'm asked which is my favourite book of all time *The Thorn Birds* trips from my lips without hesitation.

Not only was it an introduction to love and sex that was not syrupy or sanitised, it was the first time I had been enthralled by a book, entranced by a book, taken over by it . . . I wasn't just reading about the searing Australian midday sun; I could feel it. Taking every step with Meggie, the main character, I knew that if I could ever write a story that made someone feel as Colleen McCullough had made me feel then I'd die happy. But how, how could I go from recumbent, broken teen to bestselling author?

The answer came quickly. I couldn't. I hadn't lived. Hadn't travelled. Hadn't stood unaided for the longest time, what on earth did I have to write about? This realisation filled me with sadness. I continued to pop my stories into my mental filing cabinets, getting them out occasionally and losing myself in them when the night felt long and it was too dark to read an actual book. Walking was a problem, shimmying was impossible, and now my dream of becoming a writer felt entirely out of reach too.

Chapter Five

'A Period Drama'

When I hit fourteen, I'd put on a bit of weight due to my inactivity, but wasn't overweight and in truth, having a less than perfect body was something I was used to. The fact that I could barely walk was far more pressing to me than the size of my waist. I was just glad to be at home, out of hospital and able to socialise a little and go outside. I got highlights in my hair and thought they were fantastic. They might have been no more than a few measly streaks of blonde in my rather mousy mop, but in my mind, I was practically Debbie Harry.

I did, however, continue to compare my jiggly thighs with the thighs of girls in *Jackie* and *Blue Jeans* magazines. And I started to look at the bodies of the girls at school when we went swimming and realised that I was not tiny like them, but was in fact chunky, wider, big-framed and still clumsy . . . I didn't like looking like that but wasn't quite sure what I could do about it. Not that it stopped me swimming and indeed diving – which of course came naturally to me as it was how I had entered the world. Swimming was something that between surgeries I could do with ease, the weight-bearing nature of it meant I could exercise without damaging myself and I loved it. Plus, when I was in the water no one could see how I walked or wobbled; in fact they saw a swimmer like any other and it really boosted my self-esteem.

My mum and dad continued to tell me that I could be anything, do anything, achieve anything and go anywhere I could imagine. That the sky was the limit, and it was all within my grasp if I worked hard enough to make it happen. No one mentioned the fact that it was going to be jolly hard to achieve a fabulous life if I kept getting dragged back to the operating table for lengthy operations that would see me immobile for months. It seemed my family were painting on a happy face and trying to help me see the positives, and this too I understand and when I became a parent, I did something very similar, as if with enough positive reinforcement and cups of tea, I could magic everything better.

And what I didn't admit to at that point was that what I wanted to *achieve* and would regularly *imagine* was being as thin as my friend Helen and having a straight-up-and-down-shaped body and not the curves that had started to appear at my hips, waist and bust.

I was fourteen and back in school after some gruelling surgery, when I became desperate, *desperate* to start my periods, looking at girls in my year who walked with a swagger to the girls' loo, asking in not so hushed tones, 'Anyone got a tampon?'

Oh! A tampon! How exotic! How glorious! I had no idea what you did with one, but the word itself was so grown up, so cool. I wanted to fit in. I wanted to be like every other girl, and I longed to be a tampon-toting teen and finally shake off the last vestige of childhood. That would be some day when I could walk with my shoulders back, head held high and a sanitary towel and tampon or two chucked into my satchel (I'd finally ditched the briefcase) for good measure. And if one happened to roll out down the aisle of the bus? No worries, I'd stride confidently forward, retrieve it and hold it aloft.

'Oh, this old thing? It's a tampon. Because I have periods.'

It wasn't only this outward, physical sign of maturity that I awaited, but also the fact that I could legitimately – and this was kind of a big deal – ask my mum to scribble me a note excusing me from cross-country, in which I was still expected to participate when able, even if it was only at a slow walking pace. As no one in their right mind would run or even walk with a period, right? Was that even legal? And obviously these questions did not apply to the women in the panty liner/tampon commercials – when they came on the television my grandad would leave the room. These beaming, bouncy, beautiful women were period superheroes, who not only ran, but roller-skated, skydived and laughed as if this bloody reminder of their fertility was a gift and not like they were suffering from cramps, bloating and low mood.

Not that I was falling for it.

Urgh, cross-country! While I was studious, trying my best to catch up on what I had missed academically, this was an event I would take any opportunity to avoid. This has nothing to do with the fact that I wasn't that sporty. I didn't dislike PE – not at all. At my own pace and when in reprieve from the pain of my condition, I liked gently trotting around the gym or throwing a netball and was a more than proficient swimmer, if I do say so myself. I particularly liked putting on the PE kit as it made me feel 'normal' and I always tried to adapt and do *something* while my peers tore around with their black slip-on gym shoes stuttering on the varnished floor. But for those like me who were body conscious and not rake thin, the cross-country run was nothing short of torturous, brutal. The only way to be 'excused' the lesson was if you had a period and more importantly, a note from your parent/guardian, explaining that you had a period. My senior school was a stone's throw from an arterial route that now links up with the M25, and even the words cross-country were enough to put a quake of fear into my limbs. Why? Where to begin . . .

The early eighties were a time before health and safety had been invented and many adults were yet to locate their moral compass when it came to the rights of the young. A hangover I guess from the generation who with one foot in the war years, were raised by parents who had been weaned on the rather barbaric Victorian idea that 'children should be seen and not heard'. It was a time when teachers smoked in the staff room and pupils smoked in the toilets, when, cruelly, the cane was given (at my school only to the boys) for misdemeanours such as insolence, not bringing in money for a school trip or forgetting their PE kit. The fact that some parents couldn't afford a school trip or PE kit was neither here nor there. A world where the soft loo roll we take for granted was non-existent and we had to wipe our bums and down below bits with squares of tracing paper dispensed from a cardboard box with a gap in the front. Actually, wiped is the wrong word . . . smeared. Yes, unfortunately, smeared is the word I need and anyone of a similar age will know exactly to what I refer. A world where primary school kids were given, in my humble opinion, a gut-churning small warm bottle of milk in break time, the little green straw of which was plonked satisfyingly through the silver foil by a smarmy milk monitor. And if you claimed to be a vegetarian in the school canteen they might, if you were lucky, put a bit of lettuce as a concession on top of your Spam fritter. I can still recall the smell of the place on Spam fritter day: a heady meat fragrance with undertones of rancid frying oil and the whiff of old chips.

Oh, and we had to run in big, tight knickers. I can see, for professional runners, the knicker method is vital to streamline performance and offer uniformity across teams, but we are talking about a bunch of teens clod-hopping their way towards the finish line on a damp Wednesday afternoon. Completely different. I should also point out that this was in the days before big knickers were worn under sheer skirts for a night out, before bralettes and micro shorts and before we were used to seeing a thousand bikini shots in the sidebars of shame in digital newspapers. Our bodies were pretty much under wraps for the majority of the time in the cold climes a little north of London in which we lived, only revealing our skin to allow it to burn at the start of the summer holidays, in order to cultivate a Californian tan after the oil and peel phase. Yes, I know, I know . . . my stomach flips to think of slathering my face, MY FACE! It's as horrific as it is upsetting to remember. Turns out that when it comes to sun damage on our skin, ignorance was most definitely not bliss.

And yet, despite this rather modest life, when it came to cross-country all the girls were herded into the stinky changing rooms where we stepped into our big knickers, bottle green with a gold stripe up the side, in case you were wondering, and a yellow Airtex polo shirt. A whistle would then blow and we had to run, or in my case walk, up the side of the main road, not that there was a pavement or a path, no sirree! We had to navigate the clumpy grass verges and at pinch points dip down onto the tarmac or run across laybys, before heading across a field, through a housing estate and back through the school gates. Now, when I say a main road, I mean a main road, a busy road where 7.5-tonne trucks, articulated lorries, transit vans and coachloads of London day trippers heading home, raced past, all of them keen to honk their horns, shout obscenities and leer lasciviously at a gaggle of schoolgirls running along in their knickers. Can't think for the life of me why . . . but I remember feeling the hot tears of shame gather at the back of my throat every time I had to do the walk.

And so yes, the prospect of not being able to run, all down to that legitimate, hastily scribbled scrap of paper from my mum declaring I was on my 'monthlies' – I couldn't wait! Not only that, but the note was also the best and most public way to announce the arrival of your periods and what was the point of getting your periods if no one knew about it? It felt to me like everyone in my school year had 'started' so why not me? I prayed to the period gods to give me the gift of menstruation. And on one sunny June day in 1982 they were listening. I woke to spotting and the small suggestion of a gripping pain in my gut. This was it! I was about to board the period train and I couldn't wait to see where it took me.

I loped down the stairs, heart hammering as I hollered at my mum, 'Mum! Mum, help me! Help! I've got my period!'

I think my dad raised his newspaper over his face, the oldest of my brothers pulled awkward faces and there was a pause around the breakfast table while everyone tried to figure out how to continue, Cocoa Krispie-laden spoons were held aloft mid-mouthful.

'Okay, darling, well, congratulations!' She knew how much this meant to me. 'Now, let's pop upstairs and get you set for the day.'

I flounced back up the stairs as far as I was able, yes flounced. Probably stopping to pose, hand on hip. Only the night before I might have been a young girl, munching on cola-flavoured Spangles, wearing hand-knitted Aran jumpers made by my nan and watching *Why Don't You?* while I waited eagerly for my subscription of *Bunty* to drop through the letterbox, but as I climbed those stairs, I shucked off that skin. It was a glorious and triumphant moment. I was in the race; I was invited to the party! I knew I was permanently trading *Bunty* for *Jackie*, would be swapping Spangles for Hubba Bubba, I'd wander into Chelsea Girl and pick my own clothes, and I would, finally, have sanitary protection in my satchel. Why? Because I had started! HALLELUJAH!

Flippin' 'eck. Four hours later and I knew exactly where the period train was taking me: off to bed with a hot-water bottle and a slack handful of Feminax. I changed my mind, *instantly*. A gift? I could see why they called it the curse! It was uncomfortable, sticky, slightly painful, messy and under no circumstances could I, according to my nan, who like my aunt and half the neighbours, had been informed of the latest development in my downstairs area, go swimming or wash my hair! Yes, really.

I don't know what bothered me most, not being able to swim in the public pool on the other side of the park or not being able to wash and style my hair, which was at the time somewhat of a preoccupation, as I struggled, in the days before serum and straighteners to tame my locks and perfect my Farrah Fawcett flick. Well, no swimming meant my summer activity of choice was scuppered. It occurred to me then that maybe my nan was right; if I did have my own swimming pool no one could ban me from swimming, any time of the day or night, period or not. And swimming was important to me, often the only place I could move easily. I looked out of the bedroom window at our postage-stamp-sized lawn where the rabbit run was moved twice weekly to a new patch of grass, where the bike lay on its side and our old stunt ramp sat in pride of place and knew there was no space for a swimming pool, even if funds had allowed.

Not being able to wash my hair or swim was a setback, but was small fry, however, compared to what happened next. I'd learned all I needed to about how my body functioned as a young girl, via regular chit chats with my mum and a small cardboard-covered book recommended by the school nurse. The book was preoccupied with periods and getting pregnant and was crudely illustrated. I remember crying myself to sleep one night, worrying that I was a yellow arrow short of perfection as one picture showed just this thing pointing downwards from the stomach and ending at the word 'vagina'. Now, I don't know about you, but I grew up in a house where the word vagina was rarely used and certainly never in polite company. Instead, my vagina, indeed *any* vagina, was referred to as, but not exclusively, privates, noony, twinkle, Mary, front botty, girl's willy, fanny and on one odd occasion: tuppence. How ridiculous is that? Apologies to all Marys out there and all Tuppences. I did meet a Tuppence in my twenties and even though I was a fully fledged adult, it took all my strength not to laugh. The only thing that halted my hysteria was the thought of having to explain to Tuppence why I was laughing.

This crucial centre of reproduction and sexual pleasure was never called by its name, which as a young adult caused me no end of issues. And not only then, but in later years when I visited the family planning clinic or my GP with questions of a delicate nature. This is such an erosion of self and bodily acceptance, the dumbing down, the embarrassment. But as I say: different times. Now, I say it loud and proud, VAGINA! I have a VAGINA! Although I must confess to still being a little shy around the topic in polite company.

So, the moment had arrived: I was with period! Toll the bell! What came next, however, was not as I had imagined it, not at all. My mother was, quite unlike her, a little flustered.

'No, darling, you can't use a tampon.'

'Why not?' I was flummoxed. 'Julie and Sarah and Michelle use them!'

'And if Julie, Sarah and Michelle jumped off a bridge would you do that too?'

I always took my time in answering, knowing that if it meant I was as pretty, slim, popular, sporty and cool as them, I might just consider it.

'But *why*, Mum?' I whined.

'Because . . . Because I think you need to have . . . or at least had one or two . . . They are not for little girls who . . .' she gabbled, landing on her favoured cover-all that was as definitive as it was irritating, 'because I said so.'

My brain raced; what did she suggest I use in lieu of the coveted tampon? What was to be my period protection of choice? Not that there was any choice about it. God, surely not the bag of rags my nan had had to endure. Or worse, the moss and bark I had read about in the far reaches of the earth? No, it was a contraption of a different kind.

Ladies, one word: sanitary belt.

Okay, two words, but you get my point. My mum produced a pale blue elastic belt from which hung two long straps and on the ends of these straps sat two little plastic anchor shapes that dangled ominously. *Where did they go?* I imagined one possibly going up my bum, but the other end? Nope, no clue. I then watched, fascinated, horrified, as she opened a small, flat cardboard box with Dr White's written on it and pulled out a flat, gauze-covered pad that had two crudely sewn loops at either end. These loops fitted over the plastic anchors (phew!) and the whole thing was designed to go around my waist with the pad sitting on its stays inside my pants, nestling against my privates, my noony, my twinkle, my front botty, my girl's willy, my fanny, my tuppence . . . Oh, for the love of God! My VAGINA!

I was silent, traumatised and fascinated in equal measure. What was inside this pad exactly? Curious, I dismantled one and was surprised that the inner core was no more than folded cardboard-type fibres that looked and felt very much like packaging, but certainly not something I wanted next to any area of my body, least of all such a delicate area. The cardboard innards were wrapped in a thin cotton-wool layer and that was covered in the kind of gauze/netting you might see over a strapped-up wound.

Still, what did I know, a mere novice in the world of menstruation? Surely my mum knew best on this topic if no other. She had been having periods for a hundred years at least (she was thirty at the time. Ancient). So, I put my faith in her suggestion and shoved her out of the bathroom. After a warm bath, leaving my hair unwashed, obvs, I gingerly stepped into the elasticated contraption, pulled up my knicknacks and tried to walk normally. Now, without getting overly graphic, have you ever tried to walk with a pack of playing cards lodged sideways in your panties? No, me neither, but I imagine it to be similar.

I walked John Wayne style into school on the Monday morning, feeling none of the swagger I might have imagined, but instead grubby and insecure, expecting my cardboard sanitary towel to ping loose from its plastic anchors at any point and fire across the chemistry lab, knocking out a flaming Bunsen burner and landing on the head of the model skeleton in the corner, who wore our school tie. At least *he* was adhering to one of the items on the uniform list.

Luckily it didn't happen, but what *did* happen was I told Julie, Sarah and Michelle that I was now one of the gang and asked them how they coped with the uncomfortable contraption threatening, with one false move, to rocket out of my knickers. They produced a paper-wrapped tampon with the word slender on it, commenting that they had wondered why I was walking a bit funny, or funnier than usual.

So, off to the girls' loo we trooped, where someone in my year was having their ear pierced in the corner with the aid of an ice cube and a cork with a needle in it, sterilised by the flickering flame of a disposable lighter. I didn't mention the illegality of the act, not when I had more pressing issues to deal with.

And with my classmate's patient tuition, one leg up on the loo seat, one planted firmly on the floor, a few tears and the hot poker of shame lancing my pride, I left the cubicle quite changed. I'd lost my virginity to a tampon.

The sanitary belt was unceremoniously dumped in the bin. My street cred was high. And with my walk restored, my Farrah Fawcett hair flicks had never been so mercilessly swished. In that moment, I was like every other girl. I was not that girl with the crutches. There were no taunts, as there sometimes was about my walk. No cries of 'spastic, spastic, hips are made of plastic' – a catchy tune and quite inventive too. And one that cut me to the quick every time I heard it chanted by a certain group of boys whenever I hobbled by. The arseholes. No, in that moment, I was just Mandy and I had used a tampon.

I might now have been in the period club, but was actually far from one of the gang. I lost count of the times I sat in front of various medics in the numerous follow-up appointments, 'post' the last and 'pre' the next operation, usually on a chair between my parents, who smiled and winked at me, trying to reassure me that everything was going to be okay, nothing to worry about.

But it turned out I had plenty to worry about. The congenital defect in my pelvis had two major impacts on my life. First, I still walked/walk a little like a listing pregnant duck. I gave up the idea of ever sashaying. Second, I was informed, in rather hushed tones, that I would be unlikely to carry a baby to full term as my slack pelvis and dodgy joints were not strong enough to sustain a pregnancy. The doctor looked at my mum and dad as he spoke, as if what he had to say was between the three of them and I just happened to be present. In a way it helped curb my embarrassment a little; maybe this was why he didn't address me directly. He was after all talking about sex and babies and all that it entailed, and I was sandwiched between my parents! It was the equivalent of watching Sunday night TV en famille when a rudey nudey scene came on and you would suddenly need to go to the kitchen for a glass of water, waiting outside until the moment had passed . . . Only there was nowhere to go. No kitchen to escape to. I was stuck, while the conclusion was reached that the whole matter was in the future and could be addressed as and when.

'We'll just have to wait and see . . .'

In the spirit of full disclosure: I wasn't overly distressed or bothered by the fact. Not then. It felt surreal and so far from the life I lived, almost too hard to contemplate.

◆ ◆ ◆

Part and parcel of becoming a fully fledged 'teenager' was being able to work and earn my own money. This thought motivated me: no matter I might be held back physically, I was still intent on being like my dad and driving away from the house each day with my music playing as I set off to go and experience the big wide world outside the front door. I couldn't wait to be well for a long enough period to get a job, to start grafting and watch everything fall into place. Easy peasy!

It was a different world, where jobs were readily available for my peers and me, who were willing to work. It wasn't a question of could we get a job, but more a question of what job did we want. I rather liked the idea of working in a shop or a café, figuring I would have to wait until I was a grown-up to become a writer. That is, if I ever experienced enough to write about, wondering if anyone would ever be interested in a chapter about me staring at a ceiling with staples along my bikini line or my introduction to tampons . . .

I was fourteen and beyond excited, delighted in fact, when I got myself a Saturday job on a market stall selling plastic homeware and other tat.

The man who owned the stall was the cousin of someone my mum vaguely knew, a woman who lived in the neighbourhood; I'd babysat for her a couple of times. My parents no doubt felt confident that I was being looked after, as he kind of knew my family and should anything be a little beyond me, heavy lifting, standing for too long, he would understand. I don't think there was a person known to us who wasn't aware of my circumstances.

His name and every detail about him are burned in my brain. The way his long fringe fell over his eyes, his small teeth and his inability to say the letter 'R' properly. He gave me the creeps. This was based on no more than a small voice of instinct that tapped me on the shoulder and sent bolts of concern into my gut, but what exactly I was afraid of would have been hard to voice. He was friendly and smiley, a joker. If I had to summarise it, I would say he was a little starey. But was that a reason not to take a job? Because I felt he stared at me a bit?

And what if I was imagining it? I was naive, young and immature. I was also, however, keen to work and a market stall felt like a proper job, far more sophisticated than watching TV while kids slept upstairs. I chose to ignore that little voice and tell myself I was being ridiculous.

It was a job I loved – one which started at 5 a.m. and where I worked my socks off, unpacking boxes, setting up displays, standing in the cold, putting items in paper bags, counting out change, perching on a little stool when I ached badly and taking painkillers so I could push on through the afternoon, chatting to customers and revelling in the market atmosphere. We backed onto a fruit and veg stall and the family who ran it were wonderful and funny, keeping up a constant stream of hilarious banter. I felt like a grown-up. A working woman who had a life outside the front door, bring it on!

The first couple of weeks he drove me home and we spoke about the day or listened to the radio.

After my third weekend on the job, we travelled home.

I was happy.

It had been a busy day.

It was summer.

The inside of his battered van was hot and a bit grubby.

There was litter cluttered in the little dip below the windscreen – old food wrappers, paper bags and empty cigarette packets.

It smelled musty with an underlying note of diesel.

The boxes of stock were packed away in the rear.

I was wearing a denim pinafore dress and sneakers.

He drove slowly.

It was a few miles from the market to home.

He told me there was a problem with the gearbox.

I told him my dad could probably fix it, as he was good at fixing cars.

He told me to stretch out my right leg and place my foot in the gap behind the gear stick and to tell him if I felt hot air coming out of the gear stick, as that meant the engine might blow up.

I was scared. I didn't want the engine to blow up on a busy main road.

I sat with my legs wide apart, one leg twisted and with my sneaker hooked behind the gear stick, waiting to feel hot air that would mean danger, and I planned to shout out when and if I felt it. It was an angle that made my scars pull.

I never felt hot air.

I saw him unzip his jeans.

I didn't shout out.

I felt otherworldly like I wasn't really present.

I went numb and could feel my limbs shaking.

I couldn't speak.

I looked away.

I crossed my legs and I looked out of the window until we were home.

I didn't cry.

I felt my insides churning like I might vomit.

I was very scared.

I could hear my breathing in my ears like I was underwater.

I didn't really care at that point if the engine blew up.

That's what happened.

After the incident, the moment the van stopped outside his house, I ran home and went straight upstairs to hide in my bedroom. I didn't cry even then. I didn't do anything or tell anyone, didn't know what to say or how to say it, didn't want to admit to it, didn't really know exactly what had happened, but I spent weeks, months in fact, trying to process it. It was odd, confusing and scary.

I didn't turn up for my Saturday job the next week. My parents asked why I'd left, and I said I didn't like it, didn't want the job. They said it was a shame, but that it was up to me.

I still think about him on occasion, the bastard. I now know he was masturbating. Smiling and chatting to my mum and dad if they met him and his partner in the street, as if he hadn't watched me run from his van with my heart feeling like it might burst out of my chest and his grubby ten-pound note nestling in the front pocket of my pinafore for a day's work well done. I remember feeling torn, again listening to that little voice of instinct that told me to kick him in the bollocks and run, but also wanting to be polite as he was a grown-up and I was a kid, he had given me a job and he knew my mum. What a shitty thing.

I hate that it happened to me, but I know I was very lucky. I never went back into that environment because I didn't have to. I crossed the road if I ever saw him and made out he didn't exist. It was how I coped. I shut what happened away in a filing cabinet and I locked the drawer. But still, at the sight of his van my heart would beat a little too quickly and I felt sick.

I never told a soul apart from my mum, and even then, only a couple of years ago and only because we were talking about abuse and it felt timely. I swore her to secrecy. She was of course fuming that I had not told her at the time because she would have taken action. But I didn't tell her because I didn't want her to take action, didn't want her to have to conjure the horrible images that lived in my head, didn't want to give her another thing to worry about. Didn't want to cause a ripple where we lived, the nice place with the ducks, river, neat lawns and shiny cars, where everyone knew everyone else, I didn't want my dad to kill him and get into trouble.

And even all these years later, I have absolutely no doubt my dad *would* have killed him and got into trouble.

It was, however, yet another thing that put a small brick in that wall that was getting higher and higher, the one I built in my mind and hid behind. I felt a little guilty, a little dirty and I didn't know why. I felt scared, on edge and I didn't know why. What I *did* know was that I had to put the whole sordid episode behind me or there was the possibility that I might tumble into a dark place. That was how I saw it; I had two choices. Option one: stay upright, don't think about it, mention or dwell on it, and keep climbing that ladder of independence. Option two: allow yourself to face it and mentally fall right through the carpet – through the floor, through the dirt, through the rocks and water and down until you hit the darkest centre of the earth – into a place I might never be able to climb out of.

I chose option one.

Aged thirteen. Out of hospital. With Paul and Simon in our house, which was all colours of beige, a lot like living in a biscuit. A full smile. Before I stepped into that van.

Chapter Six

'The New Girl'

When I hit sixteen life was, for most of that year, on an even keel. I managed, much of the time, to consign what happened in the van to the darkest depths of my filing cabinet and was happier than I could remember, more confident than I'd ever been, thankful to be upright and mingling. My recovery after surgery was quicker, my pain not so severe and my movement much improved. This in part due to the fact that I had stopped growing.

It's a weird thing and quite hard to explain, but I only realised how much I had 'hurt' physically when the discomfort started to ebb. Unsurprisingly, with the easing of my physical discomfort came a lift to my mood and demeanour. Whenever someone asks, 'How much does it hurt?' I find it almost impossible to answer. 'Erm, more than when I got a staple in my finger but less than when I shut the same finger in the car door.' I DON'T KNOW HOW TO DESCRIBE IT! Learning to live with discomfort every day certainly normalised the sensation, even though I was never at peace with it.

I mastered the art of steeling myself to move, taking a breath before each step, tensing at times and trying to soften the muscles at others, as if I rode a roller coaster, training my body to respond accordingly and minimise the pain. The only time I couldn't manage this was when something caught me off guard, a trip, fall or misstep that would see me yell, or if someone made me jump or I moved awkwardly or quickly in my sleep. But overall, it finally felt like my body was responding to all the weird and wonderful foreign objects that were being used to lash my crumbling bones together, and I was delighted. For the first time I understood the bigger plan: that I would eventually have something in place that would mean stability, the growth of new cartilage and most important it would mean no more going under the knife, no more operations or staring at a hospital ceiling. I couldn't wait.

There were moments when the consultant's words revisited my thoughts: the fact that I would probably be unlikely to carry a baby to full term. I started to think about what this might mean, the significance of it shading thoughts of my future with a little blue. But, as I had been raised to think and my nan was fond of telling me, 'No one gets all the gifts!' Quite unlike my mum who aged sixteen was only a couple of years or so away from getting pregnant with me: that event, that *life* felt a long, long way off for me. I put it out of my head, away in another drawer of my filing cabinet, not to be opened. Not to be peeked into, not until I had to.

Some of the kids in my year were leaving school at sixteen: one to have a baby, some to go to work. One to work in her parents' takeaway, another told me he was off to sell golf equipment over the phone with his dad; he was excited. It was around this age that I began dreaming of boys who weren't dreaming of me, boys in school and who hung around in the park where we all met up. Books and boys were my preoccupation.

To be an author was still my wish, although it felt like a lofty ambition. It wasn't so much that my older family had intimated that it might be beyond me (although yes that too a bit), but more that *I* didn't truly believe it was possible and this cloaked the whole thought in embarrassment. But it didn't stop me from wishing it. In the same way I wished that I was not five foot four and that my pelvis wasn't knackered . . . I not only devoured books, but also studied the way they were written, loving nothing more than to get lost in the rhythm and pattern of the words. Hours and hours could be lost practising stories in my head, the moments of high drama, the dialogue, the settings, running them through in my mind like a movie until they were right. I still do this. Every time I read a book; I would think one of two things:

How I WISH I had written that!

Or

I think I can do better than that!

This self-belief was based on nothing more than my desire to create something as good as *The Thorn Birds*. My frustration became a secret anxiety and all because I couldn't figure out how to get out of the blocks. My parents were supportive, encouraging – 'You can be whatever you want to be!' – but this was not quite the instructional blueprint I was looking for. And did they mean this was possible in the arts too? *How* was it possible to be *whatever I wanted to be* without the first clue of how to start? If I'd wanted to work in manufacturing I could ask my dad, hairdressing or shop work, my mum. You get the idea. But publishing? Did I even understand what that was?

Not that I knew it at the time, but what I needed was a strategy for achieving, a flowchart with arrows I could follow until I arrived at point A, direction on what to do if I veered off course – jeez, didn't we all? The trouble was, among my family of dockers, engineers and stay-at-home hypochondriacs, no one had the first idea about how to write a book or get one published. Why would they? It has only been age and some small acquired wisdom that has taught me I have to create my own blueprint, design my own flowchart. Although in fairness it's more of a circular diagram that looks a lot like this:

Set your goal

If you fail, try again

Keep going, work harder

At sixteen I had a small group of friends from school who knew of my writing ambition, although I doubt they took it seriously. They knew I was good at English, it was my thing, but they, like me, were a little clueless as to how that might translate into a career. I would spend free time with them on weekends – this mainly involved gathering in any green space we could find, be it park, garden or riverbank, hanging around Camden Market trying to look chi-chi, lying in the sun at every opportunity and sitting in pub gardens trying to make our single drink last as long as the landlord's patience, as we cluttered up his establishment and spent very little cash.

It was the first time in my life that my brothers and I had entirely separate lives. I saw them at the breakfast table and in the bathroom while cleaning our teeth, but mine was a life lived outside the house whenever possible and they were, in my view, still babies. Sweet Mother of Betsy, they still played outside, did stunts and eagerly awaited the sweets Nan and Grandad bought us every Tuesday. I, meanwhile, knew the words to every Smiths song, had smoked a cigarette, dyed my hair even blonder and regularly got the Tube on my own or the bus to Brent Cross shopping mall where I'd sit outside Fenwick's department store with my mates and look at boys. I know . . . living the life.

The boy I liked went out with a willowy girl, one who walked with a shimmy. I was not and never could be her. At those moments, it felt like small consolation that I was upright at all; what was the point of all that surgery if I was always going to be part snail? But these moments of solemn introspection were brief. I'd started taking a greater interest in my appearance and decided to really look at what I was eating, understanding that if I desired willowy, the way to achieve it was not munching my way through my nan's puddings like a locust. Any flickering thoughts of inside that van, any consideration of heading back into hospital and the whisper of not being able to have kids like my friends, sent a bolt of cold right through me that could be plugged if not silenced, with grub.

I wanted to be thinner. I believed that slim was what boys wanted and I wanted them to want me. I also started taking an interest in fashion and invested in some vintage finds from Camden Market of which I was very proud: a white, pin-tucked, grandad shirt, an oversized navy, moth-eaten cashmere coat, several black items to layer and a softened, pre-loved studded belt. I thought I was the bee's knees.

Me aged sixteen. In my very favourite belt and courtesy of Sun-In getting blonder . . .

Around the same time I started to go out to the clubs of Camden, Dingwalls and the Electric Ballroom, fascinated by the emaciated-looking cool girls who hung out with the punks and the new romantics. I felt confused and conflicted about my food intake. I loved to eat, *loved* food, but didn't want to be that big girl who ate chips with the lads I hung out with. I wanted to be petite like some of my friends, as this was my idea of 'feminine' and it has, rightly or wrongly, been one that has stayed with me: the thought that the smaller I was the more feminine and attractive I would be and I wanted to be feminine, thinking I stood a better chance in the dating stakes if I was no longer a little fairy elephant. Again, I think this view was reinforced by the conversations around our dinner table, the women generally describing other women they met or saw in two ways: 'She was beautiful, really slim. A tiny little thing, elfin . . .' with narrow finger movements to demonstrate just how tiny she was.

OR

'She was a big girl, you know . . .' This accompanied by bloated cheeks and wide, splayed hands.

And yes, I did know, because I was one of them. And it filled me with shame.

Throughout my childhood and teens, my mum had music playing, usually her beloved Motown, but also one song that used to make me die a little inside. 'Fattie Bum Bum' by Carl Malcolm.

When I first heard this song, I remember cringing and feeling that the lyrics were directed at me. I know, I know, these thoughts are at best narcissistic and at worst delusional. And yet when this song used to come on the radio, which hit the charts in the mid-seventies, but was on the mainstream playlist throughout the eighties, I would feel my face colour and my pulse race at the lyrics. And the irony is not lost on me in that when I heard this song, I was not overweight, far from it, but this belief, bolstered by my admiration of the skinny girls at school, my own slim mum and the general commentary at school and among my friends, that fat was bad, and my belief that I *was* fat was taking root in my mind.

Looking back, I can see that I had already lost perspective of what I looked like and what size I actually was. Lying flat in a voluminous hospital gown no doubt added to that. It's no coincidence that the clothes I chose were baggy, loose-fitting, disguises really, as I had no idea what might fit me or what shape I might be.

My super-smart dad was offered a job with a company called Armstrong in Teesside, an area between County Durham and North Yorkshire. To make his commute possible (in his company car: a flashy metallic, mint green Audi 80 Sport) the family, after much debate, was on the move. Only this wasn't a mere hop from Essex to Hertfordshire, oh no; it was a move of such magnitude the thought of it left me winded. We were packing up the suburban life we knew and shipping off to the wilds of North Yorkshire.

In the mid-eighties, this might as well have been Antarctica. We were still awaiting the invention of FaceTime, Skype and texting, all of which would no doubt have made the maintenance of friendships easier. But at the time, I knew that even *had* my friends and I been into letter writing, it would have been no substitute for hanging around Camden Market, sitting in beer gardens laughing over nothing and quite frankly, even if they were to write and tell me all of what I was missing, I'm not sure it would have helped!

Alienation was no stranger to me, but it felt like a gut punch to be giving up such a lovely time in my life. The thought of staying in St Albans without my family never occurred to me. I still felt like a baby in so many ways and my family, the safe nest they created in which I knew I was loved, well, nothing could substitute that no matter where it was.

◆ ◆ ◆

Our house in North Yorkshire was about as far as you could imagine from the three-bed terraced homes I had known and loved. It was a detached, extended cottage, sitting on top of a hill in an acre of land, with a tall forest as our front garden, and a winding drive that cut a bumpy track through it. The first time I saw it, standing alone among rolling green hills with nothing but fields as far as the eye could see, I couldn't imagine how you lived in a house like that, one without neighbours, shops, life . . . I feared loneliness would be my constant companion, but one thing I was well versed in was spending time alone and I knew that as long as I had a book to hand, I'd get through it.

Saying goodbye to my friends, who felt hard won, was gut-wrenching. Even now, some thirty-seven years later, I remember the last time I left our old house and the feeling in my stomach like everything had drained out of it and I was hollow. I can't pretend I wasn't relieved not to be living anywhere near the pervert with the van, but it felt like I was just getting started with the capital city on my doorstep, a comforting routine and a social life.

Bereft at leaving my school year to carry on without me, just as I had my first primary school and my second primary school, I consoled myself, knowing it was good for my dad's career, good for the family and quite possibly the adventure I had said I wanted for so long – I'd always said I'd wanted to travel, hadn't I? I dug deep and tried only to show positivity, knowing how infectious worry could be in a tight family unit, remembering the faces of my family crowded around my hospital bed, each taking their cue from the other, as fear of the unknown and group sadness rolled around them like mist. It was another salient lesson that to stretch your wings and push your horizons came with consequences and required more than a little courage. I was distraught about leaving the life I now loved but knew that as a wannabee writer, I had to put myself out there and LIVE!

We arrived in August and spent that first hot summer exploring, introducing ourselves to the sheep and horses who stuck their inquisitive noses over our fence, no doubt intrigued by the scent of these newcomers, out-of-towners no less, who talked funny, travelled in a pack and were so noisy! Dad worked long hours, running the factory, while Simon and Paul went off in their wellington boots, roaming until their hungry bellies guided them home. Nicky liked to sit and watch the farmer along the lane fixing things.

Summer in North Yorkshire. I'd ditched the studded belt and opted for colour! Our little family . . . Simon, Paul, Dad, Nicky, Me and Mum 1985.

I meanwhile got a job in a café in the nearest market town and made a friend, a girl I worked with. I quickly learned that everyone in the area went to the same school, and this was a novelty after commuting across town for so long, the only person, apart from my brothers, who did so from my street. The commute in North Yorkshire was a little different too: a clunky school bus toured the villages, gathering kids as it went. That daily bus ride was an adventure in itself. Driven by a patient, invisible man, the crappy engine struggled on the hills and on more than one occasion got stuck in the snow, the like of which I had never seen. The powdery stuff, very different from the dark slush that lay in the gutter where we used to live, sat in high drifts along the lanes.

As the new term at a new school dawned, I was so nervous, but equally a little excited. This was, as my mum reminded me, like shedding skin; no one knew anything about me. I decided I was not going to be the girl on crutches, the girl with the dodgy pelvis who was always in and out of hospital. I was going to be Amanda – new girl. And I was. No one spoke like me. Everyone had a strong Yorkshire accent, which I loved. The novelty of my southern vowels meant kids would gather around, asking me to say bath and path, while they laughed. Their laughter was good-natured, welcoming, and I felt instantly at home. I might have been different from them, but no one ever, ever made me feel 'smawl'.

Life in North Yorkshire was different from anything I'd known. Among the farming families with whom I mixed, they cared little for aesthetics or fashion, as they roamed their acres in fancy off-roaders, didn't give a shite what brand someone wore or whether they were trendy or not. Everyone listened to the music they liked rather than the music they felt they should, no one checked to see what band name you had inked on your school bag, and I liked it. It was a way of life that dulled any preoccupation with my looks or weight: not only was I fairly happy with my size and the shoving on of jeans and any old T-shirt each day, just like I had when I was a little kid, but crucially, if no one else cared, why should I? It was a mentally healthy time for me. We, as a family, transitioned well to the different pace of life, a rural life with stunning views and wide-open uncluttered skylines. It felt a lot like freedom and was a feeling that stayed with me, an association, no matter how deeply buried, that a rural, quiet life was one that was good for my health, both mental and physical.

My beloved grandparents, now retired, came to see us regularly, rattling up and down the motorway on a five-hundred-mile round trip in their little Peugeot with the windows down, stopping for lunch en route – they loved the excursion. It was a holiday trip, each and every time. And yes, they always brought sweets. It changed the way they spent time with us, no longer nipping over for tea or a cuppa or meeting up for a Sunday out; they came and stayed for at least a week every couple of months and became a strong part of the community in which we lived.

My grandad and dad would hold court in the pub, a whole new audience for their tired jokes, and my grandad made friends with men of the same age as him who had never left the county. They were fascinated by his life story, an East End Jewish boy who went off to fight a war and whose family survived the Blitz and they regaled him with similar tales of horror, my favourite being how a stray bomb, unloaded from a German plane on its return trip from Hull, had hit a cow. The whole village turned out to pay their respects.

My little old grandad – pedalling off on one of the boys' bikes in North Yorkshire to fetch the bread. He would do this humming the Hovis theme . . .

This experience of swapping tales was a reminder to me of the importance of storytelling and how it could build connections between the least obvious people. It was mental kindling that I gathered, knowing that one day I just might light the fire and write that book. Meanwhile, I stored away the sights and smells of our rural landscape, popping them in a drawer of my filing cabinet in case I ever needed a setting like this for one of my books.

People treated me a little differently than I was used to, and it made me behave a little differently. I realised it was because they didn't see me as someone who was made of glass, poorly or requiring special handling, I was just one of the girls and this was how I acted, shaking off some of my timidity that I felt in social situations.

I missed my old group of friends, but somehow found it easier after a while not to write to them. It felt simpler to commit to my new life and not hanker after all that I couldn't have, a different life so very far away . . . I was also wary of old friends and new friends meeting and my new group learning of my hospital stays and the fault line running through my life that meant the whole shebang could crumble at any time.

I got my first proper boyfriend, introduced by someone I knew in the next village. He was a boy who didn't seem to mind that I wasn't stick thin. It was obvious he liked my confidence, confirming in my eyes it was far easier to love someone who loved herself.

I told him about the van man. The first time I'd shared what happened.

The retelling of it was emotionally draining, far more than I might have imagined. I sobbed about it, possibly for the first time. It felt entirely necessary to explain my slight reticence physically, my nerves, and that I was dreading him seeing the state of my lower body, my ugly pink scar tissue. His reaction to the van, fuming mad on my behalf, was welcome, confirming that I had had something done to me that wasn't my fault. It eased misplaced guilt and diluted the grubbiness I carried like a weight for the longest time, despite trying my best to shut the incident away. And as for my scars, I mentioned them only that once and he, never. It was a relief. Our dalliance was entirely without the foundation needed for a deep and meaningful coupling, but it was a nice introduction to romantic life.

The moment I hit seventeen I learned to drive. If I think back to then, it's hard to recognise that girl: I was fearless, driving across the winter moors alone in the early hours with no phone, no street-lights, attacking the remote, winding lanes in a rusty red Fiat 126, powered by a less than reliable motorbike engine. I liked the feeling of doing something daring and scary, pushing my boundaries as far as I could. I felt free. Waking up to the sun high over the fields, birdsong, the bleating of new lambs and with a sweet-scented breeze whistling through the house as all the doors and windows were thrown wide open, I felt a long, long way from London and happy, oh so happy!

And then one day in class, on an ordinary day, about to be made so extraordinary, I stood to leave the lesson, bent sideways to pick up my bag with files and books inside and the next thing I knew I'd hit the deck. It took me entirely by surprise. Face down, I lay on the floor between tables, with my eyes closed, I pleaded, prayed, 'No! No! No! No! No! No! No! No! No! Please not again. Please not here.'

But the universe wasn't listening to my plea. My old friend pain smacked me right between the eyes. I had forgotten the self-ish nature of it, the all-consuming single note of despair that plays in your mind and holds you fast. Aware of panicked activity and scurrying around me, I welcomed passing out. So much easier than dealing with the fact that my shitty pelvis was again in bits and all that I knew would follow.

What did follow was predictable: experimental surgery, long stays in hospital, the falling away of friends and another great big chunk taken out of my happiness. I have horrible memories of being in that hospital, more so than any other. The staff were won-derful, the surgeon clever, but I can only picture that stuffy ward where I cried a river into my polyester flat pillow over all the things I was not and did not have.

Life had been so great and all good things within my reach; to be reduced to this again was horrible, a blow. I cried because I wasn't thin, and I wasn't pretty (yes, these two factors again rearing their ugly heads when my guard was down), I wasn't brilliant. I was now not the girl the girls wanted to be friends with, and I don't blame them, not that it hurt any less. Nipping off for long hospital stays every five minutes made me an unreliable friend. It made me temporary, just when I had begun to feel permanent. I had always known further surgeries were on the cards, but thought they would be at my own pace, planned and not this drama, this injury, this panic. It felt a lot like going back to square one and I was resentful.

Once again, I was stuck. I couldn't make a plan. I didn't have a goal. I didn't have a fucking clue how to become the person who was hammering inside me to get out – the real me. The writer who didn't have to spend so much time in hospital, but who could run around and grab life! I longed to be at home in our cottage on a hill. Wanted to sleep in that pretty bedroom. Wanted to reach out to flick off the lamp with the faux onyx base and tasselled lampshade, sitting next to a little green leather alarm clock with a gold rim around the edge where it folded in onto itself to allow for ease of packing if you ever took a trip. I didn't need it to fold. I never took a trip.

I would lie awake, listening to the traffic, the rain, the shouts of people in the street, life in a northern city right below my window. I'd think a lot about how I didn't fit. How I hated the way I looked, hated my build, my scars, my crappy bones . . . I didn't know where my place was or what I really, really wanted to do. Write stories? Yeah, right. How would someone like me ever write a story? I'd never been anywhere or done anything. What was I realistically going to write about? Hospital ceiling tiles I have known and loved? My thoughts and frustrations would slip down the gloss-painted wall and pool in a sticky mess of disappointment that I would watch the cleaners mop up in the morning. My dreams were fierce, in them I loved, laughed, ran, succeeded and failed, and I'd wake up feeling the pressure of not knowing how to 'be' sitting on my chest with such weight it threatened to crush me.

I'd been out of hospital for a few months and made tentative trips back to school, but largely worked remotely at home – it felt safer and was easier than hobbling on and off that rickety school bus at the beginning and end of each day. Plus, I felt different, school felt different, everything felt different. I was once again the girl made of glass, who needed careful handling. It was a retrograde step about which there was jack all I could do.

Life was quieter, but getting back on track when one day my clever dad came home and . . . you've guessed it, in his late thirties with three little kids and a wife to support, yada yada . . . He was offered an executive job with STC Newport, Wales, where he would be working on the manufacture of fibre optic cable. With his new company car – a nifty top-of-the-range champagne-coloured Audi 100 – the family, after much debate, was on the move again. I could feel the tension in the air. This family upheaval was wearing thin, but my dad was a career man who went where the next opportunity was, each time raising our standard of living and proving that a boy from a council estate could achieve whatever he set his sights on with hard work, self-belief and no small pinch of risk-taking.

We'd been in North Yorkshire for four years and I knew we'd miss the quiet peace of our rural home; the whole thing, despite my hospital stay interlude, had felt very much like being on holiday. So, we packed up and moved out.

Our next destination was Thornbury, just outside Bristol. My health was good, the last operation holding fast, and yet I withdrew a little, deciding not to get too attached to the place, figuring there was little point in building friendships or getting to know the landscape, as you could bet your bottom dollar that we wouldn't be there that long . . .

It seems that fate had other ideas and I made wonderful friendships and fell deeply in love with the West Country, spending long summers and holidays in North Devon, Salcombe in particular, a place very dear to my heart. We moved into a fancy seventeenth-century house with spare bedrooms! I know! It was quite a jump from such humble beginnings. My dad's career was going from strength to strength and materially we were comfortable. We could eat out and there were holidays abroad, all as wonderful as I thought they'd be, although this all came at a price. My dad worked long hours and travelled a lot, often in the US or in Europe on business. I think he thrived on the lifestyle, but his absence bothered me. In some ways I kind of missed the early days in Collier Row, where he was home every night, when I saw my nan and grandad a lot, where we all ate at the little table in the tiny kitchen, and I fell asleep safe in my bed because I didn't yet know my pelvis was going to crumble and my mum and dad were just along the hall if I needed anything.

Our higgledy-piggledy house in Thornbury – my dad in the corner polishing his car! The little wing on the left which led to a flat roof where we'd climb out to drink and sunbathe!

We, as a family, loved that big old house, amazed by our new home. The crumbling plaster, damp outbuildings, rickety staircases, wonky walls and resident ghost, we loved it all! Simon, Paul and I were in our teens and we became even closer as siblings. The house was the base of what was to be a fantastic social life. Within walking distance to the pub, it was *that* house: the one all our friends flocked to when out and about, the one everyone met up in, hung out in and where laughter bounced from the ceiling and chased us around the narrow corridors. My dad began to sail, something that transformed his life. I can only imagine the freedom that boy who had grown up in inner-city London must have felt as he roamed the seas. He moored his beautiful boat in Millbay Marina, Plymouth, where we would descend en masse to mess about on the ocean. Thornbury is embedded in my memory with nothing but fondness and yet, as soon as I finished my education at the local comp (my final school!), my heart yearned to be back in London. With lingering memories of my pre-North Yorkshire life, the excitement of the capital and the buzz of the city, it felt like me and old London town had some unfinished business. And I was right.

By the time I reached my early twenties, my pelvis was stable. My walk had improved and my confidence that it was, finally, finally healing was at its highest.

My grandparents had told me repeatedly that my school days were the best of my life, and while I took their advice on most things, I really, really hoped they were wrong. Refusing to believe that the highlights of my entire life were once winning a German verse-speaking contest, having a bit part in *Grease* and being injected with enough anaesthetic over the years to fell a herd of wildebeest. If those were the best days then I was in deep, deep trouble. It's only with age that I have reflected on that phrase, *the best days of your life*, and I'm beyond glad my school days were not the best of my life: who wants to peak at fourteen? I said this often to my own kids.

It's fair to say the structure of school life didn't suit me, especially not with my constant health interruptions and school swapping. I attended five schools in five different parts of the UK between the ages of five to eighteen. Nothing I learned gave me confidence that I could fulfil my dream of becoming a writer. It was simple to me: when an establishment or group is disinterested in you because you don't fit into the neat package of how they measure success it is very hard to be interested in them in return. I was bursting with stories! Ideas bubbled in my mind, filling up the filing cabinets in my brain. I was desperate to write plays and star in plays – writing dramas in my head daily and using life as a research trip, mentally noting characteristics, quirks, accents and peculiarities of everyone I met and the landscape of everywhere I went, so I could regurgitate them onto the page and make the people in my stories real. But this burning passion, it seemed, counted for little when I couldn't get my head around simultaneous equations, recite the periodic table or, as was actually the case, correctly label a diagram naming our internal organs. I might have got my liver, spleen, stomach and pancreas in a muddle and had frankly no clue as to the purpose of a duodenum, but I could have quickly and confidently pointed out the mons pubis – no Googling required.

I was average. I *felt* average and yet knew that you had to be way above average to succeed or so I thought. Everyone in my family and all of my friends had always told me how pretty or beautiful my mum was, and she is. This had a huge impact on me, as the one thing I knew was that in my youth, I looked nothing like her and if she was the beauty standard, I didn't even come close. It made me wish I looked like her. My family was very good at examining new babies and claiming any bit of them:

'He's got Barry's nose.'

'She's got Elsie's mouth.'

'That's Joe's smile!'

'Ivy's laugh . . .'

But not once did anyone ever tell me I had any aspect of my mum in my face, no matter how much I wished it.

As I hit my early twenties however, and my cheekbones sharpened, my lips were full and my skin was yet to display the obvious signs of sun damage and general neglect, I quite liked the face that stared back at me from the mirror or was captured in the odd photograph. My face gave me confidence.

I mastered the art of the make-up I had for years admired in others and found my style, opting for heavy eye make-up and little else, a throwback no doubt to the Marc Bolan and Dusty Springfield inspired ideal of beauty that I had held for the longest time. Confident enough to hold people's eye line and smile, I liked the connections this made. I think it was the first time I felt that I was in control of my life: no school routine, no hospital routine and no parents looking over my shoulder. It was down to me to go to the big city, find a job and somewhere to live. My adventures were about to take a fabulous turn . . .

Chapter Seven

'Up West'

Waving goodbye to life in Thornbury, the market town where I had worked in wine bars and waitressed in pubs and hotels, I arrived in London aged twenty-two with a couple of boxes, my fake Gucci clogs, a bag of clothes and a tummy full of excitement. All set to share a flat in the very fancy Lexham Gardens, Kensington, with a wonderful girlfriend I'd met in Salcombe and a couple of strangers: a very well-spoken girl and a beautiful Italian man who was a security guard.

My parents dropped me off. Mum reminded me that my nan and grandad were only across town and held a tissue under her schnozzle, before warning me not to talk to strangers, crying because I was flying the nest, and my dad moaned about the tiny juddering lift that was only wide enough for sharing with someone with whom you were in a very close relationship. I took the stairs.

Surrounded by beautiful architecture, I loved to walk the streets, taking it all in. It felt like I had achieved something great, to have survived so many operations, to have left home and be fending for myself, sharing a kitchen and being self-reliant. My cooking, however, was terrible and I either ate toast or made vague attempts at pasta, which my Italian flatmate refused to eat. I wished I'd paid more attention to my mum and nans when they toiled lovingly at the stove creating masterpieces!

It was a time of huge personal growth, finding a job, paying the bills; my whole life now rested on my shoulders. It was as exciting as it was scary. Tentatively, I stretched my wings and prepared to fly. Standing there on the balcony of our top-floor flat at night, where I could see across the rooftops and chimneys all the way to the Albert Hall with the twinkling lights of the capital spread out like a canopy, it felt like a long way from my nan's house in East Ham, but Mum was right, it was in fact only on the other side of the city in an almost straight line from where I was born, you know the place, the one with the blue plaque.

The truth was my family hardly ever went 'up West'. Why would they when everything they needed and everything they loved was in the streets and immediate surrounds of where they lived? I managed to find two jobs, both secured via ads in the *Evening Standard*. One was with a taxi and courier firm, where I stayed for four years. It was hard graft and good fun, working in just about every department from bike despatch, booking and PR. To arrive in the office just off Tottenham Court Road and be part of the crew where long hours, robust humour and coffee on tap were the order of the day felt wonderful. I needed a job, and this fitted the bill. No longer was I preoccupied with writing a book, recognising that while it was my dream, this was all about earning the money needed to *live*, and in the face of this, all thoughts of writing were relegated. I'd climbed on to the hamster wheel of life and I started running.

My other job at evenings and weekends was selling advertising to the *Yellow Pages*. I hated every single monotonous second of it. Making endless calls and reading from a script where every call, every word and every missed sale was analysed and turned into a learning opportunity. Our sales were put on a large board, and we were ranked in order of revenue success. I sat somewhere in the middle, a place I was familiar with. Average. Not the worst, some people never made a sale before unceremoniously grabbing their coat and leaving the building with their head bowed, knowing they were not going to return for their next shift. And I wasn't as good as some of the top sellers, one of whom was sleeping with the managing director of the sales company and was given all the large accounts with hefty budgets. Bitter? *Moi?*

I largely enjoyed these carefree years, the ones I had been dreaming of when I lay in a hospital bed and wondering if I was ever going to have any sort of life. My walking ability was the best it had been and this freedom of movement without pain made my unsightly scar seem almost worth it. It was very easy, when my bones felt stronger and my body able to do most things, to forget what I had been through, a bit like the week after a bad toothache; you remember it, but it no longer troubles you and you put it out of your mind and move on.

All grown up – or at least trying to be. Me aged twenty-one with my mum and nan.

It was at this time I had my first proper, proper boyfriend. He was a City boy who was part of a whole other world where money, frivolity and travel were the norm. We met in a pub, and I was ridiculously flattered that he picked me. I'd wait for his phone calls and replay the time we spent together at my leisure. I never felt quite part of his world and never really wanted to, while doing my best to fit in. It was obvious we were cut from different cloth, had different values.

It was love I thought, or at least something masquerading as love, but he didn't love me. This was evident in the way he treated me, was unfaithful to me, strung me along, made promises he didn't keep – just often enough and convincing enough to keep me on the hook – and with alarming regularity would dump me after a spurious row before we started up again. It was on and off and off and on for years, and all the while I was meek, grateful for the outpouring of love he showered me with and just as anxious about the change of heart which I knew was only ever around the corner. It's as humiliating and demeaning to admit as it was to live it.

His behaviour slowly eroded the strength of feeling I had towards him until in the end I had no interest in being snared again just to be cut free when the mood took him. Like a fish, caught and thrashing against the bank, it was exhausting, predictable and damaging to my emotional well-being and it took me years to feel any level of trust again in a relationship. The adult me would have told him from the off that it was just not good enough and I wouldn't put up with being so mercilessly toyed with, but in my early twenties, unconfident and grasping at life to see what held fast and what slipped through my fingers, *grateful* almost for the interest from this wealthy, clever boy, convinced he must know stuff I didn't, well, that Amanda, I'm ashamed to say, put up with a lot of shit. Those experiences, however, weren't wasted; they went into the filing cabinet.

With a regular wage coming in I was finally able to travel and set off alone on many an adventure. I had been fortunate to holiday abroad with my parents, but spending weeks on remote Greek islands alone, driving across Turkey, mooching around the South of France and exploring Spain by myself was new. All without a phone or any means of contact. Travelling alone and travelling light, was for me preferable; I've never felt freedom like it before or since, the sensation of not knowing a soul in a country and yet there you are!

To wake up and see the sun rise in a new place with the sights, sounds and smells of a foreign landscape all around me is something I still treasure. On grey days, I sometimes mentally escape to a small metal table on a sun-warmed harbour, eating charred fish, freshly plucked from the ocean with a good book spread open in front of me and no timetable, no schedule, no disturbance. It was paradise. My grandparents in particular were always horrified by my escapades asking what would happen if I got into trouble and I was all alone. The fact is I experienced only kindness and friendship that gave me faith in human nature. Too many examples of this to note, but an old Greek man on Andros gave me honey from his land to cure my hay fever and a Turkish family on the outskirts of Konya offered me the spare room above their garage for a couple of nights and brought me a sumptuous breakfast. Such kindness, such love for a stranger. It made me realise that there might be people like the shitty van man, who had done a very good job of shaking my faith in humanity, and my ex, who treated me on occasion with something close to contempt, but there were many, many more kind souls out there whose motives were good. I think I healed on these travels, took time to breathe and think, doing my best to put, what was in hindsight, my difficult teenage years behind me.

Back in London, for the first time ever I had a *great* social life. This was largely down to the fact that I had a new best friend, and her name was alcohol.

It wasn't the first time I drank: I'd been sipping lager and lime and the odd glass of plonk like most of my peers since I was sixteen, and I had never been overly fussed about the taste or the way it made me feel, but this time it was different. I meant business. She became my wingman. I learned of her magic power, that after one or two glasses I could shake off my anxiety and shimmy with sexual confidence across a room, becoming a different person altogether.

And I liked the person I became, I liked her very much. She was everything I'd ever aspired to be: loud, confident, go-getting and fun! Unaware of the dangerous path I walked where the false promise of confidence meant making a pact with an adversary that rarely lost once it got you in its grip, I forged ahead. Not that I cared, I was loving the life I lived! When I drank, I didn't care about the wobble to my bum, that my arms might be less than athletic, and as for my scarring, what scarring? Who cared? I was blinkered, and only on the very edge of in control.

I thought I was happy.

White wine spritzer was my tipple of choice and after much practice I could sink a fair few, maybe eight or nine. Drinking became so intertwined with my social life that if I wasn't drinking it didn't feel social. I drank often, thinking that by mixing my wine with soda water on a night out, while others took it neat, I had my drinking firmly in check.

Skinny and drunk. Early twenties.

My routine was about as unhealthy as it could be. Sleep was for the weekends and the couple of hours I could grab between getting home after a night out and leaving for work in the morning. Living centrally in the early nineties meant we were in the thick of it. My colleagues, friends and I enjoyed endless nights at the Kensington Roof Gardens, where shouty rich boys bought bottles of fizz. We'd then head to Break for the Border in Soho to down jugs of sour margarita, because they were often the last place to close. The country might have been in the grip of rising unemployment, but we were in a bubble, spending every penny we earned, as if we knew that soon enough responsibility would come knocking and that fiscal freedom would be a long time in returning. I found the whole atmosphere fascinating – this world of intoxication, exaggerated laughter and a quest for hedonism – as if I was on catch up. I knew it was all fake, but liked the excitement of it; being caught up in the heady whirlpool of life was intoxicating in itself.

I encountered people who had moved to London and were desperate to be 'Londoners' because of all they thought it would be and all they had dreamed of being in the Big Smoke. Many thought the streets were indeed paved with gold, whereas even in an upmarket suburb like Kensington with our view of the Albert Hall, they were paved mostly with blobs of chewing gum and dog shit. My situation wasn't that dissimilar to my bus rides to school where I got to peer through the windows of people's houses as we passed by, but these people I could watch close up, intrigued to see how they acted and marvelling at their values that seemed so very different from mine. I might have been a Londoner, but this was a London that was new to me, a whole other side, literally, to the city I had been born in.

I can't pretend I didn't feel guilty to be spending cash on a social life, bottles of plonk and the odd cab fare home, when my great-nan had worked so hard as a cloakroom attendant, taking the coats of people no doubt like me, out enjoying themselves with money to spare. On a couple of occasions, I went out around the Barbican, knowing my nan had worked there during the war and the whole place had been bombed. She told tales of emerging at daybreak to see many of the landmarks by which she navigated her way home, gone, aflame, destroyed. I wondered what she might make of the whole carry-on but knew that the message from all the generous-spirited women who had raised me would be, 'You bloody enjoy yourself, darlin'!'

I rarely ate. Yes, it's as ridiculous as it sounds. My body had little spare fat and I got by on the odd slice of toast, adrenaline and the calories from alcohol. I wanted to be as thin as I could be and can even now recall the feeling of success and self-congratulation at a day spent in calorie deficit, and running the flat of my palm over my pronounced hipbone made me feel almost euphoric. It gave me a kind of high that almost negated the many side effects. My breath stank. My mood when not drinking was low. My poo was disgusting, and I felt nauseous most of the time with a pounding headache that I laughingly put down to a hangover, and which I cured by popping paracetamol with my morning coffee. It made me feel powerful that I could survive a day with little food, and I can't pretend I didn't like the feeling of being 'empty'.

It was a dangerous path to walk, and I didn't realise that my relationship with food and alcohol was becoming toxic. Looking as 'healthy' as I did and receiving many compliments on how 'slim' I was only served to confirm in some warped way that what I was doing and how I was living was a good thing.

I would regularly return to my nan and grandad's, a Tube ride away, or to our family home in Thornbury to collapse and recover. My nan would make me eat smoked haddock, as if it were the cure to all ills, before I fell asleep on her sofa, and my darling mum would make me warm food and pull the duvet over my shoulders, happy to have me back and worried about how hard I was working. My dad would kiss me on the cheek when I left and give me some money, always making sure I had enough.

Leaving their houses, I would feel 'cleaner', my fuzzy head somewhat restored and with the clarity of thought that maybe I needed to calm down a little in my social life. Their lives and environments felt wholesome; my conscience jabbed me in the ribs as if to remind me of how far I had fallen. I would vow to drink less, eat more, go out less, sleep more and generally take better care of me.

The moment, however, I arrived back in town, I'd be making arrangements, reaching for the plonk and kicking off my shoes ready to resume dancing. And how I danced! Me, the girl who had learned to put one foot in front of the other on more occasions that I cared to count.

A couple of boys came and went. None I loved, but a few I liked. They were a nice diversion but were no longer the validation I needed. With alcohol sloshing in my veins and having come out the other side of a toxic relationship, I felt like a survivor who knew my worth. In my early teens I had thought a boyfriend would mean I was good enough, now I knew I was more than good enough with or without a man on my arm.

My flatmates were glamorous and trim, and I envied their body confidence. They would walk around in their pants while I, sober, would wrap up in a dressing gown or my PJs, nervous that someone might see my scarred bits and pieces. I wanted to be more like them, but without the false bravado of drink, didn't know how.

One particular week lives in my memory. I'd run out of clean clothes, having missed launderette night. This was a weekly occurrence where we would load up the machines and tip in our cup of detergent, purchased from a grumpy woman with a knotty beehive and a cigarette hanging from her lip who would scoop the powder from a big industrial box of detergent. We'd then nip to the Devonshire Arms while the washing machine did its magic, returning home some hours later with freshly folded clothes and a little sozzled. I was fretting and ferreting around on the floor looking for a skirt. My flatmate, a Devon girl who was incredibly beautiful inside and out, suggested I borrow something of hers. I felt the familiar flare of hot shame and embarrassment. There was no way anything of hers was going to fit me. It was as I mumbled all the reasons why I couldn't and didn't want to that she shoved a little black skirt into my hands, one I'd seen her in countless times, looking fantastic. I sidled into the bathroom and locked the door. More out of wanting to appease her than anything, I pulled it on and . . . and . . . it glided over my hips and the zip went up with ease. I couldn't believe it! There was even a gap in the waistband. What wizardry was this?

I turned sideways to look at my reflection and patted my flat tum. I knew I wasn't carrying fat, but the fact that her skirt fitted, it was astonishing to me. It's no exaggeration to say that if I'd had to guess I would have said I was twice her size.

If anything could prove to me how far the image I carried of myself was from the reality, it was that little black skirt. Walking into the bedroom my friend smiled and said it suited me and she called me 'skinny arse'! It was a moment as impactful as the time I'd been called an ugly duckling. I felt the power of being slim, of feeling attractive, and there was strength in it. I wanted to be like all those girls I had feted over the years. I wanted to be like one of the girls in my magazine, I wanted to not be the clumsy girl with the knackered pelvis and ugly, puckered scars, a girl who couldn't be trusted to carry the salad to the buffet table because she would surely drop it. I wanted to bottle that feeling of pride I felt in my appearance for the first time ever and carry it around in my chest, sipping from it whenever I felt my confidence flag, and I did. For the next six years.

My newfound confidence directly influenced my self-belief when it came to earning a living. It seemed the advice I had always been given by parents to work really, really hard and never, ever give up until I got where I wanted to be was good advice. I was twenty-four and working hard in my new job with a computer-training company. This job I got quite by accident, phoning them with a query in my old job; they liked the way I sounded on the phone and asked me to pop in for a chat. It was a boring atmosphere, but better money and so I jumped ship. I'm sad to say the idea of writing was one that had slipped from my priorities. It was hard enough to work, socialise and head home when I could to recover or go sailing with my dad, let alone pick up a pen and write too. I cringe at how much time I wasted when I could have been writing and putting in the yards to make my dream a reality. But the truth is I almost put it out of my head in these years. It turned from something that drove me, a deep-seated desire to pen a novel, into nothing more than a fantasy. It was during this time that I read less too. Not filling my mind with new and wonderful books meant my brain kind of stagnated.

Finally, aged twenty-four, I rented a flat of my own in Clapham. With a new, better-paid role in the training company, as an account manager (which made my grandparents incredibly proud even though I was so bored it nearly killed me) more ready money and a whole new postcode in which to socialise I found myself in the popular club. This popularity was predicated largely on how I looked and no matter how shallow, I cannot deny it was intoxicating.

Invited to lots of parties, I was always the last one to leave the dance floor, saying yes to everything! I had a widening circle of friends in London, the West Country and on the north Devon coast, and weekends were planned far in advance just to make sure I could cram everything in. This appetite for fun and meeting new people felt very much like catching up on all I had missed while my schoolmates were at the school disco snogging boys called Darren and Dean.

Also, I liked belonging. I liked not being the girl in the pork pie shoes with the dorky briefcase who had no one to talk to at lunchtime. I liked being popular. I didn't think twice about walking into any room, as if I almost believed that I would always receive a warm welcome. Like one of those champagne-drinking, raven-haired lovelies in the skinny jeans.

Compliments about how I looked buoyed up my fragile self-esteem and I revelled in being told I had great hair (I was still dyeing it blonde), a nice face, a good figure – jeez, who wouldn't? Even if I didn't quite believe it, but that was what my best pal alcohol was for – to convince me that I was great, my life was great, and everything was going to be . . . great. How could it not be when I was having such fun!

I picture one Saturday in the early hours, as a lilac sunrise kissed the buildings, haring around Parsons Green in a vintage Morgan with the wind in my hair, barefoot, my eyes closed, arms above my head and Jon and Vangelis's 'I Hear You Now' blaring so loudly! I was drunk, but knew if I could bottle the moment, I could forever sip liquid joy.

Reading this back, I hate how important it felt to me at the time, and how ridiculously *unimportant* the size of my waist, the length of my lashes, the circumference of my thighs is to the person I was inside and all that I had to offer. It demeaned me. Reduced me to no more than a face and some boobs. But at the time, important it was. I don't like that for a short while this was the person I became, pandering to the standard set by whom? My beauty regimen was extreme – tanning, buffing, moisturising, waxing and preening. It took up every bit of spare time and every spare penny.

It was during this period that I had a couple of more serious boyfriends: one an actor I met at a theatre and another a musician I met in Marbella, hanging off their arms like a bauble. When sober I became quiet in their presence, as if something I might say would reveal my flawed inner self, put a crack in the outside that seemed, to them at least, flawless, if you discounted the ugly scars lurking in my pants.

During this time, I even did a bit of modelling, yes, me! A photographer who worked out of a studio in Greek Street, Soho, approached me. His business and list of clientele were impressive and it was a boost to think people might want to see me advertising everything from jeans to toothpaste. This came to an abrupt end when on one job a different photographer manhandled me into position for the shot, not in a sexual way, there was nothing suggestive about it and I had, as always, taken along a friend, but in a way that made me feel like . . . meat. My body reduced to no more than limbs and bones for him to push and pull until he was satisfied with the look. His action took me right back to the front seat of that van. I could smell the diesel and I felt physically sick. I knew then that even though it was never going to be more than pin money, it was not for me.

A modelling job aged twenty-five. This is the face that lived on next to nothing – I had to wear several layers just to feel warm enough to function.

Along with being a popular girl came sexual attention. I didn't know how to handle it when the person I was presenting to the world was so very different from the girl I was inside, still trying to figure everything out. The confident, laughing girl wasn't me – that was just what was on the outside; inside I was coiled, afraid, hiding behind my wall and missing home. It was conflicting. This was what I had always wanted, to be desired. To be like those girls at school with the low-slung bags and air of nonchalance. But when attention came my way, I didn't always like it.

It was a time when 'feminist' was a radical word, the #MeToo movement no more than a pipedream and the inequality gap in pay, education and opportunity between men and women even wider than it is now. That concrete ceiling still sat dauntingly above our heads. Speaking out against unwanted sexual advances or moments of threat was not something I considered, fearing that at best it would be futile and at worst would have negative consequences for me, certainly in the workplace. These incidents of sexually inappropriate behaviour are something that not only I, but *all* women I know, have experienced. I would say it is harder to find a woman who has *not* experienced it than one who has.

My examples?

I shall pick a few:

I hadn't eaten and fainted while working a temp clerical job in the City and came around on the floor of a break room to hear the circle of males around me laughing and agreeing that they should definitely take my top off. I was horrified and left soon after. And up until that point it had been a job I loved.

Making a sales call to a builder at my evening job selling advertising, to be told if I met him and made him happy . . . he'd take the ad. I laughed it off in the office, but cried all the way home, looking over my shoulder in case, impossibly, he had found out where I worked and was following me home.

Calling a cab and after the driver confirmed my name, I jumped in the back. It was only as the car drove along the Embankment (I was heading to Greenwich, south-east London) that I realised there was no radio and no license number. These were always visibly affixed to the dashboard of any taxi. I asked if he was the cab I had called and he said, 'Don't worry about that, I'll take you home.' My heart nearly shot out of my mouth. I smiled, calmly, not wanting to panic or panic him. Willing my legs to stop shaking and swallowing the desire to cry. I waited until he stopped at traffic lights not far from Hungerford Bridge that runs over the Thames. I opened the door, left it open and ran. I ran as fast as I could back up the Embankment until I thought my lungs would burst. He jumped out of the car and called me all the names under the sun. I didn't look back but got a good description of the car and the police told me the guy listened in to taxi radio frequencies and would get there first. Without giving me any details, they also said that I had been very lucky. I still remember how scared I was, how my legs shook, and my heart raced.

Like all the women I know who take the Tube, numerous incidents of being on a crowded train and feeling men press themselves up against me while looking over my head or in the opposite direction, as if nothing was amiss. Every time I was back in that bloody van with that despicable creature.

Being heckled in the street and leered at lasciviously only to be told I should consider it a compliment when I reacted negatively by telling the man and his chortling mate to 'Fuck off!'

And even in my fifties, after co-presenting a late-night radio show, catching the last overground train home that was rammed with football fans returning after a win. Many were paralytic drunk and in the crowded corridor where I stood by the window, one middle-aged man, who was miffed, as the way to the loo was blocked, unzipped his fly, took out his penis and pissed on the floor behind me. Much of it went down the back of my jeans and into my Converse. I complained to the train staff who were apologetic, but clearly intimidated and overwhelmed by the crowd. I wrote to the train company when I got home. I emailed the customer complaints division. I sat and explained to the young train steward who told me as a gay man, his abuse was almost daily. I cried again, this time for us both. I left the train when it pulled into Bristol station with a familiar sick feeling in my gut, how horrible it is to be subjected to such behaviour and how powerless I felt.

I could write another ten examples and I am sure that you, dear reader, could easily add ten of your own. How this breaks my heart!

The taxi incident on the Embankment changed things for my twenty-five-year-old self. I didn't feel quite so invincible or quite so comfortable going out and about on my own, this in the days before personal GPS, mobile phones, reliable CCTV and the connectivity of social media. I hated that someone did that to me, took my sense of freedom, made me grow up a little, and before you say it or think it, I know that far, far worse things happen. And all I will say is this: far, far worse things *did* happen, things that put me right back in that bloody van in my denim pinafore dress, just wanting to magic myself anywhere else. I began to recognise the fact that when I was drunk, I couldn't always keep myself safe and it started to scare the shit out of me.

It's fair to say that life began to feel a little overwhelming, and in truth my social life a little pointless. Running on that damned hamster wheel without stepping off or looking up, I became aware of a mental fragility that made me question the people I was hanging around with: did they really have my best interests at heart? Would the same people who loved me when I was drunk and funny also love me when I was not? Was I really having a good time if I had to keep *telling* myself (and everyone else) that I was having a good time?

I began to watch them more like an observer of a play than a participant. There wasn't much kindness, not much kinship. All conversations were about meeting up, going out, planning the night, laughing at in-jokes and comparing hangovers, but none were about how we were feeling, what we were going through or where we were heading, life! If true friendship is a lake upon which you can sail safely and happily for a lifetime, what we shared was surface water on which even the sturdiest of vehicles could aquaplane. Too many nights were spent falling out of pubs with arms around each other shouting words of affection, and yet real love was missing. It was a club for the pleasure seekers, a group of intoxicated wind bags who, like me, without the veil of alcohol, had very different personalities. It meant our communication was fake, our interest in each other insincere and our friendships doomed.

It wasn't uncommon for some of them to take drugs and I began to feel increasingly uncomfortable. It wasn't and never has been my thing. (The drug alcohol was more than enough for me.) The first time I was aware of it was at a dinner party with a member of the England Rugby team, a notable actor and a singer with a chart-topping pop group (the rugby player did not touch the drugs) when an arty type in a silk cravat asked me if I wanted some coke. I replied that it was too gassy for me and I'd probably stick to wine, thinking he must mean Coca-Cola – I felt stupid, although I shouldn't have been surprised really.

The lure of dancing on sticky floors and knocking back white wine spritzers was starting to wear thin. It struck me then: what was this world I was mixing in and did I really want to be part of it? The answer was no. I started to question how I was spending my time and began to long for nights at home on the sofa with my mum and dad, sober nights, quiet nights when I could practise the plots of books in my head, create characters and think again about the dream I once had of becoming a writer, now lying under the dust of crushed ambition and the froth of booze.

I did what any home bird would do. I packed up my flat and moved in with my nan and grandad, who had moved to Rainham in Essex. Or 'the countryside', as my nan referred to it, and I guess compared to the East End of London it was. It was close enough to the capital that I could still work and commute. They loved that they could walk to marshland and had a neat back garden. The fact that the windowsills of their bungalow were lined with diesel dust from the lorries hurtling up and down the busy A13 and the sirens of emergency vehicles making their way in or out of London echoed around the walls at all hours of the day and night, was neither here nor there.

It was a lovely time for me, a bit like returning to the nest, which was feather-lined, warm and with a ready supply of worms. Swap worms for roast potatoes and buttered cabbage and you get a truer picture. My grandparents were delighted to have me 'home' and beamed every time they looked at me.

Moving in with my grandparents was, I could see, entirely necessary for me to feel grounded, connected and safe. But living with them also felt a lot like failure. In the great race of life, it felt like friends from school and my parents' friends' kids were creating homes, having babies, travelling, climbing the career ladder or dancing till dawn, yet I was curled up in my nan's back bedroom while she peeled spuds, listening to Matt Monro's greatest hits, stopping only to let my grandad whisk her around the kitchen while she laughed and muttered, 'Silly sod!'

No longer stretching my wings, I felt a little like I was being left behind, not that I could compete in the having baby stakes – that was never going to be me. This thought sat like a dull hum in the back of my mind. It didn't exactly sadden me, but I knew that there might come a time when it would require greater acceptance, if and when the desire for motherhood ever bit.

The first thing my nan did was feed me. And the last thing my nan did was feed me. There were constant shoulder squeezes, tuts and comments issued from my various ageing aunties who visited on a Sunday about how skinny I was. I swallowed their words as if they were compliments, not concerns, and let them line my hungry gut.

How I loved spending time with these older matriarchs whose wrinkled faces, liver-spotted hands and whistling dentures would be of the least significance to anyone who spent time with them. What you would remember, however, was their generosity, their weighty judgement on all things they had never experienced, their raucous laughter, wisdom, warmth and, vitally, their appreciation of a good fruitcake. I adored being in the bosom of their love; it was healing and forgiving, but I could never imagine being *like* them. Yes, I'd returned to the fold to reconnect with all that was important and to take stock of the person I was in danger of becoming, but still I did not want to live their lives, lives which to me felt 'smawl'.

My nan (second right) and her sisters and brother: Winnie, Gwennie, Davey and Elsie.

I remember them chortling into their teacups, wearing Crimplene trousers and ill-fitting bras, as I lay on my tum on the rug with my face inches from a portable face-tanning machine I'd bought from Romford market. It really is as gruesome as it sounds, like the sunbeds people lie under, but a mini version with the ultra-violet tubes behind a little glass sheet that I would practically press my face against, thus ensuring a year-round tan and a lifetime of skin damage – what was I thinking? But I liked the result – that sun-kissed, holiday vibe that made my teeth look a little whiter and seemed to slim my jawline. They similarly laughed when I waxed my top lip, plucked my eyebrows to within a spider's leg of thinness, fake-tanned my entire body before going to work (I can still recall that yeasty/biscuit smell and how the stains never budged from the white pillowcase) and daily blow-dried the bejeebers out of my dyed hair, God forbid I might be seen with my natural brown curls.

These rituals and procedures allowed me to feel more confident as I religiously followed all the grooming tips I could hoover up from *Marie Claire* and *More!* magazines. What a treat it was to buy something glossy or informative, rarely both, from the kiosk on the station platform and to sit with my legs curled beneath me on the sofa with a cup of tea resting on a coaster, thumbing the pages until I had devoured them whole. They just didn't get it, these old, old women . . . naive at best to the ways of my world. I might have now known I didn't want to live a life of bright lights and bars, but I sure as hell was not about to consign myself to a life of sitting around discussing the neighbours and what we might have for tea . . . I wanted more! I was becoming aware of a new breed of woman popping up in my glossy magazines – one who told me I could have it all – a family, a career and time for myself! YES, PLEASE!

This brings to mind one of my favourite Mark Twain quotes:

'When I was a boy of fourteen, my father was so ignorant I could hardly stand to have the old man around. But when I got to twenty-one, I was astonished at how much the old man had learned in seven years.'

My nan sat me down one night and told me that I needed to slow down a bit and that rushing around was no good for me, that she was worried . . . and that money wasn't everything – I needed to think of a life outside of work and she told me how happy her childhood home had been with very little materially and yet daily they would laugh until they cried. I felt my muscles soften and my tears flow.

She was right. Who was I kidding? There was nothing 'smawl' about the lives of these relatives of mine. These glorious matri-archs had survived a world war, lived among the ruins of bombed-out streets while their men were away, fighting. They had fed and clothed their children on a pittance, taken in the children of neigh-bours, acted as midwife to anyone in need, buried babies born too soon or too late, washed and wrapped the bodies of their own parents and sent them on their final journey. They had danced in the streets on VE Day and wrestled with a new life when the boys they had waved off came home as men and changed, all no doubt trying to navigate the new world they lived in and the people they lived with. They had had precious little time for eyebrow grooming and fake-tanning – 'somewhat preoccupied' would best describe their formative years.

But I was of that age and mindset when I thought my gen-eration invented – everything! And the thought of my parents or grandparents having the first clue about what it was like to live my life and the challenges I faced, was actually laughable. They couldn't *possibly* know what it had felt like to dance until the sun came up, to fall madly in love, to have your heart broken, to want so badly to fit in with the crowd that you could play the part of a completely different person . . . a person who would disguise their true self behind a mist of alcohol. It was only my own advancing years and life experience that made me realise it was *me* that was naive at best.

Living with them was a lovely hiatus to the madness. I liked how my grandad always kissed my nan good night and always made her a cup of tea in the morning. I thought this was real love. I began to see that actually, a life lived in service, dedicated to the well-being of their family was quite possibly the greatest gift they could give. And there I was, benefiting from that very thing, finding myself and regrouping in that safe space.

On trips home, Mum and I spoke about my life and the pace at which I lived it. She too voiced concerns about my mental and physical safety, drawing on her own experiences. It broke my heart to hear her confess to my adult self that *she* had flirted with anorexia, striving for emaciated and filling her tum with ripped up tissues to get through a day of instruction at the Lucie Clayton modelling school in London. Her dad, my beloved grandad, had found out that aged sixteen she had been scouted by a modelling agency when 'up West', and fearful of the less than glamorous side to the industry, promptly sent her off to Lucie Clayton where her alumni was Joanna Lumley and Jean Shrimpton, The Shrimp (two of the top models in the sixties).

I think it was here that my mum's view that beautiful meant thin and elegant meant tall was, if not formed, then certainly confirmed. I hated that she had experienced the same body obsession as me and vice versa. It's easy to see that her attitude to food and thinness affected me at some level. And I know that she adores me and would be mortified to think this was the case.

From my mid to late twenties, I actively pursued thinness, desperate to maintain that flat tum and skinny arse. It was ridiculously easy to change my body shape. If I wanted my jeans to be a little looser on the weekend, a couple of days of rigorous discipline and I could achieve my goal – now it takes weeks to even notice a ripple! I never binged. I never made myself sick. And I never told anyone. I simply ate very, very little, drinking glass after glass of water instead of the wine that had if nothing else, previously provided me with calories, as I tried to abate the gnawing hunger that made it hard to sleep. My breath once again stank, my periods, once so longed for, were sporadic. My daily calorie intake was well below what is necessary for optimum function.

I found it hard to concentrate at work; I was now working for a computer company in Covent Garden and had a cleaning job at night. I constantly felt a little confused and nauseated and still with that pounding headache. Apples were my meal of choice, and I would pick at the vegetables that my nan would lovingly put on to boil for me at least half an hour before she knew I was due home. But other than that? Not much. I would occasionally indulge in a 'big' meal, a celebration or a feast for a birthday or Christmas or if one of my nan's legendary roast dinners was prepared. My family, therefore, saw me eat and I could see the looks of relief between my mum and nan, which made me feel rubbish, hating that I was worrying them at all, having worked so hard to convince them that everything was '*fine!*' Afterwards we would apply the same post-match analysis to the food as we always had:

'*So, Mand, how was the gravy?*'

'*Were the carrots good?*'

'*Did the stuffing have a decent crust?*'

'*How about another helping? You'll waste away, my girl . . .*'

Yes, I was their girl, but at that point in my life I was not having another helping. I stared endlessly at pictures in my magazines of Naomi, Cindy, Christy and Claudia, noting their rangy limbs, carved cheekbones, sharp décolletage and was in awe of their physicality. These women were supermodels, mega stars the like of which we had never seen before. It was the first time I was aware of women, who were not actresses, writers, musicians, politicians or nobility, launched into the stratosphere in terms of fame and stardom and it was all down to their incredible bodies and perfect faces. It was another reminder that fat on my body would be bad and fat on my body would be unattractive and fat on my body would mean failure and as for an aged face? Forget it. Wrinkle-free perfection was where it was at. Not that I had to worry about that. I was in my twenties with a fresh, sun-kissed, freckled mush and not a crow's foot in sight.

Living at my nan and grandad's, I didn't socialise nearly as much. I kind of slotted in with their routine of early supper, early night and early rising. And when I did go out it was with quieter friends and a lot tamer. It meant I could save money and after a couple of years I had the deposit needed to buy my own flat.

It was 1994 and I was twenty-six when my bank offered me a mortgage that was three times my salary, meaning in those days, property ownership was possible. I bought a one-bed flat in Blackheath, London. Nowadays, even if it *were* possible to get a mortgage that was three times that equivalent salary, it wouldn't buy a garage! I moved out of my grandparents' and into my little Georgian hideaway, a stone's throw from Greenwich Park. How I loved that flat! I felt a swell of pride and gratitude every time I put my key in the door. Even when in the spate of six months, I came home to find a messy burglary had cleaned me out and then when a small fire due to a faulty wire devastated the kitchen, still it didn't dent the affection in which I held the place. Grandad and I would sit on the hill on the brow of Greenwich Park and look at the skyline of the Isle of Dogs, visible over the river. He used to tell me how the land around his wharf was sold so they could build the big towers. He liked to drive me to the construction site to marvel at the fancy flats, which now overlooked the council housing in which most of his mates lived.

'Although I can't for the life of me see why anyone who wasn't from around here would want to come and work and live out here . . .' was his dire prediction for the area now known as Canary Wharf. I often wonder what he'd make of the place, a whole impressive silhouette of skyscrapers that have changed the face of that side of London. And with the lure of the shiny urban lights and waterway walks, it turns out that quite a few people from 'not around there' want to work and live in its confines. It's strange for me to visit the area, and I can't help but think of it as the industrial warehousing it once was, with timber wharfs and shipping companies, which my grandad knew well. Every time I smell sawn wood, I am taken back to the timber mills, stacked high with wood unloaded from vast ships that had sailed from Russia and Scandinavia, now the site of those impressive skyscrapers.

With my own flat and a steady job, I started to go out a little again, and while not teetotal, I never again hit the town with the full force of drinking and dancing that had shaped my earlier life. I learned I could have the odd glass. It was enough. Living more soberly was like peeking into an alternate universe and I very much liked what I saw. No waking up with headaches, no planning every evening around where we would drink and dance, and no choosing friends based on who was the most 'fun!' No being sick in the loo and slumping face down on the bathroom floor. No waking up with random bruises, missing shoes and wine-soaked jackets, no blood-shot eyes, no crying alone when the music stopped and I arrived home to a quiet, empty flat, no gaps in my memory and no feeling like I was hurtling through space with absolutely no idea of where or even if I would land safely. My thoughts were clearer, my sleep settled, and my routine allowed for calm planning and not the frantic jumping from place to place, party to party, event to event, scared I might miss out. I felt . . . better. It was nice, however, to be able to socialise with colleagues in and around Covent Garden on a sunny evening.

On one such evening I met a man, a lovely man, a computer whizz and sailing nut who made me laugh. We talked about boats and very quickly he moved into my little flat. It was a happy time.

And then something happened that I had not banked on. In the latter part of my twenties, after our whirlwind romance, I fell pregnant. We were a new couple, and this was one hell of a way to get to know each other!

The many surgeries I had endured, and the fragile nature of my pelvis meant I had made peace with never carrying a child, and yet that little stick I had peed on in my bathroom told me differently and I felt joy flood my veins. I was pregnant!

It was my pregnancy that made me stop drinking entirely. I just stopped. Gave it up. I was twenty-seven and bar the odd sip of bubbles at a wedding, an occasional drop in celebration and a cup of something fruity once or twice on holiday, I've not really drank since. The longer I was totally sober, the more I could see that alcohol only confused my life, adversely affecting my mental health. Giving me a false sense of security and masquerading as an ally, I didn't like what it did to me: providing me with a mental crutch made of nothing good. She was a false friend who urged me on and stood back, enjoying the spectacle while I teetered on the edge of a bubbling cauldron in killer heels. That's not friendship, it's the opposite of caring, and I think the very best thing I ever did was to stop boozing. Still, decades later, even in recent times when I refuse a drink, I get called boring, lightweight, a party-pooper or am met with a sour expression of disappointment or dismissal. Shockingly, even today that pressure is still there at social situations and in groups, but I think I'm still funny with or without white wine spritzer sloshing in my veins and I've even been known to dance.

At only ten weeks pregnant, I was still very much in the sur-prised/excited/stunned phase. My nan had gone into overdrive and begun knitting and Mum made good friends with the women who ran the baby department in John Lewis she was in there so often, browsing. The women in my family had a new game of 'name the baby' and at every opportunity sent me names they liked or didn't like – I can't remember many of them, but know Horatio and Isadora figured somewhere; both were under consideration.

All my focus was on this pregnancy – thinking how I could work around it and what might be best for this unexpected and precious gift. I smiled a lot, felt smug and so very, very lucky.

It was around this time that I set up my own business with my new partner. There were many large companies who had invested in computer hardware and needed their employees trained in the software to bring their operations into the twenty-first century. This was the mid-nineties, when companies were making the switch to Microsoft Office for Windows and all their staff needed train-ing. Without premises, cash or any discernible skill set, I managed to organise training courses at the clients' own premises, which they paid for in advance, via a bank of verified freelance trainers to whom we paid a daily rate. The trainers, who travelled there directly, we paid above the odds, so they were keen to work for us and do a great job. All I had to do was administer the courses remotely and book the training days.

This was a short, golden window of opportunity, as pretty quickly big companies set up and equipped their own training departments, which in the long run was often cheaper than out-sourcing it. Smaller companies did not have the volume of training requirements to make the business work. It was a failing business, but it provided us with an income for a couple of years and taught me that if I used my head and put the hours in, I could make a living for myself, if I was never afraid of grafting hard, being flexible and doing what was necessary. It was about as far from my dream of writing books as it was possible, but it was that old hamster wheel again; I was on it without time to look up, running faster and faster to keep all the wheels turning, working hard, trying to iron out the kinks in this new relationship, knowing we needed to be a well-oiled machine before this baby arrived.

I read all the articles I could on pregnancy, as excitement grew in my wider family at the prospect of a new baby who would be the first grandchild and great-grandchild! My partner was delighted. We bought tiny pairs of socks, little vests and I even walked around the flat with a cushion stuffed up my jumper, beaming at how I would look in just a few short months. I invested emotionally in the tiny seed that had taken root in my womb and I allowed myself to think ahead to a time when I would become a mum.

But it was not to be.

I started bleeding in the middle of the night and lost that first baby at a little less than thirteen weeks, walking around the flat with a cushion of tissue stuffed in my pants and not knowing what I was supposed to do next, how I was expected to act. Physically, for me, it was no worse than an average period. But don't think it was anything like as easy, because my hormones were raging and I was distraught, upset, although not entirely devastated. In the back of my mind, I'd never fully believed it in the first place. Having a baby had literally felt too good to be true. I was not only tearful, but also disappointed and dare I say it, guilty that I had let everyone down. To watch my dad's face crumple in sadness and my mum hold me tight and tell me it was all okay and that I could try again, was hard. I felt like I'd let my partner down too, who was wonderfully understanding, kind and supportive, but I still felt like a failure, and this was not the first or last time that as a woman, as a person, I felt less than . . . I put another brick in that emotional wall and crouched behind it.

The medical team assured me I could carry a baby and that there was no reason for me not to conceive again. I was keen to know if there were things I could have or should have done differently. The medic told me, 'These things just happen.' So, I gave away the little socks and vests, balled the list of names and threw it in the garbage and got on with my life.

We got married. Yes, someone *had* asked me to marry him! In the wake of our loss and with our attentions on the business and keeping afloat financially, it was a lovely distraction and something really good to look forward to. All around us things had felt as if they were slipping out of reach: our pregnancy, business, money and even how we felt about each other. Marriage felt like the next logical step, and I thought it would make us stronger as a couple.

I forged ahead without really stopping to ask if this marriage was right for me, for us. Still only half emerged from my sobriety chrysalis, and figuring out exactly what I wanted in life, I should have remained single until the process was complete, and I should have understood that a wobbly relationship is rarely made stable by the addition of a gold band and a signed wedding certificate, but hindsight, my friend, is, as they say, a wonderful thing. He was a great guy and things were *okay* and I figured that would be enough for a happy life, wouldn't it?

We moved to a Kentish village to live in a terraced cottage with rickety wooden stairs and a room we could use as an office. Married life began for the lovely man and me. I felt calm, sedate and settled, but not euphoric, excited or ecstatic about our future. Everything was a little muted, a little pale, and I was a little lonely, far from my family and my friends in London. I told myself this wasn't a book or movie, and that I had no right to expect fireworks and roses, this was real life, and I was pretty sure it was as good as it got. We worked together and lived together, and it was 'fine'.

It was with great caution that I informed my nearest and dearest when I fell pregnant again. The announcement was tinged with apprehension for me that sadly removed a little of the joy and excitement. Having walked this road before I could only hope for a better outcome, but as someone whose body had let her down on a regular basis, I knew it required a little more than hope.

I took great care as the weeks slipped by, and if I could somehow concentrate really hard on keeping this baby inside me then I had a greater chance of making it to the finish line. I abandoned my extreme diet and began to eat. Nothing was off limits. My body, as if shocked and delighted to be receiving any nourishment at all, ballooned. I was enormous, putting on 3 stone, or 42 lb. My baby swam in water and Greek lemon rice, my favourite go-to dish, served by a local Greek takeaway, and I couldn't get enough of it. That and fresh bread slathered with butter.

I went crazy. I was swollen and uncomfortable – no shit! My old aunts would tell me it was okay as I was eating for two. They were wrong, I was actually eating for about fifteen. But did this stop me chowing way past being full? No. I was stuck at home in the latter stages without anything other than one ghastly denim dress to wear, as it was all that fitted me. I would wash it and dry it overnight and put it on the next day. I grew to hate that dress and every picture of my pregnant self features the item. The business was barely thriving, yet I was unable to go out and find a job as I was heavily pregnant; there was no money for an extensive maternity wardrobe or fancy-pants jeans and cover-ups.

I truly loved being pregnant, knowing that with every month that passed I was getting closer and closer to becoming a mum, allowing myself to believe it was possible. And as my belief grew, so did my excitement, but having worked so hard on my 'thinness' for years, oh my goodness how I felt challenged by my pregnant body. Lying in the bath, I would watch the water ripple with his kicks and internal fist bumps that were thrilling. Finally, my body was doing something great – it wasn't broken or shattered to pieces, failing or smashed, it was successfully growing a baby. Bloody marvellous!

I had seen pictures of my pregnant mum with her tiny little bowling ball of a bump sitting inside her hot pants and resting inside her slender manicured hands – well, if she sported a bowling ball, I had a bloody space hopper! It was conflicting: the vast swollen barrel of my stomach was a thing of disgust, despite the utter wonder of creation that was going on inside. My stomach, however, was no more a concern than my vast veiny boobs, bloated ankles, moon face or sausagey fingers.

I was not in a good place mentally. It became clearer with every passing month that my marriage was failing, but we battled on, fighting against the instinct that told me we were about to hit the rocks, heavily pregnant and losing interest in the business as it sank. Money was incredibly tight. We eked out the pennies as we worked together, lived together and were expectant together. But when one domino was pushed, it felt like everything fell down. The idea of giving up on my marriage was painful, especially when the examples of my parents and grandparents were of long, strong marriages next to which I failed in comparison.

My pregnancy wasn't easy, largely because of my self-inflicted weight gain and the reality of living a life with someone who you weren't sure you wanted to be married to, which was understandably horrible for us both. There was no blame, no hatred and no solution. We were very different people who found it hard to communicate and it felt a lot like living with a stranger, which only added to my (and his) loneliness. The arguments between us were fierce and left me feeling drained and oh so lonely and I am sure he felt the same. He would seek solace in a bottle of red and I would cry myself to sleep.

Our cottage felt claustrophobic. I couldn't breathe, stifled by the situation and my inability to figure out how to make things better. It was as if I knew we were unfixable and yet there we were, based remotely from our friends and family, which made me feel incredibly isolated, financially under strain and having a baby together. I hoped beyond hope that our baby would be the wonderful thread that could stitch us back together, but if anything, it was a pressure that ripped us apart, putting even more emotional and financial strain on a union that was already close to breaking point.

This period in my life confirmed that no matter what happened, success or failure, I needed to be close to the people who were my support system. It was clearly not going to be a happy ever after for my husband and me and yet we limped on, both, I think, hoping that we were wrong, that we had made the right choice and that we'd wake up with sunshine in our thoughts instead of dread. My whole world felt like a pressure cooker. It was everything I had longed for, a house, a husband and a baby on the way, and yet I had never been so unhappy and desperately, desperately lonely.

Physically I was struggling too. The skin across my abdomen was tight with silvery stretch marks, which ran like tributaries down my hips and thighs. My bras were enormous. I felt sick if I saw my naked body and guilty that I had let myself get like that in such a short space of time. Crying one day to my mum, she assured me that I looked beautiful (I think I did and probably always do to her) and that my weight would drop off once I was feeding the baby and could get back to being active. I thought this too and couldn't wait to get back into shape so I could once again feel the power of that slim body and not the self-revulsion that had begun.

Despite my previous loss, I got lucky, beyond lucky! And that pregnancy, while not easy, resulted in the birth of my beautiful son, Josiah (Joshy). He felt like my reward for the loss I had experienced previously, and with my newborn child in my arms my life felt complete, and all memories of my miscarriage were swept from my mind. I knew that what I felt for this child was an all-consuming forever love.

The same could not be said for the man I had married and what came next no matter how predictable, was no less devastating for that. It took all my courage to admit and all my concentration to recognise that without the right foundation and with the constant onslaught of verbal clashing that occurred almost hourly, arguing around and around on a draining spiral, it was not a healthy way to live for any of us. The fraught atmosphere where our anger and frustration crackled in the air long after we had fallen silent was not a good environment in which to raise a little boy.

We divorced.

It was horrible, and with emotions raw and hurt on display, we knew moments of unkindness that would on reflection fill me with shame.

. . . my darling baby boy! I think my face says it all.

Chapter Eight

'THE DECADE OF DIETS!'

At nearly thirty, newly single and with a small baby to care for, I existed in a permanent state of feeling numb and scared. It was one thing to grab any job going and look after myself, as I had done for most of my life, but quite another when there was another little human depending on me. I gripped my baby, feeding him and watching him as he slept, trying through my attentions and murmurings to reassure him that no matter what, we would get through this and that he was so very loved.

Being divorced on my own with a little one and no real clue of how I was going to get by had not been in my plan – of course not. It felt a lot like failure and certainly wasn't how I'd wanted my son's life to start. I had rushed into a marriage, which was reckless, selfish and dumb. Blindly falling into plans and agreeing, as if this was my one shot and I needed to take it or else face a life of no one picking me . . . We both deserved better. My heart hurt, and it hurt all the more at the thought that I was denying my ex and Josh the everyday family life that I had been surrounded with.

With decades now passed and emotional bruises long healed, it's hard to look back at that time with anything other than gratitude, not only for the resilience and lessons it taught me, but also because we got Josiah. I would not change a thing, not now. And the lovely man is happy with a partner, who is wonderful, and a beautiful daughter, Josiah's sister, and they are very close. I love that Joshy has this wonderful sibling he adores and another family too.

But at the time, with the business and marriage so closely intertwined, everything came to an abrupt halt. We closed up shop, packed up bags and slammed doors as we left. I walked with a haunting falter, as if I'd just woken up and didn't quite know where I was. Yet again it felt safest to go where I knew there was a nest and moved to the West Country, to a little house in Southmead, Bristol. It was affordable and I was near enough to my parents, who were a lifeline when it came to childcare, enabling me to work two, sometimes three jobs, including working in a call centre and cleaning offices of an evening, while I built a life from scratch in a new place.

I would drop Joshy with my mum early or she would stay over. Depending on my start time, she would either look after him all day or drop him at the nursery on the days he went. I'd come home after a day in a call centre, have my supper with him, bathe him, put him to bed and then at least three nights a week go back out to work and Joshy would either stay with my parents or I'd swoop by on my way home and scoop him up before heading home. I was still on that hamster wheel but was running faster than ever just to stay upright. Joshy was the only joy in my life, everything else felt like a hard and exhausting grind.

Spending my days and nights away from my baby was not what I would have chosen. This was not how I wanted *his* story to unfold, thinking of my own childhood where no matter what, my mum was always on hand. It was the predictability and routine that made my younger self feel safe. I knew it was different for Joshy, but I wanted to provide for him a life that was stable and that meant paying the rent, putting food on the table, affording nursery fees and all the other things that would keep us afloat. My parents bought his clothes, his bike and so on, and helped out in ways they cannot even imagine – their support made all the difference, made everything possible.

I was and am proud of my financial independence, one thing I have had throughout my life: the ability to pay my way and support my son and myself, largely because I was always willing to do *any* job. This is true, but I am more than aware and eternally grateful that it was made so much easier by my parents providing a safety net, which would catch us if ever we fell. More often than not the roles I undertook weren't glamorous or fun, reading from a brain-numbing script under a strip light in a call centre or scrubbing bathrooms and emptying out sticky bins in an office block, but it didn't matter, it was all about doing whatever was necessary to keep our heads above water, while dreaming, dreaming of one day sitting down to write. My stories and life experiences often rattled the drawers in my mental filing cabinets, wanting to be set free. But with each year that passed, I grew more to see that Mrs Blight might just have been right, writing books was probably not for a girl like me.

My grandparents on my dad's side had passed away and my Aunty Kit died. I had been especially close to her, and her death came when I was running on empty and hit me hard. She had been one of the women who shaped my thoughts, and while I knew that she like my nan and grandad could never fully understand how I had married and divorced in such a short space of time, I also knew that she was one of my greatest cheerleaders. I still miss her.

It was at this time that my weight battle started in earnest. I fed my son, and did lose some weight, but as a single working mum who was struggling financially and emotionally, I admit I took solace in hot chips covered in salt and vinegar and slabs of chocolate while I sat alone of an evening. It felt easier, quicker to shove bad fuel into my gob and go to sleep or grab anything and get back out to work. My cupboard stocks were pitiful, and I pretty much bought produce for one meal at a time. This meant not outlaying too much money, but also that I relied on cheap snacks whenever I felt my energy dip.

My body, still at least 28 lb overweight, was to me unattractive, but I was far from obsessed with my size, shape and face as I had been when trying to retain my slimness or how I was to become in the future. The fact that I had grown a little human who owned my heart was incredible and all-consuming enough for me to be diverted from the fact that my boobs were still like melons (water not cantaloupe, sadly) and there was a pouch of skin that hung over my caesarean scar.

Oh yes, did I mention my caesarean scar? It sat, in fact sits, a shade above my surgery scars, adding to the whole crisscross, grid-like mess that is below my knicker line. Did I mind? Well, when I considered the fact that this scar was the one that had enabled me to give birth to my baby boy . . . I did not give a jot, in fact I embraced it. Celebrated it!

This euphoria over such a damaged part of me was short-lived. I was only twenty-nine and could still feel the outline of that slender girl, who was the life and soul, hiding beneath the thin cushion of fat. I could still glimpse her in the mirror if I looked at it the right way, stuck out my chin and sucked in my stomach. But what did it matter? It wasn't as if any living soul was ever going to see my naked self. I was done with all that, reeling from my failed marriage. Living alone now with my young son, I might have been far from confident in how I looked, but I had no idea how in the coming years my body shape and weight would change so drastically and as a result my self-esteem and happiness would be reduced to dust. No idea at all . . .

It was when I was thirty that I got my first proper, grown-up, clever-clogs job. Having read about a new tech start-up who were looking for admin staff, I secured an interview and put on my cheap suit. I had to drop Josh at the nursery on the way and he desperately needed a pee. I pulled over under a flyover and tried to hold him so he could wee on the ground (standing-up wees were still a little way off!). Now, as anyone will tell you, there is a skill to weeing when being held in this manner. It's a little precarious to say the least and let's just say I didn't get the angle exactly right. I screamed, as I felt the warm pee soak my left leg and prayed that it would dry out before I had to walk in for my interview. Dabbing at it with paper towels helped, but I was more than aware of the whiff of pee I carried.

Knowing this was highly unlikely to endear me to any potential employer, I more or less wrote the whole experience off and was far more relaxed than I would have been had I thought I was in with a chance. I liked the company a lot and asked questions, hoovering up all I could about the possible uses for storing/mining and analysing huge quantities of data. It was fascinating to me, a whole world away from writing books, but was something I wanted to know more about. The CEO and I got on fantastically, but I didn't in a million years think they would offer me a job. With no mention of my damp leg, much to my delight they offered me a job as an account manager – with a fat salary and a company car (a silver Audi A4 2.5 TDI in case anyone is interested).

This job changed my life. With hindsight I can see it was one of the crossroads that life put in my path, and I am so glad it did. It took courage to go for that interview, in an industry about which I knew zip and for a vague position, which I was sure I was massively underqualified for, but that courage paid off. The job brought me financial stability, it helped my self-belief and over the six or so years I was with them, it saw me work in a growing company, all over Europe and the US on some incredible projects that gave process and insight into how companies collected and best utilised data, whether for predictive modelling, marketing or whatever. I learned so much and am still fascinated by how data has become currency, for the greater good and conversely, the bad.

My life was fast-paced, chock-full of meetings, flights and hotel reservations, and with a calendar that bulged at the seams with all it tried to contain – none of it was social, all work and with my parents doing more than their fair share of helping to raise Joshy – it was all I could do to cling on to that spinning hamster wheel as it went faster and faster. I lived off hotel menus and grub grabbed at airports, always, always on the move. At school drop-off one morning, a mum in the playground said to me, 'I really envy you, being able to go and sit on a plane and fly to America, stay in a hotel . . . You are lucky. I'd love a break like that!'

I nodded. I was *so* lucky! Lucky enough to have cried all the way to Heathrow as I made another trip away from my son, heading off to stay in a faceless, nameless hotel that looked and smelled the same as the other six I had stayed in that month. Lucky enough to have missed his first step, which my mum let him recreate with me thinking it was his first . . . and feeling hollowed out when this came to light. Lucky enough to feel so torn that my insides were like toffee: pulled thin, brittle and unsure I would survive even the smallest knock.

Not that Joshy wasn't loved and adored. Here's a standard family picture of him in a wheelbarrow with my grandad being pushed by his nan!

Josh and his great grandad in the wheelbarrow being pushed by my Mum - just a standard day at Nanny's house!

Yes, it was my choice, my choice to earn a decent living, to climb a career ladder with the hope of carving a hole in that concrete ceiling. My choice to try and have it all, to set the best example I could to my baby boy, to break the mould, to show my darling nan and great-aunts that it was possible to dream of a life outside your postcode, to do what the men did. But be under no illusion, that fancy car and salary came at a cost. Not least of which having to hear comments like that when I was distraught about leaving Joshy again for a week or so.

It was inevitable I guess that something was going to give, but when it happened it was not what I had expected. I was thirty-two and Joshy was four. We had moved into a lovely garden flat in Clifton, Bristol, when the word cancer was first cast in my direction.

It was a word that in my youth meant a death sentence, but thankfully not now, not that my stuttering heart and sharp intake of breath made any allowance for that.

I was petrified. Other than fatigue I had no real symptoms, and my tumour was found by luck during a routine exam. I remember laughing initially because it had to be a mistake – this was something that happened to other people, despite it being a disease that touches *every* family, *every* person and my family and I are no different.

I told very few people. My primary concern was not upsetting or worrying my little boy, keeping life as stable and secure for him was the most important thing. No matter that it will affect one in two of the population, it's still a word that when spilled from the mouth of a medic, leaves you cold and in doubt: *surely, they don't mean me? That can't be right!*

But it was right, and I had surgery to remove a small tumour from my left ovary. I was sore from the surgery, but it was not nearly as bad or invasive as many I had previously experienced, and my recovery was good.

It was a new experience, a different kind of discomfort and after learning to deal with the sharp and acute pains of my bone surgery, this was more a dragging sensation, uncomfortable but not the level of pain that had taken my breath away throughout my teens.

The same could not be said for my mental recovery, and for years afterwards I would wait for my check-up with bated breath, fearful of every dodgy-looking mole, every unexplained bleed or odd bowel movement or tired day (of which there were of course many!). It was a fear that sat like a background note to my life, not defining me more or less than any other experience, but one that had the power to wrench me from sleep and leave me lying in a cold sweat. I've filed it in my 'life' file, which I mentally flip through occasionally; it helps me practise gratitude for what I have and where I am. Still here. My biggest worry at the time was that had I not been so lucky, it was unlikely Josh would remember me, and that struck me as the biggest shame and is something I still have nightmares about.

◆ ◆ ◆

I like to call the time between divorcing and meeting Simeon Prowse some ten years later, the decade of diets. My weight fluctuated between 150 (10 stone 7 lb) and 196 lb (14 stone). This was the first time I allowed my weight to yo-yo in this fashion. The losses and gains were incremental and was the beginning of a devastating cycle that would become my life. It was a cycle that trapped me, overwhelmed me and held me so tightly that it nearly destroyed me entirely. And if you think it was simply down to my inability to stop putting food in my mouth . . . oh my friend, I wish that it were. Trust me when I tell you there is nothing simple about it, about any of it, because if it were, I would have done these 'simple' things and not consigned myself to an existence of internalised distress over my appearance. I'd not have wasted some of the best years of my life, not missed out on some incredible opportunities, not woken with regularity in the wee small hours trying to figure out how to move my life forward while reaching for something to eat.

Throwing myself with gusto into a whole array of regimens and restrictions that promised results, I grabbed at the promises these diets made and believed the hype that they would CHANGE MY LIFE! I wanted to change my life, didn't I? I wanted to feel less self-conscious, wanted to not feel so awkward about my size. The dream was to sling on some tight jeans, a halter neck and let my cheekbones do the talking. Not necessarily because I wanted or felt ready to date, but in the firm belief that it would help me not feel less than. The sad truth is my self-esteem fluctuated almost in direct proportion to my body size.

As you know, dear reader, I've had an unhealthy relationship with food since my teens, using it to plug the holes that had sprung in my emotional and mental well-being and to stopper the gaps in my self-worth. And by now as I hit my early thirties, there were a lot of holes. I'm also aware that there is so much more to being a citizen of value on the planet than the size of one's arse and how many wrinkles you may or may not have on your forehead. And I will strive until my dying day to dispel or at least question the assumption that beauty, youth and slender bodies mean high value and anything less than this is the very opposite.

I'm passionate about this, knowing what it's like to feel without value because of the number on the scales and all associated perceptions, as if my IQ, point of view, eloquence and any other achievements somehow diminished as my fat content increased. Yes, it's a weird dichotomy that this fast-paced world we now live in, a world where popularity is a nice little earner, where self-worth is sometimes measured in ticks, likes, mentions, comments or shares, is also a world where it is now vital to question everything, from designer handbags, virtual love affairs and our news to the many flawless images of women and their beauty – as all are sometimes fake. The bigger I got the more invisible I became or at least the more invisible I *felt*. Diets promised to break the cycle and set me free – yes please!

The sad truth is, yes, I wanted my life to change, wanted my body to change, but I didn't really want to put the work in. I wasn't ready, finding it easier to retreat into my PJs, eat whatever lay at the bottom of the fridge and concentrate on Joshy, who was the centre of my universe.

Josh aged three – and me thirty-one – I can close my eyes and remember what it felt like to hold him like this.

Some of the diets I tried were weird and wonderful, some of them felt like torture from the get-go and some were pleasant at first, yielding short-term results that were exciting, a boost to my sense of well-being and my confidence. To drop a few pounds, which is actually very easy when you have a lot to lose, as the first thing you lose is fluid, meant I quickly saw the loosening of waist-bands, the slightest emergence of a hint of hip bone and a sparkle in my eye at the thought of all the wonderful reward that would be coming my skinny-arsed way.

But ultimately, it was a battle of wills and often the strong pull of the carb was greater than my ability to say no to it. This weakness did nothing to aid my self-esteem. I thought often about what the matriarchal figures who had raised me faced, battling poverty and world war, and they did so with strength and for this I felt a great deal of shame. Why did I not have similar resolve? I'd given up booze in a heartbeat, neither lamenting nor dwelling on it, so why could I not do the same with food?

It didn't take much to push me off track, to give in to my craving. My will and promises would crumple after a hard day at work, a lonely evening, or a sleepless night while I mentally chased greater financial security, planning how to tackle what came next in my calendar and how to better carve up my time so I could give Joshy more of it. Yes, these aspects all played their part, and it wasn't long before, using the above as the excuses I was quick to lasso, I could be found with my nose in a biscuit barrel or my chops around a chunk of cheese. And the weight I'd lost, and a little bit more for good measure, would ping back on before anyone could say, fancy a doughnut? The diet book/printed sheet/rulebook would then be consigned to a large plastic storage box under my bed where my bloated self would sleep soundly with relief, knowing I could wake up tomorrow without the fear or dread of the diet I had placed myself on. Giving up on a diet brought instant relief, the same as if an appointment or event you've been dreading gets cancelled – it felt wonderful in the short-term, but the long-term effects of this constant failure were anything but wonderful.

As my weight crept up, I began to further lose my bearings when it came to my physical self. And having yo-yoed between starving and bingeing for most of my life, I forgot what success in terms of my health and well-being actually looked like and couldn't imagine how I could get back on track. The previous interest I had taken in my face had stopped. It was hard to see anything great in a face that was doughy and swollen. The one small ounce of confidence in myself physically that had been centred on my face was gone. That plastic box got fuller, and my mattress sagged further until all that separated me from the promised world of weight loss was mere millimetres and yet in reality it was as far out of my reach as it always had been.

If I managed to lose a few pounds, it was as if I could justify my actions with the warped logic that because I had lost some weight, maybe as much as a couple of kilos, I was *owed* the good stuff that had been denied to me. A reward if you like. I'm now acutely aware that this binge and starve is just an eating disorder by another name and that the 'good stuff' I refer to is of course the bad stuff.

Joshy and I lived in the middle of the city and had a twenty-four-hour supermarket, every take-away restaurant you can think of and fast-food outlets within strolling distance, meaning I could fix my hunger or heed the call of a craving, give in to my greed and have the sugar soaked, fat-laden snack in my podgy mitts within minutes. Hurrah! Although it wasn't a cause for hurrah – it was a damaging, demotivating, self-worth-sapping cycle that held me in its clutches and no one had the hammer with which to break the cycle but me, but I was too weakened by my nutritionally poor diet to even pick it up.

This repeated sequence felt hard if not impossible to break. I've tried to remember the diets I have been on in my time. Most yielded short-lived results and felt a lot like punishment. Some were great but the moment I resorted to 'normal' eating, I would quickly put on the weight I had lost and more. Here are some (but not all!) that I have tried:

The Cabbage Soup diet.

The Cambridge diet.

The LighterLife plan.

The F-plan.

The Rosemary Conley plan.

Fasting.

Juicing.

Slimming World.

Weight Watchers.

The Mediterranean diet.

The Banting diet.

Starving myself – yes really.

Drinking only water with honey and cayenne pepper for three-day periods.

Only eating everything with a very, very tiny spoon – I can see your 'eye roll' from here!

Only eating things that fit into a ball in the palm of my hand . . . I know. I know . . .

The Slimfast Plan.

Atkins.

Keto.

The Alkaline diet.

Paleo.

There are most definitely others . . .

I always applied the same skewed logic around starting and maintaining a diet, which I can now, with hindsight, see was only an excuse not to start/persevere/succeed. My rules on dieting were very strict. For example, I could only start a diet on a Monday, so that I could have a good 'whole' week of eating 'right'. Which for me meant the week or weekend before I embarked on my latest weight-loss venture, I could indulge in all the things that were going to be denied to me when dieting. Ridiculously and predictably, this meant I usually began a diet a few pounds heavier than I would have been without the period of indulgence that preceded it.

I didn't say it made sense.

If I 'broke' a diet by going off-piste I would then consider it properly 'broken' and so a cheating biscuit or a square of cheese would lead to a fatty lunch of a mayonnaise-filled sandwich and fish and chips for supper, followed by chocolate because in my mind I may as well, why not? The damage was done with that one biscuit . . .

The best way to describe it is this: in my mind breaking my diet was like firing a dark ink splat onto a freshly painted pale wall – it was ruined and therefore I might as well go crazy! One ink splat or ten, who cared? The wall was going to need repainting anyway, right? And of course, if I 'broke' my diet then there was no way I could get back on the wagon until the following Monday – see above.

These self-imposed rules and rituals were of course just another way of giving in to that voice of self-sabotage: the thought that I was going to fail anyway sooner or later and so why bother? It made sense to me at some level: by failing quickly and spectacularly, it kind of put me in control, which made it slightly easier to bear. But only a little.

I was feeling well, Josh and I had a safe little home, and yet my whole life felt like it was poised on a teetering rock, as I lived one pay cheque away from trouble and it didn't feel good. I felt like I'd screwed up: no husband, no partner, not enough time with my son, no support other than from my parents and not the life I had planned, I wanted to be a writer! Some chance. No matter how loudly I shouted this to the universe – the idea was laughable. I was far too busy chasing my tail, and racing around trying to keep all the plates of my life spinning, in the way my mum had when I was younger . . .

All the food-restrictive diets, the cutting out of food groups or any other of the weird and wonderful weight-loss strategies that I signed up for, followed a similar pattern. I call this my 'Diet Cycle'.

Euphoria at the thought of starting. This was going to be IT! The solution I had been looking for. I'd often buy the book or register and allow myself to start picturing the slender me – a confident go-getter, able to shop for clothes I liked in High Street stores, rather than covertly hunting down sack-like, floaty garments that would hide my shape. A me who could pop on a swimming costume and frolic in a pool rather than avoiding swimming altogether (and this was nothing to do with my period!). I would lie in bed and before I fell asleep visualise the new me that would emerge from the chrysalis of flab in which I was encased. I would feel happy, keen to get going. Motivated! Excited!

The first couple of days were always the hardest. I, like everyone else, do not like feeling hungry and having filled my face with such regularity, whether my body needed food or not, I was unused to the feeling of hunger.

I would push through feeling utterly, utterly miserable. As if part of my life joy had been removed. Having thought about, pondered and obsessed over food for so much of my day, without it, my life felt a little empty . . . like a much-enjoyed hobby or interest had been banned for me. The initial and inevitable weight loss could no way justify my low mood, sugar withdrawal, fatigue, headaches, hunger and sense of deprivation. I am embarrassed to admit that I would, on occasion, feel murderously resentful of those not on the diet and able to eat all the things I wanted to eat. Then I'd begin to eye up the bread, the cheese, the cookie, the crisps, in fact anything I could get my hands on, often unable to think of anything else.

A bad day, or indeed any small event, like not being able to park the car, or the arrival of an unexpected bill, or just feeling overwhelmed or tired would see me give up. Give in. Eat. Fail. And eat some more. And the sense of failure coupled with being back in the grip of an unhealthy food obsession would leave me feeling worse than if I hadn't bothered.

I would swear off diets. Completely. Promising never ever to do that to myself again. Until the next time when I'd feel euphoria at the thought of starting. This was going to be IT! The solution I had been looking for . . .

The very worst thing for me about trying and failing at so many diets was not, as you might suspect, the wasted money on all these promised cures or the misery of restrictive calorie intake, and not even the complete removal of the enjoyment of food or indeed the *damage* this yo-yo dieting effect might have been having on my body and mind. Yo-yo dieting, we now know, causes the body to increase appetite and cling to its energy storage, meaning you often gain back more weight than you lose.

No, the worst thing for me was the shame I felt at my failure to maintain my weight loss or to lose weight at all – the reverting to type the moment my regimen slipped. I can't bear to calculate how much weight I have lost and gained on the terrible merry-go-round of bodily abuse that was my life, but it has to be hundreds and hundreds and hundreds of pounds. My husband, Simeon, and I recently sat down to do the calculation and when I saw the five-figure sums he was totting up with a pencil, as if checking any other kind of measurement, my heart sank. It was as sobering as it was mortifying. When looking for any reason/excuse/justification to abandon the diet – all it would take was the sage words from a friend, colleague or family member, who would unwittingly give me the get-out-of-jail-free card I was looking for.

'*Don't go too far now, darling!*'
'*I don't think you need to lose weight, Mand.*'
'*You're gorgeous just how you are!*'
'*You have a pretty face, don't worry so much about the rest!*'
'*You don't seem fat to me. I love you how you are.*'

And without further ado, I would be tipping my tofu and spinach into the nearest bin and heading for the closest purveyor of thick shakes. Again, was this abandonment of my goals and the giving up so easily the fault of all those who sought to reassure me? Make me feel loved, no matter how unhelpful? NO! The fault was mine and mine alone. No one was popping Revels in my gob while I watched a movie or sprinkling sugar by the tablespoonful onto my cereal.

I was thirty-seven and got to the point where I felt so unhappy about my size that I began to dread leaving the house, looking for any excuse not to have to go outside. My career was affected. I became a little withdrawn at work, didn't put myself forward in the way I had for trips or extra responsibility, preferring to hide away.

Leaving that job, I decided to take out a loan and open a shop with my mum. This was in part down to the fact that I could hide away in a shop, sit behind a counter and not have to squeeze into a suit every day. Don't get me wrong, this wasn't the only reason. I also liked the thought of working for myself, spending time with my mum, not travelling and being able to play a greater role in Joshy's day-to-day life. He was eight and was struggling at school; he started to show reluctance to go in and wasn't keen to go to parties or have friends home for tea; he seemed a little isolated and it tore at my heart. I figured having me on hand might make him feel more settled and I would have done anything, anything to make his life the best it could be.

We opened a beautiful shop in Clifton Village, Bristol, selling French furniture and homeware. Mum and I chose the stock and every day we would drink coffee, chat to customers, arrange displays, order stock and on the odd day we even sold something!

Unhelpfully, I began to compare myself with everyone, particularly every woman. If I saw a slim woman, I thought she must be disgusted by me; if I saw my reflection, I cringed at what I looked like. I hated that this was how my mind worked, it was narrow-minded and self-obsessed, but I was stuck and miserable and I loathed myself. This plummeting self-worth and sense of revulsion sent me straight into the arms of food where I sought comfort, which of course only exacerbated my situation.

When I was slim, I was party to the nudges and finger points if someone very, very overweight was in view. I heard the snide comments about such people ordering and eating fattening food. I heard the sharp intake of breath when a large person got on a train/bus/plane and was about to squish into the seat next to you. A friend had once said to my slim self, 'I often worry about airplanes and the weight limit – how do they calculate for people who weigh the equivalent of two of me? Is that even safe? I flew from Glasgow to London on a flight when a very, very fat woman sat with her arms and body hanging over the chair. Her flesh pressed against me. I was uncomfortable and embarrassed to be that close to another human, squashed against her.'

That's the trouble with my impeccable filing system. It doesn't only store all the great or encouraging memories and thoughts for perfect recall, just ask Mrs Blight.

I knew how society whispered, and when I was overweight I could hear those whispers as loudly as my own heartbeat. Having to go to parents' evening at my son's school or any event would see me crying before I left the house, fretting for hours if not days in advance, as my thoughts raged in a self-absorbed and inward-looking way, what would everyone think of the size of me? And it wasn't my size that bothered me per se, but rather what it said about me, my lack of discipline, lack of control when it came to food groups and portions. I disgusted myself and could only imagine that this was how everyone who saw me felt too.

It is only with clarity of thought and free from the grip of food addiction that I can see that 99.99999999 per cent of people couldn't give a flying fig about what I looked like, if they noticed me at all – people are generally far too preoccupied with their own life and troubles to be overly concerned with mine! But my view of myself was skewed, I pictured myself as if permanently in one of those inflatable sumo suits that meant people had to jump out of my way for fear of getting bowled over by my bulk.

The best way I can describe how I felt to be overweight and in public is this: imagine you were off to a concert or a lecture or a pantomime or the theatre or a school play or meeting . . . and you arrive late and it's very busy, crowded, but you see some spare seats and your heart lifts and so you settle down, only to receive a tap on the shoulder from someone informing you that those seats are actually reserved for VIPs. Oh my goodness, the humiliation of having to stand and endure the tuts of those around you, whose view you are now blocking, as if to say, 'Huh! You thought you were a VIP, did you! Now try finding a seat!' Yes, that red-faced moment of publicly getting it wrong, of being unwanted or in the wrong place or taking up space that wasn't yours – THAT was how it felt for me, every single day.

At the checkout: 'I am so sorry!'

On a train: 'I'm sorry!'

On a plane: 'Gosh I am sorry!'

In the street: 'So sorry!'

So, what was it I was apologising for? My size? My overeating? Actually, yes, both.

Our shop was popular, with regular customers who liked to pop in for a cuppa, but margins were tight. We got by and it was wonderful to spend time with my mum. We made great money at Christmas and were known for our fantastic festive displays and decorations, but it was becoming increasingly hard to stay in business when we only made money for one month of the year. Rents and business rates in Clifton were rising.

And then one day we had something much bigger to worry about than business rates, something that pulled the rug from under all of us.

I dropped Joshy at school while my darling mum had gone to an art shop on the other side of Clifton to pick up some brown luggage labels that we used as price tags. My dad called out of the blue to tell me that she had been involved in an accident.

It's words you never want to hear, words you might imagine, but the reality makes you stop while you try to process the information pinging around your brain. My blood ran cold, but I was massively reassured when he explained, quite lightly, that she had stepped onto a crossing to get to her car on the other side of the road and had been hit by a cyclist. His voice was incredulous, only Mum could get hit by a bike ON A CROSSING!

Phew. I matched his tone; the relief was sweet and instant. There was no urgency, it sounded minor. He couldn't answer any of my questions, asked with a gentle tease, what kind of bike? A kid's trike? A chopper? How fast was it going, two miles an hour? What has she done? Banged her arm? Fallen over? I arranged to meet him at the hospital where she'd been despatched to A&E, thinking of jokes I could make when I saw her and worried that the shop would be shut for a couple of hours – I mean, a bike, ON A CROSSING! How did that even happen?

The central Bristol hospital was busy. I parked and took my time in arriving, walking via the ambulance bay. The first thing I saw was my dad leaning on a wall with both palms flat against the bricks and he was being sick. *Oh, great that's all we need*, I thought, *Dad to be going down with a bug at a time like this . . .*

There was no bug. I walked over and he took a second to compose himself before telling me tearfully that they didn't know if my beautiful mummy was going to make it.

I laughed then, a small and embarrassing sound that left my mouth. It was made partly in nerves and partly because it had to be a joke, right? She was due at the shop with the labels; we were going to get our morning coffee.

He took me inside where two police officers and a doctor were standing in the waiting room who *could* answer my questions:

What kind of bike? *'A mountain bike being ridden by a six-foot tall stocky student.'*

How fast was he going? *'About thirty miles an hour down the hill.'*

What has she done? *'Fractured her skull, eye socket, cheekbone, shoulder, arm, fingers, ribs and heavily bruised her thigh, knee and shin. But that's not the worry; it's her head that's the concern. She has sustained a massive brain injury.'*

How did that even happen? *'He was wearing a helmet and with his head down was keeping up with a bus and the bus pulled in and he saw the crossing too late, she turned to face him. Witnesses say she was smiling, and he hit her full on, head-butting her with his helmet in the face as the bike hit her body, knocking her back onto the road where she hit the back of her head. She's in a coma.'*

My knees felt soft. I didn't cry. I asked to see her. I just wanted to see her. It felt like the world turned in slow motion. The doctor pointed down a quiet corridor and I walked along it but couldn't find my mum. There was only one trolley outside an X-ray room with a person on it. It was hard to tell if it was male or female. Their face looked like (and it's hard to describe) bunches of black grapes: and so swollen, everything looked flat. I felt sad that someone could look that way but was more intent on finding my mum. I walked back, saying I couldn't find her and this time the doctor guided me and stopped at the trolley.

'Here she is.' He spoke softly.

'That's not my mum.' I smiled, embarrassed on his behalf at the mix-up.

But it was.

They moved her into ICU. Dad and I sat by her side. Her pillow was covered in red dusty sand that I kept brushing from the sheets and our clothes. It was everywhere. I didn't realise it was her dried blood. Her hair was matted, and I've never seen a person look so physically broken.

I shan't ever forget it. Her lifeless, bruised and smashed body with tubes and God knows what else coming out of her. I wished I could swap places with her, rather me go through it than the mum I adored. The mum who had danced to Motown in our little kitchen before making us a tent under the table so we could eat our sandwiches in it, the mum who had dedicated her life to her kids and Joshy so I could go out to work. I realised this was how she must have felt so many times when I was younger and recovering from surgery and would wake up to find her by my bed. It made me love her even more and topped up the guilt I felt that she had to go through that at all.

Dad and I sat quietly and helplessly, as one by one my brothers arrived, a little behind us in their shock and there was nothing we could do, as they too went weak-kneed, their distress instant at the sight of her. Our mum.

'She'll be okay. She'll be okay,' my dad repeated as if he believed if he said it enough he could make it so.

I left to pick Joshy up from a school hockey match; he was playing on a pitch outside town. I went home first, got changed and washed my face, picked him up and it was only when one of the other mums asked if I was all right and pointed out that I didn't have any shoes on, that I realised I might be in shock. I've used this scenario in one of my novels, and remember looking down at my wet, muddy feet and finding it odd that my shoes were missing.

My mum survived, just. She was in a coma and hospitalised for weeks. And I didn't breathe properly in that time but spent each waking hour trying to keep things as 'normal' as possible for Joshy and trying to tamp down the hysteria and distress that sat beneath my breastbone, knowing it would help no one, least of all Mum if I let loose the rage of distress that caged my every thought. Slowly, slowly her speech returned, her movement improved as her bones healed, but it took years and years, almost eight before she was what I would call 'better'. She still suffers from horrendous vertigo upon waking up every morning and sits up with sickness and a head that swims and there are gaps in her memory. It's been a long and hard journey for her, but not without moments of humour. About a year after her accident, she saw someone smoking on the TV and said, 'Oh, isn't smoking disgusting!'

We laughed; she had been smoking about twenty a day before she was struck but had 'forgotten' this among other things. And only a couple of months ago she said to me, 'It was strange, Mand, when I was in hospital, there was no room for me in the regular hospital so when I was in a coma, they put me in an aircraft hangar.'

She stared at me for a second and then laughed, as she thought logically about her statement. 'I wasn't in an aircraft hangar, was I?'

'No, darling. You were in a cramped, overly warm ICU ward.'

But we both agreed that actually, a spacious aircraft hangar was probably preferable.

Her accident taught me that life is precious. Family is precious and her beauty became the last thing we considered at the prospect of losing her. My preoccupation over the size of my bum felt superfluous, ridiculous even, as I watched her try to sit up and use cutlery unaided. My body like her face is after all only a wrapping. Thinking about my mum and how we nearly lost her is hard, even now. But it confirmed that she had been telling me the truth all along: it's most definitely what's on the inside that counts, is of most value; her love, her kindness, her unconditional support and her ability to smile.

My wonderful Mumma post-accident – Annie, aged seventy-three.

Chapter Nine

'Cupid Takes Aim'

I was thirty-eight, had dusted myself off from the wreckage of my short marriage and let my bruises heal, adamant that I would never date again, let alone marry. And it suited me; I existed in a bubble without having to worry too much about only owning greying apple-catcher knickers and not a slinky thong – it mattered little, no one would ever see my bits and pieces, scars and all. With a young son, working in the shop at weekends and when I could, being there for my mum, who was still very much in the recovery stage, and a new job that supplemented the shop rent, meeting a partner was the last thing on my mind.

Without Mum it was impossible to run the shop alone, and with declining sales, sporadic opening and not much cash for stock, I did what needed to be done and mothballed it, opening at week-ends. After-school clubs picked up some of the slack in Joshy's care and Mum (with Dad on hand) carried on minding him. My new job was in a senior management position for an electrical company, this role offered to me solely because of the position I'd had with the tech company. The shop had become a financial millstone, but it felt important for Mum to have something to concentrate on getting back to, a goal. I did my best to keep all those plates spinning. How I hated climbing back onto the corporate ladder and putting on a suit, but hated even more the idea of not being able to pay my bills.

One thing I knew I would miss about going to the shop each day was that it gave me the opportunity to read. Between customers (and there was a *lot* of between customers, sadly) I could devour pages of a story and chose to revisit my old favourites, Maeve Binchy, Rosamunde Pilcher, Penny Vincenzi and others. These women were/are my heroes. Getting lost in these stories again stoked my desire to write, but I began to feel a new fear: supposing I couldn't do it? I'd imagined writing a book for so long, a book that sat in my imagination and was fabulous, but maybe it took more courage than I possessed to put my creativity to the test? I began to put pen to paper and wrote a couple of stories: one set in North Yorkshire and Marrakech, which drew largely on the landscapes I loved, and one the story of a rape survivor. I loved the strong female characters but was unsure of whether they were 'good enough'. I put them in a drawer, a physical drawer as well as a mental one, where they remain. So yes, I was busy or made myself busy, anything other than step out of my comfort zone and into the dating pool.

Friends, mums of other kids at school, had often tried to fix me up with this 'really great guy!', refusing to believe I was happy on my own, but that was the truth. I was. Not happy with my body or how I looked, but happy-ish with my life. Or maybe the word isn't happy, maybe a better one is 'preoccupied', and I was certainly that. Mum was on the mend, slowly. Joshy and I were in a lovely little routine and when he was asleep, I had full power over the TV remote and Barry Manilow was my playlist. I might not have been close to realising my dream of becoming a writer, but I was living the life! Heck, I didn't even shave my legs from one winter to the next and if I wanted to spend the night crying over a weepy chick flick and eating ice cream there was no one to stop me. It felt easier not to rope someone else into this strange life of mine, one where I might say no to holidays, days out, parties, barbecues, the cinema, in fact, any number of fabulous invites because on a low day I was worried about back fat.

It was, I decided, time I did something about it. A huge factor in this was having seen my mum work so hard on her recovery, how could I not do my utmost to lose a few pounds?

In early 2007 I was thirty-eight and feeling fairly good about my size. Yes, really! With Mum on the mend and in the swing of my new job, I had managed to stick to a liquid meal replacement plan for a torturous few months, drinking only shakes and water and not consuming anything solid. Not a single bite. While others tucked into breakfast, lunch, Christmas dinner, Easter eggs and birthday cake, I would empty an artificial-tasting, chalky sachet into a cup of water and give it a good rattle before popping in a straw, like the ones that went in our school milk, but thicker and they didn't require the smug assistance of a smarmy milk monitor. Motivated by rapid weight loss, it felt like the answer! I pooed infrequently, fainted a couple of times, my teeth felt loose in my gums and my breath stank, but I lost weight! Boy did I lose weight.

The trouble is the plan did nothing to address the reasons behind why I ate and didn't give me any strategies that might help me once I returned to solid food. My plan was to use it to kick start my weight loss journey and when at my 'ideal' weight, figure out how to maintain it – easy peasy. Weekly, I went to the house of a weight counsellor to pick up my haul of synthetically flavoured sachets. It felt illicit and embarrassing all at once, sneaking up the side path to hand over the cash and get my goods in a plain white plastic bag. The weight counsellor, a representative of the company, was very nice, but clearly obese. I wondered why he didn't hoover up a couple of shakes himself, but apparently, he had, and it worked wonders, and he had only 'relapsed' in recent times.

If ever there was a red flag that this diet might only be a short-term fix, it was the sight of this rather depressed man, with fat spilling over his too small shoes, pointing at slides and graphs about weight loss and asking me and my fellow slender wannabees to open up about our food intake that week, the highs and lows of our diet. Finally, at the end of the evening there would be the grand weigh-in where we would all eye each other competitively, clapping as if we were delighted at the rapid left sway of the needle on the dial, but secretly wanting to beat all the others in the great race to reach slim . . . I liked the high of feeling slender and the compliments it garnered. It felt like I was winning. I was faster, fitter and on the outside, looked the best I had in a while. And with my weight at a shade under 150 lb (roughly 10 stone 7 lb) I met Captain Simeon Prowse, love of my life, MBE.

Despite all my protestations to the contrary, sneaky Cupid had been taking aim! It was a grey Saturday when I went to watch eight-year-old Josh play rugby with his friend Ben, who had been to my house for numerous playdates. Ben was a lovely, quiet boy who told me his dad was a soldier. The military! The very thought horrified me; it was a life I did not envy and could think of nothing worse than sitting at home waiting for and worrying about my man.

Dad and I schlepped off to watch the rugby match; I was in his old wax jacket, no make-up, messy hair and wellington boots covered in mud. The match was about to start, and I became aware of someone walking towards me. He was smiling and I felt like I knew him.

Now, just to be clear, when people over the years have told me that they fell in love at first sight or that they met their soulmate, my cynical self would chuckle and think *'sure you did!'* or *'of course you have!'* and I'd assume that the god or goddess who called to them was seen through the lens of beer goggles or a firmly attached Prosecco filter. This was my firm belief . . . until it happened to me.

Ben's dad introduced himself to me as Simeon and I remember laughing and he did too. And we just stood there laughing at each other. It was the weirdest and most wonderful feeling like, 'Ah, there you are!' even though I didn't know I'd been looking for him. Instantly, I wished that I'd bothered to wash my hair and put make-up on, but there was little I could do about that on the side of a rugby pitch. Dad took the hint and ambled home, bless him.

Simeon took my number, suggesting we could take the boys bowling some time – I thought it was a nice thing to do, take the kids bowling, why not? I thought about him that evening, so out of practice at the whole dating scene that I wondered if I had imagined our 'connection' and wondered if maybe he asked all the mums if they fancied taking the kids bowling, maybe that was his thing?

The next day, however, he called me and invited me to a car park in the Cribbs Causeway shopping mall just off the motorway, where we went for a coffee. Yes, this was our first date, to a car park where we sat and drank cheap, bitter coffee out of a polystyrene cup! And in short, we have pretty much been together ever since. It felt like there was an urgent need to catch up on our stories, as if aware at some level this was necessary for us to move forward together. He didn't flinch when I told him about my failed marriage, my life, Mum's accident, my pelvis, cancer and my worries that Joshy was struggling a little at school, how he had recently been diagnosed with dyslexia and I was at a loss how to make him happier, help him feel less anxious. I just let the words tumble, my guard down. He told me about his failed marriage, his life as a soldier, some of the horrors he had seen and how he was responsible for Ben. We clicked. It really is that simple. We clicked and we liked each other. I still like him, a lot. I mean, I *love* him too, of course, but that liking bit is I think very important.

Simeon was based with a regiment in Kent, about a hundred and fifty miles away, so much of our courtship was done over the phone and when we could sneak in the odd hour for a coffee at weekends. Neither of us were in the first flush of youth and yet we were very careful not to rush, as if we knew early on that this might be something we could grow if we nurtured and cared for it at this delicate stage.

Our main concern was and still is our sons. Both boys had been through a lot in their little lives and their peace of mind was paramount. I couched things with Joshy carefully, suggesting playdates with Ben and his dad (Ben's grandparents were local and were on hand when Simeon was away), playdates where we would meet in parks or castles in the countryside, and where I'd pack a picnic. The boys would run off to play and if it felt safe, Simeon would reach for my hand or kiss me, and those stolen moments would leave me breathless. I felt a dizzying desire for this beautiful man that was entirely new to me, and I wanted more. He smiled at me in a way that no one ever had before, as if he couldn't believe his luck, as if he was proud. And it made me feel like a million dollars.

It was as Joshy and I trundled down the motorway home that I noticed he was a little quiet. I asked him what was on his mind, and he said, 'I think Ben's dad might be your boyfriend.'

'Oh!' I was shocked. 'Why do you say that?' Had he seen us stealing a kiss behind a tree, holding hands behind our backs? My nerves jangled; this was new territory, and I knew I had to tread carefully.

'Because I saw him drink from your water bottle and you never let anyone drink from your water bottle. You think sharing water bottles is disgusting!'

True and true.

It felt like the opportune moment to scout out how he might be feeling.

'Would you think it was great or not so great if Ben's dad *was* my boyfriend?' I asked, tentatively, keeping my eyes on the road, desperately wanting this kid's approval, knowing this would mean a smooth path ongoing.

'Not so great! No way! Oh no way! I'd hate that! No!' He folded his arms and shook his head.

Shit.

'Well, you don't have to worry about that right now,' was all I could think of saying. It worried me though. Joshy had started to express his dislike of school and was a little quiet, a little thoughtful. His dyslexia was a challenge and socially he felt awkward. He had a lot to deal with and the last thing I wanted to do was give him another thing to worry his little head.

I called Simeon when we got home, and he told me Ben had also expressed his extreme disapproval at the hint of a suggestion that we might be more than friends. Bloody marvellous! It was a key moment in this relationship that felt like so much more than a mere fling; we either A) called it a day or B) figured out how to make it work.

We were already falling for each other and without hesitation both agreed on option B. His mantra has always been that life will never be without problems; our job is to find a way through them and if we do that calmly together, then so much the better. I agreed, but I remember his face when he first discovered that when a problem occurs I am not calm, I am in fact a little hysterical!

I have an irrational fear of small frogs. Outside I love them, admire them, but put one in the same room as me and it's a different story! A small frog found its way into our flat and as the boys played at the table and Simeon sat on the sofa, I dropped to the floor, leopard-crawled across the carpet with a cardigan over my head, screaming, and wouldn't come back inside for three hours. But I figured it was good he knew the real me.

The boys aged eight and me at the seaside on our first family break in my beloved Devon.

Marriage had not been in my thoughts, and I was confident I would never take the plunge again, but six months after meeting, Simeon proposed one evening in his army quarter, presenting me with a thin gold ring that was to be my engagement ring and my wedding band, costing the princely sum of twenty-eight quid.

I couldn't have loved anything more. It was the same type of plain ring I had described that my nan and great-nan had worn and symbolised so much to me, the lack of bling, the simple meaningful token of love that was more than the sum of its parts. Marriage was important to him. I changed my mind; with this man and the way we spoke about the future we wanted to create for our sons, it was an easy yes! I couldn't wait to marry him, and we set a date six months ahead, slotting it in before he headed off on tour to Iraq.

We told the boys separately of our plans to marry and Joshy looked anxious when I spoke to him. I sat him down and promised him I would never, ever make a decision about his life, about *our* life that I did not think would make it better, and how I firmly believed our lives would be better with Simeon and Ben in them. He nodded and looked me in the eye trustingly. It was almost approval, but I meant what I said, if my choice had been more than he could cope with then I could not have gone ahead with it.

Our little boys became brothers and went from being friends to enemies and back again, sometimes in one day! Just like regular brothers they were either bickering or laughing. Simeon and my happiness oscillated accordingly – if the kids were happy, we were happy; when they were squabbling or upset, it heaped tension on our shoulders, both trying to navigate this new dynamic in a way that worked for us all. We did our best to manage their anger and worry at how their lives might be changing.

With our wedding date looming, Simeon and Ben moved in with Joshy and me. At this point all normal parenting rules went out of the window. Having spent the first year or so of Joshy's life wishing he'd arrived with a manual, I found myself in a similar situation trying to figure out how to parent a child I did not yet properly know. Nature gave me a helping hand in the form of unconditional love when it came to my baby, but it's quite a different story when you welcome into your home a child who has been on the planet for nearly nine years without you in their life. I didn't love Ben immediately – of course I didn't. I had to learn to love him, and I hoped in time he might love me. The same applied to Joshy and Simeon. The trouble was, I was so desperate to be *liked* by Ben and for Simeon to only see me in a good light, that the rules and boundaries I set for Joshy did not apply to Ben.

'No, of course you don't have to try the broccoli!'

'Yes, you can play with the Wii just before bedtime!'

Simeon, likewise, found it hard to reprimand Joshy, wanting to be seen as the goody and terrified of upsetting me. It felt like

I was in a constant interview for the role of perfect parent. As a result, Simeon and I were uptight, anxious and exhausted. There were evenings when I grinned instead of screaming and shut myself in the bathroom to cry into a flannel, wondering how our flat was ever going to feel like home again if we couldn't all relax.

Eventually, when Joshy asked me, 'How come you don't tell Ben off for eating with his mouth open but if I do it, you go nuts?', he was right. It wasn't fair and we knew things had to change. We explained to the boys that we couldn't compromise our standards and behaviour anymore to keep them happy, told them we were still learning and trying to figure it all out and how we were nervous of getting things wrong because it was so important to us. We asked if they had any questions and after a while Ben blurted out tearfully, 'I'm worried my dad will love you more than he loves me!'

It was a heartbreaking admission from a little boy who had experienced upheaval. His previous home life had not been without challenges and Simeon was now solely responsible for him.

'Oh, mate, that could never happen. You're his son! His baby! And you always will be. You will always be his most important person.'

Then Joshy piped up, 'Who do you love most, Mum?'

'You!' I replied, without hesitation. 'Always, always you.'

We phrased it as best we could: that while there was an infinite amount of love to go around, Simeon would always love Ben in a way he wouldn't love Joshy or me and the same was true in reverse for me.

So, were we bonkers? Possibly. Did acknowledging that truth make people uncomfortable? A little. But the fact is, it gave each boy the feeling of security. They both knew that while this strange domestic merger was going on, their position was unchanged, and it made all the difference. They knew that they could rely on moments alone with their 'natural' parent to talk through anything that was worrying them and not have to 'share' the person *they* loved the most.

The transition into our blended family has been fun, stressful, tough, frustrating and rewarding. I've cried as much as I laughed and it took years for us all to ease into it and properly, properly relax. I still remember when Ben, aged fourteen, was asked if he needed a lift home from school. I was parked nearby with the window open and heard him say, 'No, it's okay, my mum's here!' It was the first time he had referred to me as his mum, and it is a moment I will never forget.

It wasn't easy forming a little family. In my head I thought it would be more like *The Brady Bunch* but with less canned laughter and no kooky housekeeper, swishy blonde hair or knee socks. It has been tough at times, too tough, not least when I found myself sitting at home, trying to keep things as 'normal' as possible for the boys, waiting for and worrying about my man while he was away on exercise training for his tour. But the simple truth is I love him, and he loves me, and we have now been married for a hundred years and we love our kids to the moon and back and I would not change one single moment of it.

Simeon also told me he found me beautiful. And this was profound for me. He wasn't saying I was beautiful; he was saying he found me beautiful. Big difference. And this for me was illuminating. I realised in that moment that I did not have to be beautiful for everyone, I didn't even have to be beautiful for me, although that would have been nice, but the fact that there was another human being on the planet who held me in such high esteem and saw me in that way who was *not* my mum . . . it was and still is the most glorious feeling. A gift.

I felt quite confident about my body in those first months, telling Simeon I had lost a lot of weight and not holding back physically in the way that I always had. I didn't mind showing my arms and if my top rode up while I lay on the sofa to show a hint of stomach, so be it. Daring, eh? It was as if I believed that my slimmer body, apart from my nasty scars, was not going to make him retch. It was a nice feeling. And this comfort came from being at ease in every other aspect of our life. We could and still do, talk until dawn and it was that deeper connection that didn't feel reliant on the transient nature of sex alone that made me feel so secure.

When I met Simeon, I was again eating solid food after my liquid diet, and had put on some weight, a few pounds, but after nothing but liquids for six months, my capacity for food was much reduced – this the one good thing about the plan – and I was far from fat. My outfit of choice was jeans and any old sweatshirt, as every picture of us during this time will attest! It didn't occur to me to dress differently when I was slimmer; in fact, looking back at all photographs from my teens to the present day, I seem to have always worn jeans and a top that covers my bum, no matter what my shape or the weather. Trying to disguise my form or as if I have no concept of my shape or size. I've never been that interested in fashion or looking glam, always opting for comfy and low-key, trying to hide, I guess.

With mere weeks until our 'big day', shopping for something to wear for my wedding was comical. Now, I know for some brides to be it is a big deal, the frock! And I personally know brides who have spent months if not years considering the look, the material, the cut, the fit. I was not and never have been one of them and was so out of practice at clothes shopping and bothering with my appearance that I rushed into John Lewis while Simeon took the boys to choose a computer game. Picking up a pale gold coatdress that looked like it might do the job, I paid for it without trying it on and was waiting outside the game shop for twenty minutes while the kids took their time. It still makes me laugh that it took that much longer to decide which Mario Kart was worth the investment while I grabbed any old dress in which to waltz up the aisle. I couldn't see why it was important. I still can't really. I'd already started to lose sight of why make-up, clothes and the whole outer casing that made us mattered at all. I think having Simeon love me gave me confidence that this belief was the right one, he loved me how I looked, bare skin, scars and all and no amount of lipstick or mascara would change that.

I took holiday from work to get married. The electronics company had gone bust, and I had just started a new job with a PR agency in London, working in their communications division. The boys were now ten and with them moving their way through school, I commuted from Bristol on some days with after-school clubs and my parents picking up the slack, and I worked in their Bristol office on others. I absolutely hated the job; it was a competitive, toxic environment, but it was a good income and a couple of days a week in London was so much better than having to rush to Heathrow and catch a plane.

We were married in Münster, Germany, where Simeon, now promoted to Major, was posted pre-tour and was one of the places my dad had worked, setting up a factory for an American firm, and there I was in the same city, with my soldier by my side. It was a simple, low-key ceremony without guests, music, flowers or fuss.

We discussed at length the possibility that Ben, for several reasons, might have been prevented from attending, as permission was required from his maternal family, whom he hadn't seen in the longest time. It would have been divisive for us to have one son there and not the other, and neither of us wanted the fallout from that. And if the boys couldn't be there, we didn't want anyone else to be there. We could not, would not, risk their feeling excluded or left out. Besides, it wasn't about a fancy display or a party, but simply us taking the step to unify our family, to give us both greater freedoms when it came to childcare arrangements . . . and to say the vows that meant the world.

On the day itself, Simeon had a day off and we were eating scrambled egg on toast at the kitchen table in the army quarter, where the hallway and lounge were littered with his camo-clad stuff waiting to go to Iraq. I casually asked what time we had to leave the house. Simeon looked at the clock and said, 'In about twenty minutes.' I thought he was joking until his expression told me otherwise. This is another example of me not being calm in a crisis, as I ran around the house trying to find my shoes, shoved my hair up and put my coatdress on which fitted, kind of. And off we went! Two strangers from his office were our witnesses and afterwards we went home for a cup of tea and to share a pizza from the freezer.

The next day he left for a tour of Iraq – so at least one of us got to go somewhere hot and sunny for a honeymoon. I laugh, but as I returned to the boys in Bristol, I felt his absence like a hole in my gut. It wasn't the start to marriage I had envisaged, and I felt a little adrift, admiring the little gold band on my finger, but missing him until my bones ached. I still feel like that when we are not together. What I said to Joshy when he was so anxious about the new pairing was absolutely true: our lives are much better with Simeon and Ben in them.

Our wedding day! Hair needed a wash and I had a blob of ketchup on my vest under my frock. Nothing new there, then.

Chapter Ten

'THESE THINGS JUST HAPPEN'

I was knocking on the door of forty. It had been a while since my body had let me down, the surgeries for my pelvis were thankfully behind me and with my weight more or less under control, Simeon and I decided, with one child each (although we only ever think of them as *our* boys) it would be perfect to add to our family with a child of our own.

I fell pregnant quickly and we were over the moon. Caught up in the excitement, full of hope, and still posted in Germany, we planned for the arrival of our much-wanted baby. I got carried away, letting Simeon talk about the future with a little one in tow, an addition that would be the glue to unite Josh and Ben. We spent hours marvelling at the gift of conception and planning the next nine months: Simeon would be back from tour, and we would be in new quarters by the time my due date came. I fell asleep after those conversations feeling like the luckiest woman in the world.

A mere nine weeks later, I woke up in the middle of the night with a familiar cramp in my stomach. I thought that if I lay very still and tried to go back to sleep, make out it wasn't happening, I could stop it, but I couldn't. Of course I couldn't.

It was a situation that was familiar to me although no less upsetting for that. I'll never forget creeping from the bedroom on all fours and lying on the bathroom floor, weeping for our loss. It felt worse somehow because I was older and knew that it might be hard to fall pregnant again, that and I so, so wanted to have a baby with the man I loved. Simeon held me tight and told me that we already had so much to feel thankful for; this was a sad, sad thing, but we could try again. And we did.

Now, I don't know any woman who conceives preparing to lose the baby she's carrying, and yet this is exactly what happens to an estimated one in four pregnancies, with many more miscarriages happening before a woman is even aware she is pregnant. Three or more losses in a row (recurrent miscarriages) are uncommon and only affect around one in a hundred women.

Turns out I was one in a hundred. All those years I had longed to have one statistic that put me above average – why did it have to be this one?

I fell pregnant again quite quickly, only for this pregnancy to end in the same way with a miscarriage at eleven weeks. I felt hollow, cheated and watched my dreams of new motherhood slipping through my fingers, but also slightly numbed, as if it was just what happened to me and therefore shouldn't keep affecting me in this way. I felt guilty for feeling so affected, as if I really had no right, it was no worse than a heavy period and yet I was falling apart, weeping and struggling to find the silver lining – what was wrong with me? Meeting Simeon and falling in love had removed a brick from my emotional wall, which let in a chink of light, but these losses put it firmly back in place. Yet another brick in the wall of worthlessness I had been unwittingly constructing for the longest time and any knock, any setback saw me mentally reaching for the mortar.

I remember coming home from the hospital after the procedure to remove what they termed 'the products of conception' – a phrase that still makes me shudder, and thankfully one that is being phased out. A kindly neighbour who was not up to speed on proceedings rushed over to say hello. He pointed at my stomach and said, 'I believe you have something wonderful going on in there!' I stared at him, quite at a loss what to say without embarrassing him and opening the floodgate to my tears.

The first loss was disappointing no doubt, the second upsetting, but then, and I write this with no small amount of sadness, it was what I came to expect. But it was a predictable cycle: fall pregnant, pray with every fibre that this baby would stick, bleed. Fall pregnant, pray with every fibre that this baby would stick, bleed . . .

And my reactions to the losses were accordingly muted. I stopped crying, stopped feeling sorry for myself and I became almost resigned. A self-protection mechanism of sorts. By expecting my pregnancies to fail, the impact of another loss was lessened, as if my hardened shell could better stand being knocked sideways.

And it worked, to a degree. I'm also ashamed to admit that I remember talking to a friend who had suffered a miscarriage at six weeks, and she was bereft, but I could barely comfort her, not when that was my norm. It wasn't that I was blind to her hurt, her loss, but I simply couldn't take it on. I sometimes wonder how I must have come across during this time; another loss garnered no more than a nod in public before I went home and howled my distress into a pillow before calmly carrying on.

Simeon didn't know how to comfort me or what to say and I didn't like that this was the case. As a couple, despite being bound by love, we were still finding our rhythm, our explicit trust and our best way of communicating and I can't pretend that this merry-go-round of baby loss didn't put the most enormous strain on our relationship. We made the decision early on not to tell the boys of our attempts to provide them with a sibling, not until there was something certain to share with them, thus avoiding dragging them with us on the uncomfortable, emotional voyage too.

We also avoided telling my family and my colleagues in Bristol and London when I fell pregnant, thinking it best that they too did not have to live the highs and lows of baby loss with us. It became a journey that Simeon and I travelled alone, bound in something that felt a lot like shame, holding each other tight when the world crashed around us, and celebrating cautiously when we were given reason to celebrate. Even to have the conversation with the man I loved and explain another miscarriage sent out long shadows of sadness that only exacerbated my heartache.

The disappointment and sense of failure were exhausting. My pregnancies therefore became like a dirty secret, hidden until I could guarantee, almost, that we were home and dry. Pregnancy four, five and six all ended in miscarriage, at a little over six weeks, the others at twelve and fourteen weeks respectively.

Each time I was told 'these things just happen.' This I understood, but why did they keep happening to *me*? It quietly broke my heart. And I didn't know how to fix it. Simeon was right, I had two fantastic sons, a lot to be thankful for, was I asking for too much? What was it my nan had said? 'No one gets all the gifts.' Maybe she was right.

I quickly got to the point where there was little joy in discovering I'd fallen pregnant, which is such a terrible thing to admit and an even harder thing to write, the beautiful event and moment of high emotion marred by anxiety at what might, and in my case usually did, happen. A positive pregnancy test was always met with muted joy, not only because it was a reminder of the last time and the time before that and the time before that . . . but also because we dared not hope. Dared not dream.

The last time I fell pregnant, I had a good, good feeling. We were back in England, living in our third house in three years; the army did like to move us around! The one constant was the boys' school, where they could stay, meaning that no matter how turbulent our home life, they had the knowledge that their routine, their base was constant. But I'm sure that they, like me, longed for one house where they could properly settle. I was an old hack at moving. It was a doddle: pack a box, unpack a box, find the kettle, plug it in, make tea, wave to the neighbours, invite parents and grandparents over to see the identikit living quarter in a new postcode. The curtains, carpets and lampshades were always the same! Once or twice, I collected the boys from school on a Friday night and sat in the car trying to gather my thoughts, where did we live now? Once I even collected the kids and drove to our old house in Hilperton, Wiltshire, when we had actually moved to Larkhill Barracks, Salisbury – we laughed as darkness fell and I turned the car around and headed home . . .

Simeon was on tour and things felt different where this baby was concerned. It was no more than a sixth sense, but I was optimistic, excited and determined. It was as if after all my losses, we were somehow owed a lovely outcome. I suffered with chronic morning sickness, which was unusual, and every resource told me this was a very healthy sign, an indicator of a *strong* pregnancy, and I wanted so badly to believe this. I *did* believe this. We finally told the boys that if all went well, they would have a little brother or sister. They received the news coolly, with the question, 'Can we get a dog?' Their eyes were wide.

'Pleeeease! Pleeeease!'

I think they thought it was an either/or thing, a baby or a dog. We explained that we weren't ready for a dog just yet, but one day, *one day* when we had space outside, a routine that allowed for walks and cuddles, we would get them a dog.

'Can we get two dogs?' Joshy asked.

These boys knew how to push it. It felt easier to agree than rail against it. They didn't really mention my pregnancy, as if I'd told them what we were having for supper or anything else of minor consequence, which made me laugh. I hoped their enthusiasm might be a little more evident when the new baby arrived.

There was certainly no fanfare, no gender reveal, no pop of a champagne cork. It was pretty understated and actually this is kind of how we are about most things, it certainly makes it easier when things don't go according to plan. I had waved Simeon off for work, he was again travelling to a hot and dusty place and as ever I didn't want him to go. His deployments varied from six-month-long stints to quicker 'trips', which were unnerving for me, but we were happy, because even though we were going to be separated by oceans, our baby was growing inside me and what better connection could there be to the man I loved?

I had been cautious about telling people about this pregnancy for obvious reasons, but at my twelve-week scan when I was told that everything looked 'really great' I nearly jumped for joy! We were home and dry. I could *feel* it. I knew it. Eating healthily and exercising right, I once again bought baby clothes, excitedly filling up the chest of drawers with Babygros and little cardigans knitted by my nan with ribbon threaded through them. I talked to my baby, convinced it was a girl, I told her all about her daddy who was far away, but who was going to be the best dad to her in the whole wide world! I wrote to Simeon daily, on tissue-thin 'blueys', giving him every detail of how I looked and felt and planning all the wonderful things our little girl would do. My sickness subsided and I felt on top of the world! Due to my history, I went for a routine scan at twenty-four weeks.

It was a Wednesday, a grey day. I dropped the kids at school and caught the bus. I lay on the couch and watched the screen, excited to see our baby. The sonographer was chatting to me about nothing much, chit chat, small talk, army life, we laughed about nothing of consequence . . .

And then she went quiet.

And her face dropped.

And I knew.

She clicked to take photographs of the image on the screen and, avoiding eye contact, quietly told me she was going to get a colleague, as she wanted a second opinion. But I already knew what she was going to say. Outwardly composed, but with a rising panic inside, I was, in this crisis, surprisingly calm. I climbed from the bed and wiped the gel from my stomach, as my spirit sank. I put my clothes on and held my handbag on my lap, waiting, concentrating on reading the posters about pregnancy-related matters and any other signs around the room:

KEEP THIS WINDOW CLOSED.

CALL THIS NUMBER AFTER HOURS.

KEYS FOR CUPBOARD ARE IN RECEPTION.

WASH YOUR HANDS.

Anything to distract my mind. She returned with a doctor in tow. It was a terrible moment. I closed my eyes and wished that I were anywhere other than in that little room with an image of my baby girl, captured on the screen, which they both studied. My little girl.

'I need you to get back on the bed, Amanda.' The doctor spoke softly, kindly, yet firmly. The sonographer couldn't look me in the eye. Like an automaton, I slowly pulled down my jeans and pants and clambered up on the sticky tissue that lined the couch, feeling the slight roundness of my baby in my stomach, the size, I had read only the day before, of a large grapefruit. The atmosphere was sharp, weighted, and I braced myself for verbal confirmation of what their faces told me. There I was again, staring at a hospital ceiling, but this time it wasn't my pelvis that had let me down, but my womb. Again.

Our baby's heart had stopped beating at twenty-three weeks. I'd had no clue, no symptoms, no bleeding.

I felt devastated, cheated and responsible. Was it something I had done? Not done? We had been so close I could almost feel her in my arms!

They wanted to take me straight to the operating theatre, but I asked to go home and spend one more day with her, knowing it would help me to say goodbye in my own time while she was still with me. I arranged to go back into hospital on the Friday.

I remember being quiet and calm. Mum and Dad collected the boys, who were thankfully a little oblivious, distracted at my mum's by a lovely supper and treats. She kept them overnight. I didn't put the radio on or the TV. There was no music, no adverts, no chatter or laughter, just my breathing and the voice inside my head, talking to my little one, apologising, telling her how sorry I was and how I had been so looking forward to holding her against my skin. I drank tea, dozed, cried a little, but not a lot. I was contained; holding it together for fear of what losing control might look like.

Simeon knew I was having the scan and managed to call from Iraq. I held the phone and the moment I heard his voice, I broke down, properly broke down. My sobbing left no space for words and so I didn't try. I fought for breath and howled a little and sank down onto the floor with my baby, the size of a large grapefruit, asleep inside me.

And then without warning, the phone suddenly went dead. My heart leapt into my throat – had something happened to *him*? The thought was more than I could bear. I had a warm bath and looked at the swell of my stomach and then spent the night and next day chatting to her and telling her everything I had hoped and dreamed for her.

Thoughts of the abrupt phone call ending kept me awake. Simeon had always told me, however, that one thing was certain: while he was away, if ever there was bad news, it would reach me very quickly as the army had a slick system for notification of accident or emergency and I took comfort from that. I reminded myself that the connections were sketchy, the internet unreliable and a thousand other reasons why the call might have failed, doing my best to quieten the dread that he might be hurt. Even the thought was more than I could cope with. He had already come under fire from rocket attack and dealt with IEDs, but I chose not to let this enter my thoughts. I only had enough energy to think about when Friday dawned, knowing I'd go back to the hospital for the pregnancy to be brought to an end.

It is a day that is ingrained in my memory. It was also coincidentally my beloved grandad's birthday. I'd packed a small overnight bag and woke early to the sound of heavy knocking on the front door. Putting on my dressing gown, I walked into the hallway and there, staring at me through the glass panels of the door was my Simeon. I couldn't believe it. The sight of him . . . it's something I will never forget.

Still in his desert combats and with sand in his hair, he had abruptly ended the telephone call, as he knew that every second would count if he were to get on the only flight leaving that evening. I opened the door and he said to me, 'I told you I would always come to you if you needed me.'

And he was right: I did need him. I fell into his arms and closed my eyes, handing over the reins mentally, physically leaning on him as he guided me to bed where I slept, and he watched over me.

He stayed by my side during the procedure, holding my hand. I won't go into detail. It wouldn't serve anything other than to maybe put the pictures in your head that I would rather were not in mine, but the process was life-changing, with images that endure.

I dream about it sometimes. I find it hard to talk about all of my losses, but that one was the toughest.

The recovery was difficult, with my hormones going crazy and my body producing milk for a child I was never going to feed. I didn't even know what words to use, let alone how to grieve. I disliked the term 'failed pregnancy', and miscarriage put it on a par with the many early losses I had encountered that had been nothing like this. I'm still stumped when I try to find the words. It again made me feel like I had done something wrong. Another brick.

I went home and folded away the baby clothes for the last time, knowing I would not, could not put myself or Simeon through this again. I placed them quickly in a bag, without really thinking about what they were, no more than unwanted garments taking up space and not needed. Actually, that's not true, they were very much wanted, just like the baby we had lost, but I couldn't think about it, about her, about how she'd left my body, knowing that if I hesitated, I might fall . . . And I had two boys to look after, a job to get to, a house to clean, supper to cook.

I dropped the bag at a charity shop without saying a word to the lady behind the counter. It was easier not to have the reminders around, easier for me anyway. It didn't occur to me to ask Simeon if he wanted to keep anything. I regret that. We gently told the boys we had been mistaken and there was not going to be a baby. They reacted just as coolly as they had to the initial news and this time, I was relieved. I erased all the dates for check-ups and markers from my electronic diary, wiped it all out with one click of my finger and I got on with daily life and work, albeit with a little bit of sadness lurking in my crappy, useless womb.

Simeon didn't know what to say or what to do to make it better, and his hesitancy made me feel awkward in a way that was new for us. Up until that point there had been nothing we couldn't say or discuss. When pulling together two fractured little families it had to be that way, nothing off limits. I believed and still believe that communication is everything and yet there we were, sleeping on the furthest edges of the mattress, smiling weakly at the other and sipping our morning coffee in silence while the conversation was calm, offering a thin veneer of normality. *What did we want for supper? Have the boys got their sports kit? Can you pick up some milk?* It felt formal, like we were reciting a script, and I focused on the words, fearing that if I didn't, I might yank my hair, punch some glass, crouch on the floor and scream until my veins popped and my throat became raw.

The sorrow filled every gap inside me; thoughts of what had happened were all-consuming. Sleep was the only thing that brought me respite, those few minutes or hours when I could submit to it, close my eyes and escape to a world where I hurt a little less and my heart was not shredded, my eyes were not red raw from crying and my gut didn't ache, my head didn't throb. Yes, grief is a personal journey and one that changes everyone who walks it.

My grief transformed over weeks and months until it was a ball of rage, of sadness that I made small and swallowed until it was no more than the size of a pea and something that small could easily be shut away inside my filing cabinet in a dusty drawer. And there it sat, next to an image and smell of a white van interior, next to countless images of hospital ceilings, beneath which a scalpel, drill and saw had been taken to my tender skin and bone, my numerous miscarriages, too many to count, all pea-sized too now, my lovely mum, bruised and broken on a trolley, images of my husband on tour: these red-ringed with fear of what *might* happen, and a baseline worry over my Joshy, who still didn't want to go to school and who told me he felt sad but didn't know why. I couldn't stand the thought and shut it all away and carried on. Just like I always had.

When I met Simeon.

And me aged forty.

Chapter Eleven

'An Author'

Time was the salve to the pain of my loss. Not enough to heal me completely, but certainly enough to allow my thoughts to settle and for Simeon and me to find a way back to each other. It was a slow process, but one that started with physical reassurance, the holding of a hand, the stroking of hair, gently, gently allowing us to return to a point where our emotions were not so jagged and revealing them didn't mean the other got cut. My body felt less frail, and my sadness, like smoke, was carried away on winter winds.

I spent a lot of time by the sea, sitting on a bench on the headland in Woolacombe, North Devon, wrapped in a soft pashmina and welcoming the healing touch of sun on my skin. A place I had visited often when living in Thornbury and with so many happy memories of walking on the firm sand in winter and sitting in the car with a hot cup of tea as my brothers surfed, Woolacombe was also the place where my dad had proposed to my mum in the original Red Barn over half a century before. I love it there.

The boys were fourteen and had grown into fabulous teenagers who took over our lives and home completely. If we weren't running them around in the car (one of them always had somewhere they needed to be) we were feeding them and their friends on weekends, washing their clothes and sports kit or shouting at them to turn down the TV/computer game and tidy their room. They never did either, but how we loved their company. There were funny nights spent eating pizza and playing board games, there were caravan holidays in Woolacombe where the boys lay on surfboards and ate fish and chips at night. They were finding their feet in that bruising twilight between boy and man, and we were keen to let them discover what they wanted to do and be at their own pace. Ben was very sporty, smashing cross-country times at county level with one eye on a career in the military, and Josh was quietly studious and inventive.

My boys on one of our Woolacombe trips X.

Neither Simeon nor I were fully aware that it was more than a little sadness that dogged one of our boys. Josh had started to slip a little off course; he was at times withdrawn, quiet, seeking solitude, and his clear-cut route to academic stardom was starting to become entangled with vines of mental illness and a thicket of depression that would eventually, heartbreakingly, halt his progress. This journey Josh and I have spoken about it our jointly written memoir, *The Boy Between*.

Ben and Josh were part of the same friendship group, which meant things were either a party or there was conflict. Both boys were feeling their way through the haze of teenhood and both dealing, in different ways, with Josh's declining mental health. Having grown up in a house with three brothers, I knew enough to ride the wave and not give too much credence to any disharmony. My brothers were now in their thirties. Simon a dad to my darling niece Amelie, Nicky had baby Noah and Paul was travelling the world.

Simeon and I had by this point had eight addresses in five years! In hindsight it was farcical – every few months, sometimes less, packing up our lives and moving to an identikit small house with paper-thin walls so Simeon could take up his new posting and I could plug in the kettle in another new street. The novelty of moving had worn very thin, and I resented the constant upheaval, plus I think there was some lingering mental sadness over my disrupted teenage life, when moving had made me feel rootless, but I'd married a military man, and this was part of that.

The houses were all very similar, square and utilitarian, but with subtle differences, so I would regularly get up in the middle of the night to visit the bathroom and walk straight into a cupboard or turn left instead of right and smack into a wall. It always took me a little while to get oriented, it's that old clumsiness thing again! Don't get me wrong, I was more than grateful for those paper-thin walls that gave my family shelter.

The level of disruption was unprecedented, with operations in Afghanistan and Iraq. And with all the associated training and movement of equipment and people, Simeon was given new postings with very short notice, often to cover gaps that could not be foreseen. Little did I know that Josh was so very unhappy, not learning this until he had left school. I too hated him being away at boarding school and would have preferred this not to be the case. The guilt I feel at this is immense and I suspect I'll always feel this way.

It was an odd life really. Living at the beck and call of my husband's employer was like nothing I had experienced before, but to try to separate the man from his career, well, that would be like someone asking me not to read a book! I was forty-two and for a few months, a stay-at-home army wife while I recovered from illness. Another tumour had popped up, a small malignant one between my bowel and womb, which was removed.

This diagnosis sent us into a tailspin. It was one of my worst fears realised and it floored me and Simeon. We spent a lot of time sitting quietly, holding hands, crying and vowing to make the most of every single day for the rest of our (hopefully) long lives. It brought us closer and was another reminder that life can turn on a penny and how none of us knows what's around the corner. I am, however, more than aware that with the Big C taking aim at me more than once, it feels like only a matter of time before I have to face it again, but that is actually something I find too hard to talk about.

It was also an opportunity for me to take stock. For most of my life I'd fought to have a career, to survive and provide for myself and my boy, and yet there I was, an army wife and dedicated mum, keeping house, moving house and yes, recovering, but it was not enough for me. For the first time in my life, I had time on my hands. I had stepped off the hamster wheel, albeit not by choice, and began to think in earnest about writing that book.

Holding down well-paid jobs in recent years had given me confidence that I wasn't dumb and that I could, if I followed my instinct and worked hard, make a success of things that might in the beginning seem insurmountable. If anyone would have told me when I was cleaning offices that I would be shipped out to Chicago by a tech firm to help set up their North American office, I would have thought it was ridiculous, waaaaay beyond my capabilities, a joke! And yet that's exactly what I'd done, so wasn't it time I put my pen where my mouth was and had a go at that damned novel?

Simeon knew it was my dream, had *always* been my dream, to write a book. As someone who had been a soldier since he was sixteen, he understood how life could lift you up in its fast-flowing current and carry you along, where all you could do was concentrate on keeping your head above water, powerless to change course, clinging on to whatever life raft had been put into your hands and hoping for the best. Not that he didn't LOVE his career; he's an army man through and through. Without hesitation, he told me not to go back to the job I hated and to write that book.

'Do it, Mandy!'

'Really?' I laughed loudly with a feeling of excitement that I hadn't felt for the longest time for any project. It was much more than him saying, *follow your dream, I'll pay the bills, we'll figure it out*, it was also a show of support. He believed I *could* do it and that was all the motivation I needed. I know that I would never have done it without his unconditional love. Euuch! Just read this back and I have to say that Cupid got me real good!

Giving up my job meant I didn't have to travel to London or work in the Bristol office. I spent more time in the shop, which was limping towards the ends of its days as we ran out of both money and steam. Mum still loved to while away her days there and the social life that came with it. I strongly believe it helped her recovery. It was also the perfect place for me to write. I'd travel there from our army quarter and without the cash for my own laptop, I borrowed a little word processor that Ben had used for schoolwork. It had a tiny eight-inch screen, and the letter 'S' didn't work, so I used a dollar sign instead. I wasn't entirely sure what story I was going to write, but I knew that Sophie, Simon, Samuel and Sally were not going to be big characters and it wasn't going to be set in Singapore or Scarborough!

Opening it up with trembling fingers and placing it on my knees while I perched on a wide step inside the shop window was a moment I had waited for my whole life. I'd always said I thought I could do it, always wanted to do it, but in that moment, I realised that talk was easy, now was the time I put myself to the test. I was going to open up those filing cabinets, I was going to mentally delve among the good, the bad and the darn right terrible of all that I had lived, all that I had felt and all that I had encountered. And I was shit scared.

Writing Poppy Day *on the step in our shop, dreaming, hoping of getting published one day.*

The thought of writing a book had been nearly four decades in the making, what did I have to lose?

Quite a lot, as it turns out! Simeon had gone back to Afghanistan for a month or so. I no longer had a proper job and going from two incomes to one is never easy. We made drastic cuts to ease our outgoings and enable me to write. We sold our car, nearly all our furniture and my precious collection of books and ornaments. Selling my books was the only thing I regret and I'm slowly buying them all back. We maxed out our credit cards and as a family ate pasta in an extra jumper and thick socks, as we were reluctant to put the heating on.

At first this felt like the first steps on my bohemian journey, all very arty-farty and exciting, but very quickly the novelty of living this way wore off. We had both lived with hardship at times in the past and to see a huge drop in our standard of living, while dragging our kids along for the ride, at times, quite frankly, felt nuts. But we persevered, fuelled by nothing more than the idea of what life might be like for the kids and us if my dream came true.

One question, however, a big question that had the potential to throw a spanner in the works, rolled around in my head and threatened to extinguish the flame of confidence that was about to ignite all the emotional and mental kindling I'd been collecting for years: '*What on earth am I going to write about?*' The same question that had dogged me since Mrs Blight had laughed at my confession of wanting to write stories when I was only a little girl. I had drawers and drawers in my brain full of stories, and had even penned a couple of tales that had never seen the light of day, but were they any good? Were they the books I *wanted* to write?

It occurred to me then: I had to write about what I *knew*, so that spurred the next question: what *did* I know? It was as I pulled back from the keyboard and took a deep breath, closing my eyes, concentrating on clearing my mind and thinking only about those filing cabinets in which my ideas had been neatly placed since I was a small child that my thoughts became clear. It was a rush of information, a whoosh of realisation that carried me along on its crest, elated by the clarity of thought and able, finally, to make a plan:

I knew motherhood.

I knew families.

I knew what it felt like to be an army wife.

I knew the East End of London.

I knew what it felt like to have my husband away on tour.

I knew my fear was of him being taken hostage or coming home injured.

I knew love.

I knew loss.

I knew friendship.

I knew the restorative power of a good cup of tea.

I knew what it was like to want more out of life.

I knew the type of books I wanted to read.

And *Poppy Day*, my first novel, was born.

It's the story of a young girl, a hairdresser living in London with her nan, whose husband is taken hostage while he is on tour in Afghanistan and it's about her efforts to bring him home, as she knows that no one, no one has the same vested interest in his return as her. There was no clear plan when I began to write, no strategy. I simply wrote the story that played in my head like a movie. But was this correct? Was this how I was supposed to do it? It was more a case of responding to the compulsion that bloomed inside me, a deep, almost visceral desire to tip the contents of my head onto a page.

It was a great leap into the unknown. It felt wonderful to be writing, and very natural for me, I didn't have to overthink it. For the first time, I sat quietly and let my creativity run free. I got lost in the story, crying and laughing, as if I was reading it for the first time. I took Poppy into my heart and, truth be told, even now, a decade later, she lives there still. I learned that I could happily write for hours and hours a day, translating into words the scenes that danced in front of my face. And not only could I write happily, but I learned that writing was the thing that *made* me happy, happiest! Days would slip into hours and hours minutes and minutes seconds, and it would often take me by surprise that so much time had passed, and I would have pages and pages or rather page$ and page$ of a story to read.

The habits and superstitions I formed in those early days are still with me. The obsessive falling into a story and not really looking up until it's finished, if a word is duplicated erasing the 'newest' word as it had no right to be there, putting in page numbers (and they have to be in the centre, bottom of the page) and only when I have more than sixteen pages! I have a favoured font that all my drafts appear in and then a different font in which I send the finished book off to my editor. And if a character is in a sticky situation, or sad or anything else that isn't glorious and I have to stop writing because it's bedtime or any of life's other inconveniences, then I write: '. . . *and she/he found themselves on a beach where the sun was shining, and they didn't have a care in the world!*' Just because I can't stand the thought of leaving them in a bad situation until I can next get back to them and I erase that line before plunging them back into misery! But at least they've had a lovely little holiday.

My books have different tones because they are essentially written by the main character I channel – so it's how *they* see and feel the world, based on all their experiences, that dictates the tone and style of the book. The rhythm of my writing is very important. If I can find a rhythm it doesn't matter where I am or how I'm working, I can fall back into it, like banging a drum with perfect precision;

I can then carry that drum anywhere and can still bang it in the same precise way whenever I need to.

I write anywhere: trains, planes, floors, waiting rooms, cafés . . . It doesn't matter to me. I think growing up in a busy house always packed with siblings, friends and noise has stood me in good stead. As a child I became well-practised in grabbing a book and having to zone out, ignoring the chaos all around as I curled into the corner of the sofa. Or sitting among mayhem on the bus, lost to the words on the page. Writing is the same and it's an ability I cherish.

Simeon was still away when I finished the book. I sat back, breathless, elated, shaking and delighted, and I don't mind telling you, I cried. It felt almost like what came next was secondary, I learned then that it was the writing of the stories that's the thing I love the most. Still is. I read it through for the first time and was once again my childhood self, utterly mesmerised by the fact that pictures visualised in *my* head were now there for other people to read on the page, and again I could only think WOWSERS, it really is the closest thing to magic!

With the first version complete, I didn't dare show it to anyone. I kept it close for a few weeks, figuring out what to do next. It felt extremely exposing, like showing someone the inner workings of my mind or my diary and I didn't know if I was ready to do that. Supposing they didn't like it? I feared they might laugh or tell me it was rubbish and then what would I do?

The enormity of the situation was a little overwhelming. I'd harboured the thought for so long that I might be able to write and now, with the manuscript finished, I was about to find out whether the whole thing had been some ghastly flight of fancy and we had struggled financially for nothing more than a vanity project. It felt selfish, reckless and risky, but it was all a little too late for that. We were committed and it was time to go to phase two – let someone read it! I realised that if I ever wanted to sell a book or get a book published, this was something I needed to get over pretty fast.

My mum read it and loved it, but then she has loved everything I've ever done, said or created since the day I was born and so while her feedback and unwavering support means the world, it wasn't what you might call objective. Dad too, and my grandad – all were full of warm praise, but there was no guarantee that someone who didn't love me would feel the same. Simeon came home on R&R, and I gave him the manuscript and left him on the sofa, returning only to replace his cold tea with a fresh cup and to offer him lunch. I found him crying some hours later and I think I knew then that it was a story worth reading. I've never been so happy to see a person I loved in such distress; anyone who has wanted to evoke emotion in their writing will totally know where I am coming from. Take that, Aunt Spiker!

His belief gave me the confidence to dare to dream that I could write something that might be worthy of publishing. His financial support meant I could climb off that ruddy hamster wheel and make it a reality. And more importantly, his love and friendship made me think that if I tried and failed at it – that was probably okay too.

My beloved grandad was gravely ill when I finished the book and had been suffering for some months with cancer – which had metastasised by the time he was accurately diagnosed. His illness, treatment and care at the hands of a soon-to-be-struck-off medic is a harrowing tale too detailed to accurately convey here. My grandad was an incredible man and refused surgery that might have prolonged his life, claiming he was in his eighties and the NHS had better things to spend their cash on than keeping him going for a few extra months. This was typical of him, and it was only after he had died that we learned of the ways he had helped people, organisations, churches and families all over the East End, quietly and with no fuss, providing assistance where and when he could. I'm glad he got to read my first book. I take enormous comfort from the fact that he might not be around to see how things have turned out, but he was there at the very beginning. During the last conversation I had with him only a short time before he passed away, he told me that someone would publish my novel, he was certain of it, and that if there was anything he could do while 'upstairs' he'd do it. It made me laugh and it made me cry. Still does.

When it came to getting published, I didn't have the first clue where to start. The world of publishing was a complete mystery to me. An enigmatic, complicated, multi-faceted world about which I knew absolutely zip. I quickly realised there was a huge gulf between writing and getting something published – two entirely different skillsets. I might have felt fairly confident now in the writing, but in everything else . . . ? It was like feeling my way in the dark.

I decided to start by sending copies of the book everywhere, EVERYWHERE! Scouring *The Writers' and Artists' Yearbook*, I wrote out the names and addresses of publishers, agents, book printers, you name it. If there was the word 'book' or 'publish' in the job title, they got a copy! When I started out, it was customary to physically send the first three chapters and a covering letter, which when money was tight, was a huge expenditure. It was early 2011, when I'd watch the lady in the post office stick on the stamps and pop the manila envelopes in a pile, waiting to be whisked away to the desks of people who might just change my life. The first packages were sent out with a kiss and a word of hope whispered inside them.

All I had to do was sit back and wait for the replies.

I waited and I waited.

And I waited.

I went from longing for the post to arrive each day with a gut full of excited anticipation, to dreading it, as no response would mean the low of disappointment.

And then – one unremarkable day – the first reply arrived, and my pulse raced. I took my time opening it, sitting at the kitchen table, breathing slowly, closing my eyes and praying for the outcome I desired. With trembling hands, I carefully extracted the generic letter, telling me that I had not been successful, they did not want to pursue this manuscript. My heart sank, although realistically I told myself the chance of the very first letter being the YES! I was looking for was a little unlikely. It was a short, printed missive that had been *signed on behalf of. . .* no doubt by an intern who did them in batches. Other replies began to trickle through, more rejections and then more and more. I got a lot quicker at ripping open the envelope and did so with a lot less ceremony and a lot less hope, yanking out the printed response, casting my eyes over it briefly before balling it and chucking it in the bin.

All were the same firm, curt and resolute 'Thanks, but no thanks . . .' written in so many variants, and none were pertinent to my manuscript. I hoped for a lengthy letter about why it was not right for them, how I could improve, what made it not publishable in their eyes. But of course, that never came, only ever two or three lines of dismissal, if they bothered to reply at all.

Each rejection was a tiny dagger that lodged in the thin veneer of my confidence. I began to question why I had thought it was a good idea to write a book at all and to count all the days I had wasted tip-tapping away on that little word processor instead of working for a wage. I felt stupid, embarrassed that I had even thought it might be a possibility for a woman like me. The whole exercise felt indulgent when I would have been better off out earning money. There were a couple of days when I felt like throwing in the towel. I could see that this venture was probably going to end in humiliation, and all the doubters and naysayers were going to be proved right, it *was* too hard to get a book published. I felt like a fool.

And then my mum gave me a good talking to.

'Do you like the story you've written?'

'Yes.'

'Would you buy it if it was on the shelf?'

'Yes, yes I would.'

'Well, there we go, then. Don't forget, Mandy, millions of books DO get published. Someone has to get picked. There has to be one book that rises to the top of the pile that stands out, so why not yours?'

Her words made me think, *yes, why not mine? Why the bloody hell not mine?*

Buoyed up and with renewed vigour, I sent out more and more copies, figuring that each 'no' was one step closer to me getting my 'yes'!

In hindsight, it was my lack of understanding of how to get a book written and out into the universe that proved to be one of the secrets to my success. I didn't see and was unaware of all the many, many boulders blocking my way and the wide hurdles over which I was supposed to clamber. The alarming odds against actually getting published didn't put me off because I was unaware of them! I was staggered to learn when I first started that over 90 per cent of book manuscripts sent to publishers are weeded out, 'rejected', at submission level, meaning it was highly unlikely that my manuscript was read. The chances of a book being traditionally published was less than 1 per cent. And as if this wasn't demotivating enough, once published in print, the average book sells fewer than 250 copies a year. I'll just let that sink in: less than 250 copies *a year*! After all that hard work, all that self-belief and having made it that far . . .

Armed with nothing more than renewed faith in my story and the words of my mum ringing in my ears, I carried on. I sent copies to bookshops, journalists, editors, anyone who I thought might be able to help get my story out there. But again, after this initial burst of energy, knowing that even if a response was forthcoming it might not be what I wanted to see, my enthusiasm began to flag again. I had sent out approximately seventy manuscripts and had over thirty or so rejections. I could see my dream of becoming a published author disappearing like the rolling morning mist.

Our finances and resilience were stretched thin. The lack of money was a constant source of worry, and losing my beloved grandad put a splinter through my heart that is lodged there still; I only have to put my hand on my chest to feel it. Mum had been away caring for my grandad and the shop finally closed its shutters. My lovely nan with the beginnings of dementia moved to Bristol to be with us, so we could all care for her. My wonderful auntie Jo, Mum's sister, a single mum with a full-time job, came at weekends and when she could get away. It was hard on everyone, especially my nan, an East End girl who found herself transported to the West Country.

Simeon, now back at work in the UK, stopped asking if I had had any replies, knowing that if I had it would have been the first thing I'd have mentioned as he walked through the door, plus he'd have probably heard me singing for joy all the way over in his office at the MOD.

Understanding now that a traditional publisher was not going to scoop me up anytime soon, we decided to self-publish the book and to raise some money for a charity very close to our hearts in the process. Our logic was that my little book might not be the start of a writing career, as I had hoped, but it could at the very least raise money for soldiers who had come back injured or changed by conflict, knowing the only difference between them and Simeon was luck. We thought if we sold a few copies that would be a great thing.

I painted on a smile and readily agreed that this was the best course of action, but inside I was broken. It felt like possibility and hope that had been pillars on which all my future happiness was built were crumbling. No matter what life had thrown at me, the thought, the image and the dream of seeing a published book with my name on it had sat like the brightest light at the end of even the darkest tunnel. An escape for me, mentally, physically, financially and a victory for the girl who didn't think she'd ever amount to anything because she didn't know how to get started, didn't know how to convince anyone that she was capable of something amazing. I got a sore throat, it felt as if a lump sat there made of disappointment and sadness. My voice went croaky and every bite and every sip had to navigate the boulder of desolation that I could not shift.

We agreed that financially it was for the best that I began to put the feelers out to see what job might suit me next. The thought of putting on work attire again and sitting in an office, painting on a smile and climbing back onto that hamster wheel, filled me with dread, particularly as I knew the taste of failed ambition would be bitter, the commute longer, the early morning starts colder.

Writing had sat, always slightly out of reach, but there on the hazy horizon, spurring me on. To have tried and failed would mean I'd still be doing shitty jobs, but without the possibility of ever achieving my goal, and the fact that I'd come so close was almost harder to accept than if I hadn't tried. It had felt nice living with the possibility of becoming a writer, a thought that one day . . . but to live with proof that this was never going to happen would, I knew, be that much harder.

I reminded myself that I'd spent the best part of my working life doing shitty things I didn't want to just to put food on the table and pay rent and this was no different. It was just life! It was sad to see my dreams dashed, but as we had always agreed, it was a huge achievement to have finished a book at all and that was enough to put a tiny swell of confidence in my own ability. Simeon pointed out that it didn't mean I had to stop writing, just that I would do so for my own personal satisfaction – it was, after all, my happiest place!

I can't pretend I wasn't disappointed. I was completely gutted, but no one could say I hadn't given it my best shot and I realised I would not have swapped the disappointment for not writing my book at all. That boulder, however, remained firmly lodged in my throat and it stayed that way for months. Every weekend and any spare time, we would load up the car with boxes of my little book and go to military events, army bases and armed forces days and sell copies out of the cardboard boxes. It was hard work, but there was something thrilling about putting the story into the hands of readers, as well as raising money for the charity we cared about.

Despite my decision to find a 'proper job' and give up on my dream, fate had other ideas.

Unbeknown to me, at a social event in London, a journalist to whom I'd sent a copy of *Poppy Day*, handed it to a friend of his who happened to be Caroline Michel, the country's top literary agent. It was the kind of thing I could not have planned, envisaged or dreamed of. It was the universe working behind my back, or maybe it was my grandad giving me a little help from 'upstairs' – who knows! She not only liked the book, but also repeatedly tried to call me. Thinking it was a PPI call or someone chasing a bill, I kept deleting the number I didn't recognise. Can you *imagine*? There was me schlepping up and down the country with boxes full of books, trying to keep my spirits up, while feeling desolate that my long-held dream had come to nothing, this wish I'd had since that first trip to a library all those years ago when a lady in a turtle-neck sweater gave me my library ticket. And at that very moment, this fearless, brilliant woman who was about to change my life was trying to get hold of me AND I DIDN'T TAKE HER CALLS? She must have thought I was being cool: far from it!

With new social media accounts, I wrote all over Twitter the fact that I was going to be attending a book signing at a charity event in Selfridges, London. My little book was loved by those who read it and that alone was a delightful boost. This was a very significant day for me in a very significant place. My nan had told me that when she was younger, she never had the confidence to go into Selfridges as it was too fancy and she felt she wouldn't be welcome there. She even went as far as putting her hand on the brass doorplate before losing her nerve and walking away. My mum when pregnant with me had gone into Selfridges and bought the outfit in which I was to travel home from hospital, but with no idea of the size of a baby or just how incapacitated she would be post birth (more wincing and clenching from me), she bought white leather shoes, a cape with a down-feather-trimmed hood and cuffs and a fancy frock, spending all her money on something that would not fit me for years!

And there was I in that same very fancy store, sitting at a little table with my books in a pile and a queue of people waiting to have them signed and chat to me. It was a real pinch me moment, surreal. I felt so nervous, like it must be a mistake and any second I was going to feel that tap on my shoulder, and just like my nan, such was my lack of self-esteem, I expected to be turfed out.

And suddenly there she was in the queue, my agent to be! Caroline had come to the book event to find me, and after one conversation, where she told me she loved my story, but that it needed significant editing and she knew just the publisher, I signed with her, my fabulous agent. I can't describe quite how it felt to drive home, knowing that paper had been signed and she was in my corner. But I'll try. It was like winning the lottery. It was like finding the answer, being given the keys, shown the code, offered a seat at the table – it felt absolutely, mind-blowingly WONDERFUL! I think for the first week or so after, I expected her to call and say there had been a ghastly misunderstanding or she'd had a change of heart. She didn't. And in March 2012 my dream came true and my first novel, *Poppy Day*, much edited, improved and in a shiny new jacket, hit the shelves . . . and that darned lump in my throat disappeared and I was utterly breathless with joy!

Caroline asked me if I had any other ideas for books and I told her I had lots of stories.

'How many?' She wanted the specifics.

'Umm, about fifty?' I answered casually, not wanting to give the true figure which was at least double this.

'Fifty?'

'Yes.'

'Why have you not mentioned them?' she laughed.

'I didn't know it was important.'

I dared not tell her about my filing cabinet system in case she thought I was nuts. But I opened a new filing cabinet in my head and popped my first novel into a drawer marked 'finished novels'. It felt so good! I shan't ever forget what it was like to hold that first copy of *Poppy Day*, to open the cardboard box when the copies arrived and to pull out the little paperback edition. It was the first stepping stone of my writing journey, but the last stepping stone in the dream I had carried since I was a little girl. I had done it. I was a published author. Me, the girl who was average, clumsy, carrying extra weight, who couldn't be trusted to carry the salad, who couldn't walk properly for much of her teenage years, who didn't know what to say to Mrs Blight when she suggested I ought to have a plan B, who missed her grandad so much it hurt, who had sobbed over her babies who left too soon, who couldn't sleep if she thought too hard about how to make her son happy or replayed the horror of her smashed-up mum on a trolley, who didn't want her husband to go away fighting and who was doing her best to figure out life one awkward step at a time. I had written a bloody book!

Caroline and me at ITV Studios.

Chapter Twelve

'THE QUEEN OF EMOTIONAL DRAMA'

Life, as I hit forty-two, was good. Simeon was now posted to Army HQ in the UK, which meant not so much travelling to hot, dusty and dangerous places, and this made me happy. I could take my mind off the worry pedal for a bit, although I've found over the years that life has a sneaky habit of replacing one worry with another.

Having listened to many friends lament their descent into middle age, I didn't share their concerns and was positive, if not a little smug, that the prospect of getting older didn't faze me. In a world where women are encouraged to believe that ageing is unacceptable and we must therefore continue to spend . . . spend . . . spend, pointlessly chasing youth, I've always found it slightly ridiculous that the one thing we can all be certain of, if we are very, very fortunate, is that we will slowly decay and shrivel until we are no more than worm fodder . . . and yet we fight against it rather than embrace it.

I was carrying about an extra 15 lb and while not even close to body confident, being a published author had massively boosted my self-esteem and I was in a good place, happy in my relationship and the boys were, I thought, settled. I loved being able to write and I'd never worked harder in terms of the hours I put in.

But I had also never had such reward and I don't mean in monetary terms, although, yes, that too, eventually, but the first time I saw someone who was not a relative of mine reading one of my novels . . . it's a day that will stay with me. I climbed into a random carriage on the District Line of the London Underground in October 2012 and there was a woman with a book bag on her lap and she was reading *Poppy Day*. I thought my heart might burst right out of my chest. I felt my face blush red. I was tearful, overwhelmed, fascinated and felt for the first time in my life, successful. Not because she had bought my book or because I had 'made it', but because I studied her and she was engrossed, biting her bottom lip and turning pages, as her eyes danced across the text, the book held close to her nose. She was lost, as I had been so many times in a story.

It was a moment I will never, ever forget. I don't know her name. I know nothing about her really, but I can tell you exactly what she was wearing, her hair colour, her age. I can describe the thin gold chain around her neck, a wedding ring . . . a stranger who had the biggest impact on me. Her rapt expression was silent encouragement, enough to spur me on to start book two. If it had only been her and me in the carriage I might have had the courage to ask her what she thought of it, and depending entirely on her response, I may have introduced myself. Instead, with nerves lapping at my heels and a dry mouth, I jumped off at my stop and stared back through the window as the doors closed and the train clattered off along the tracks. She didn't look up and I was glad. My only wish was that I could have been with my grandad, with whom I'd sat on that train so many times. He would often meet me at Embankment station, when I worked for the taxi firm, and we'd travel home together. Who knows, maybe he was right by my side. One thing is for sure, he would most definitely have asked her what she thought of it and then introduced me.

The word-of-mouth chatter from readers and reading groups around my first book brought wave after wave of publicity: magazines featured it, radio shows spoke about it and the book just kept selling.

Reviewers and journalists were interested in me as an army wife, writing about an army wife. It meant my second book *What Have I Done?* was eagerly anticipated. I continued to write what I 'knew' and the response to these first couple of novels was beyond my wildest imaginings. I will never forget what it felt like to sit and watch them rise up the book charts until they reached the top spot. I was in a chart with Jodi Picoult! I was in a chart with Maeve Binchy! These were writers I loved and admired and there was I, Mandy from Stepney, in a chart with these titans! I will never get used to it. Never.

With a loyal and growing readership, the foundation was set for my career as a writer. *What Have I Done?*, a novel about a woman called Kathryn in a controlled and coercive marriage who fights to find herself and set herself free, won the Sainsbury's e-book of the year award, rocketed up charts, was one of Amazon's Pick of the Year novels and on it went. With this success came feelings of increased confidence. My phone buzzed day and night with kind messages via social media from strangers all over the world telling me how much they loved my stories, related to my stories and wanted to read more. This helped me shake off the dark shadow of inadequacy that had dogged me for much of my life. Days and days spent staring at a computer screen meant my brow became etched in furrows, my eyes were slightly hooded and my neck was in danger of becoming a turkey wattle, but I didn't care! For the first time in my life, this was not about me trying to attain approval or love through the way I looked, but about using my smarts. I was the girl who might not be able to make a decent cupcake, but I'd written a bestseller or two.

◆ ◆ ◆

2013 was the year my beloved nan died. It was a very different experience from losing my grandad, who was a mighty oak felled by illness against which he had no defence. My nan's passing was slower, longer and her final years tinged with the discomfort and confusion of dementia – not only hers, but those of us who loved her too. We faltered often, driven by fatigue, hopelessness and guilt as we did our best to keep things positive when it would have been a lot easier to watch her sink and sink with her.

'Joe's not been to visit me today,' she'd tut at the tardiness of her absent husband. We quickly realised it was kinder to say he was running late or was on his way, knowing minutes later she'd be distracted by a theme tune on the telly or the retelling for the millionth time, of a story from her war years. Nodding with mock surprise and trying not to recite the tale in your head word for word, was preferable to witnessing her heart cleaved open with distress if you inadvertently mentioned that her husband had passed away . . . this in her mind, the first time she had heard it.

Now this should be neither a shock nor a lamentation that I lost my grandparents, it is the natural order of things *if* you are very, very lucky. But their deaths, no matter how certain, left a small hole in my heart and a sadness in my bones that missing them to this very day makes a constant. I know I was incredibly fortunate to have them in my life and to outlive them, to be close to them, to gather all the wisdom, love and guidance they cast in my direction, saving them for when I needed them the most, and it's not without irony that I needed them the most when they died, when my grief was all-consuming. They were another set of parents to me and even though they died a few years apart, now strangely with the benefit of time passed, it feels like it happened at the same time. I guess because I always saw them as one entity. A couple. A single unit. Like the rest of us I have no idea what happens when we shake off our mortal coil, but I took comfort from the thought of reconciliation for them, even if it was only in moments of fantasy. A reconnection of them in some way so she could nag him, and he could ignore her and carry on reading over his glasses that had slipped down his nose. Maybe this thought is only to give myself some kind of happy closure; I think that's probably it.

One of the last times I remember them being out and about before illness struck my grandad and my nan went downhill.

I was fortunate, along with my auntie, to be with my nan, holding her hand when she took her last breath. It was a wonderful privilege, and I can tell you that not once did I, nor any of us, think about her wrinkled forehead, her thickened waist, less than groomed brows or her unstyled hair. It was a reminder to me of the unimportance of our outer casings. No, I thought about her letting me cheat at cards when I was a kid and the smile on her face as she dished up her incredible apple pie and the way she cried when she spoke about the son she delivered at full term, and in eternal sleep. His name was David, a boy who walked with her every day of her life even though he never took a step. And I too walk with a child like that every day. I understood. I took her sadness, added it to my own and folded it into my stories. Safely stored in my filing cabinet.

One aspect of being a writer that did not occur to me was the fact that to help my books fly, I needed to undertake publicity and PR. I knew very little about the world of publishing and thought that my book would be finished on the Wednesday and the next week would probably be on the shelves of every bookshop in the land! Well, it didn't work quite like that . . . the process can be slow, frustratingly so. Even today I work about a year ahead of my publishing schedule, writing books that will come out about twelve months later.

As I achieved greater book success with my third book, *Clover's Child*, my fourth, *A Little Love* and my fifth, *Will You Remember Me?* my books began to come out around the world, in Australia, New Zealand, South Africa and all over Europe. I was asked to travel to these countries to undertake book tours and events. It blew my mind. I would step off the plane in countries I'd never been to before, to be interviewed by newspapers and magazines, appear on breakfast and morning shows. I'd meet women at book events or signings who told me how much they loved Poppy, Dot, Kathryn, Peggy and others and hear how they sat with my book in their hands, escaping from the real world, as they took every step with my characters. They will never know what their words meant and how it made every step *I'd* taken to get to that point seem worthwhile. I still get messages daily from all over the world from women telling me how they relate to the issues I write about.

TV in Ireland.

We felt it was time to buy a house and make a permanent home. The boys were eighteen when we moved into a small new-build house that we had bought off plan, our first proper little home of our own. The idea was that no matter where Simeon and I travelled, the boys would have this base, this home, and us too when we were in the UK. The day we picked up the keys is one I shan't forget. No army carpet, curtains and lampshades, no more packing and unpacking of boxes, unless it was on our terms. It felt amazing. The first thing I did was paint a wall grey and buy yellow furniture – just because I could! I loved that house. It was on a new development by the Cribbs Causeway shopping mall where we had our first date, and, in terms of size and construction, was if anything a little smaller, but not that much different from the army quarters we had lived in, but the main difference was it was ours and no one could take it away from us and no one could ask us to move at a moment's notice. It felt great. It was 2014, and by this point, Simeon and I had lived in twelve homes in eight years.

And frankly I'd had enough of offering to make tea for the furniture removal men and hunting for the bloody kettle.

Knowing we could stay where we were and put up pictures, plant a tree if we so wished and make plans, gave me such a feeling of peace. It wasn't a grand or opulent house; in truth I didn't want a place like that, knowing I would not have felt at home. We had been stunned by a visit from a financial adviser who told us we could get a whopping mortgage with the rise in our income now that my books were selling so well. Excitedly, I spent a day or two on Rightmove, ogling vast houses with marble kitchens, stables, tidy shingle on the long driveway and utility rooms with shiny tiles. Trying to picture our little family in a house like that was impossible. Stables? What would I do with a bloody stable? I wanted somewhere that was cosy and where I could chat to my neighbours over the fence, like my great-nan, nan and mum had in their homes.

Also, knowing how life can turn on a penny, I still had that feeling in my gut that this success might not last, I might not sell another book, this might all be a flash in the pan and the last thing we wanted was to find ourselves in debt, lumbered with that whopping mortgage and having to move, *again*. And if we'd gone down the huge mortgage route – how much of the house would we actually own, the front door maybe? Half a stable? This new house was very affordable, meaning that if the shit hit the fan and I had to go back to cleaning at night or working in a call centre or whatever, it was comforting to know we could still afford our house.

My new solitary career, which saw me largely bound to that little word processor, which I was as loath to give up as I was comfortable writing on it, meant I spent hours and hours in a chair. No longer having a physical job or a second job, running around as a waitress or working behind a bar and not climbing stairs or even walking to a bus stop, meant my physical activity was curbed. The most I undertook during the day was to lope to the kitchen and flick the kettle on to boil and brew my beloved fuel of choice: coffee. I'd usually grab a slack handful of Digestive biscuits for good measure as I was passing and I gained weight, maybe another 14 lb.

I was now a writer. An obsessive, sedentary writer who practised her craft for hours and hours each day, sitting with my legs curled under me, while my body softened to match my surroundings. My muscles seemed to atrophy in a hunched pose and damage began to set in. This was my dream job, *is* my dream job! And if I got a bit of backache, a slight hump, rounded shoulders, stiff fingers, a permanent frown at the top of my nose from constantly looking down with a fixed look of concentration, and arthritic lumps forming on the top of my aching wrists, then so what? It was worth it, wasn't it? It was still very much my happy place and Lord knows I needed to go there often, as Josh was very poorly.

His mental health had declined to the point where we began to suspect he was suffering from depression. We crept around the house, trying not to wake him up, knowing that sleep was hard for him to come by, wary of disturbing him. When not sleeping, he lay in his horizontal world, a husk of the boy we loved, troubled, sad and with a haunting stare that made me weep. It was exactly like he had given up on life.

It tore me apart, not knowing what to do or how to fix him. He clammed up, not wanting to talk, sleeping more and more and ambling reluctantly into school where he studied for his A levels. Simeon and I were ignorant of how best to handle the situation. We kept reassuring him (and ourselves) that once he got through his exams and into university, his life could begin in earnest, he could study the one subject he loved, Biology, and his whole life would begin! And so, we did what I thought was best, and what had undoubtedly helped me at times of stress. We built a nest and did our very best to keep him safe, warm, fed, loved and prayed it was enough.

My new career was of course not responsible for my weight gain; eating too much food was, once again using it to plug any holes: my sadness, my worry, my exhaustion, but certainly my lack of exercise didn't help. Putting my work out into the public arena had an unexpected consequence and not one I had remotely considered. It seems that as soon as you have, as is the case with me, even the *tiniest* of public persona, the world appears to be given carte blanche to judge you.

As I wrote book six, *Christmas for One*, book seven, *A Mother's Story*, book eight, *Perfect Daughter*, book nine, *The Second Chance Café*, and book ten, *Three and A Half Heartbeats*, I expected my stories to be judged. I *wanted* to hear the feedback, to read the reviews – this is lifeblood for authors, knowing how to improve and crucially what my readers most related to, what they liked best, enabling me to shape future stories. What I hadn't banked on was that I would be judged for my appearance, my weight, my hair, my walk, my clothes, my . . . you name it.

I was crowned 'Queen of Emotional Drama' by the *Daily Mail* and as my books began to sell in their millions, I was asked to appear on national radio, TV panel shows and morning shows to give my opinion as 'every woman' and very often the area under discussion was one of the topics of my book: family life, loss, finding love later in life, or else it was to talk about my journey and how in my forties I had managed to make my publishing dream come true.

The first time I went on TV, aged forty-three and early in my writing career, I was petrified. I didn't want to see myself on TV and I didn't want others to see me on TV. It was one thing to have greater acceptance of myself physically but quite another to put it on television! It was an afternoon chat show, *The Alan Titchmarsh Show*, and I was so nervous I didn't think I'd be able to speak, but I did, zoning out the fact that there were cameras and an audience and remembering something my Aunty Kit had once said to me: 'We all shit through the same hole!'

And she was right: people are people and there is often more that binds us than we think. So, I relaxed, chatted as if I was chatting to him alone and before I knew it the show had ended. My agent called to say she'd been contacted by breakfast TV to invite me on. And that, as they say was that. The more I was interviewed, the more TV I did, the easier I found it. I got on well, not performing or trying to impress with a caricature personality, I'm just myself and all nerves are gone.

Being overweight on TV has been hard. Especially as the rumour goes that the television screen adds at least 10 lb to you. This in conjunction with the high-definition images that we are all used to, which magnify every imperfection, every flaw, every whisker-filled follicle, every open pore, every lump, bump and wrinkle and . . . you get the idea.

I am now a regular on sofas and panel shows where the topics under discussion range from the complexities of Brexit to the nation's favourite biscuit and everything in between. I've worked with a whole array of fabulous people, and I've learned a lot. Nearly all of them have been generous and encouraging. It was fascinating to me the amount of preparation that went into making people 'TV ready'. For some of my regular TV gigs, *The Matthew Wright Show* and *The Jeremy Vine Show*, I naively assumed you would rock up, have a quick gander at a script or running schedule and take your seat, but no, hours can be spent in hair and make-up. Every single make-up artist I've worked with has been a magician, helping to hold back the years with artistry and skill. It is a rare talent to take my tired, washed-out face and turn me into something bright and fabulous! All with no more than a swish of a blusher brush and some carefully placed concealer.

Plunged into this world of the beautiful, I always felt like the plainest girl in the room and was in awe of the celebrities who were very often flawless. Many confessed to the use of Botox or other beauty enhancements that would take years from their faces. It struck me as a shame that they felt such pressure, but there was no denying the effects were dazzling. With the right hair extensions, plumped lips and smoothed brows, they looked somehow other-worldly, but also incredibly glamorous.

I realised fairly quickly that unlike me where my job is to write – TV presenters, broadcasters and many 'celebrities' explained they have to keep up this outer casing of perfection because that is their brand. The public don't want them to age or decay like a gone off lemon in the beautiful fruit bowl of life, they want them to remain plumped and youthful! It struck me as such a shame, especially as often brilliant broadcasters who can ask cutting questions, entertain with wit and who can be just as insightful whether they have a wrinkle or not, jump on the Botox and enhancement train. And having seen it up close, it's really hard to disembark because if they do, they will reveal their ageing selves, a bit of a shock for everyone who is used to the veneer of perfection. The talk behind the scenes has taught me that it can sometimes feel like the young or the next best thing is snapping at your heels, eyeing up your job and so to give in gracefully to ageing could actually be a bad career move. The pressure to maintain the illusion of youth must be enormous.

Very often I would meet women who were older than me but without the faintest whiff of ageing, looked decades younger. It made me wonder if my choice to let my face decay like that old lemon was in fact the right one. I'd nip to the studio loo and stare at the dark shadows beneath my eyes, my wrinkles, my thinning upper lip and saggy chin and wonder if I should let an 'aesthetician' get their hands on my ageing fizzog. But after sitting on the train home for a minute or two, I'd laugh that I was even considering it. No one I loved or lived with seemed that fussed by my face and that was all that mattered.

It was no surprise to me that if you go on TV and express an opinion, of course you are going to find that some people agree with you, some are entirely indifferent to the subject under debate and others who absolutely disagree with your stance. And what better place for them to express their outrage and opposition to your view than on social media, right? I quickly learned that it came with the territory and anyone regularly on TV is fully aware that the exposure comes at a cost: that of putting your head above the parapet and allowing your opinions to be held up for scrutiny. More exposure – of course – saw my worst fears realised.

I was in my mid-forties, with books eleven, *Another Love*, twelve, *My Husband's Wife*, and thirteen, *I Won't Be Home for Christmas* out and was in the public eye a lot more, a regular on weekend radio and TV. Now, maybe I was a bit naive and had certainly come to this life of books and television later in life, but I did not expect, and was in no way prepared for the vitriol directed at me for the way I looked. I had made peace with my face, but my weight struggle was still a work in progress. I found the abuse bewildering at first and so very hurtful – trying to get my head around the fact that we might be discussing something as fundamental as campaigns for mental health, domestic violence, the climate change debate, you name it! And yet rather than engage with the conversation off-air, I would be bombarded with tweets of a personal nature that have included:

'What do you know you fat b*tch?'

'Shut the f*ck up and go back to the pies.'

And even, and most succinctly:

'You ugly fat c*nt.' (I must confess that at this point I rather wish they had used the wishy-washy term, tuppence or tinkle – so much more pleasant!)

The first time I read such a message, from a woman, who in her biography claimed to be a 'mum and grandma', I stared at it on the train home for the longest time. I wondered how she'd feel if someone had sent such words to her 'children and grandchildren'? I'd never been spoken to like that before, other than possibly in a road rage incident or maybe uttered under the breath of someone and of which I was unaware, but it was shocking. It made me feel sick. There it was in black and white, hatred directed at me, a stranger and written without the smallest clue as to who I was, what I stood for, how I felt, my history, none at all.

Simeon, monitoring my accounts, as he does when I am on-air, saw it and told me to ignore it and that I should feel sorry for someone who feels the need to send something like that. He's right, but that didn't stop all the feelings of self-doubt bubbling to the surface, didn't stop that little earworm with messages from my internal voice of self-sabotage getting louder.

They came at a time when everything that used to be smooth was starting to wrinkle, everything once sharp was getting a little slack, the hair I have always had was thinning and suddenly where I'd never had hair – great, rustic clumps of the stuff grew. Some days, I honestly didn't know whether to invest in facial bleach or a mini lawn mower. I have to confess that even though I know the whole premise is utter rot and that there is no such thing as a lotion I can slather, a cream I can apply, a serum I can dot or a juice I can drink that will take me back to the halcyon days of my smooth-faced, taut-skinned, lustrous-haired, full-lipped younger self, I had, on occasion, usually when my mood was low, bought the bloody stuff! Falling for the slick advertising with compelling 'before' and 'after' pictures promising that while I might go to bed looking like Hagrid, if I shelled out upwards of fifty quid, signed up for the app and meditated, there was the chance I might wake up as Gwynnie. If only.

Did I hanker for the face of my youth? Think about it? Mourn the loss of it? Sometimes. I saw many women in the public eye who would reduce their face to parts: 'I hate this patch of sun-damaged skin, want a smaller/straighter nose/fuller lips/no wrinkles here, wider eyes, a taut chin, smoother neck . . .' on and on it went and I found it sad. This quest for youth and perfection forced me to face my lifelong negative preoccupation with my appearance, especially as I was ageing myself and I felt conflicted. I had survived two malignant tumours, had watched my beautiful mum recover from a physically life-changing accident and lost my darling nan. I'd seen my pregnancies end before that child got the chance to grow old and I realised how bloody ridiculous it was to waste a second of life worrying about, fretting about and fighting against an ageing face when what I should be doing was celebrating it! My young face has gone! And missing it and attempting endlessly to recapture it would, I knew, not only be emotionally and financially draining, but also utterly pointless. And yet, I still found myself looking at adverts that promised to wipe years from my brow and I wondered what that might look and feel like, would that kind of intervention stop the trolls from whipping out their poison pens.

No matter how I tried to laugh it off, these nasty messages affected me, not least because I can't in a million years imagine sending a note, writing words or even *thinking* such a horrible thing about someone I do not know and then putting it out for the world to see. I also despair of a mind that decides the best course of action, instead of healthy intellectual debate or verbal jousting, is to simply point out the fact that I have cellulite, big boobs and the hint of a moustache – which neither advances the argument nor educates either party, but mainly, *mainly* I was stunned by how much these often-anonymous comments affected my already fragile self-esteem.

Why did I give so much thought to the person who tried to break or hurt me? How about concentrating on the ones who put me back together again? The lovely messages far, far outweighed the nasty ones, messages from women who related to my look, my words or both and readers who wanted to tell me what my books meant to them. So, what did it matter if someone I neither knew nor cared about had this opinion of me? But the truth is it *did* matter because despite the reassurances I gave myself to paper over the cracks of low confidence, I took those comments to heart, believing that they were possibly, if not probably, how much of society viewed me.

My mum got angry on my behalf, telling me how ridiculous it was to give credence to the words and to allow a stranger to influence how I thought about myself. She was right, of course. Some people I know with thicker skin than mine *are* able to laugh off these comments, to put them down to no more than the sad virtual ranting of some inadequate wanker who face-to-face would probably smile and shake your hand, someone to be pitied.

But sadly, I don't and never did have the thick skin required. Especially when they were so cleverly and brilliantly addressing what was obviously an issue for me, my weight. The words confirmed what I believed everyone was thinking and sometimes, depending on what else was going on in my life, they had the ability to floor me. I became a little quieter at home, a little more reserved in public and began to feel it better to decline invites than to appear at things; maybe it was easier to hide. I said no to fancy celebrity-packed events that are really only photo opportunities and networking events. I didn't want my photograph taken. So, I hid, felt low and ate more.

Sometimes though I had to venture out, and I think a lot about one evening a decade ago now. Simeon and I had been invited to a ritzy ceremony at a fancy London hotel. I'd anguished over going, glancing occasionally at the gilt-edged invitation stuck on the fridge door with a number magnet, as I peeled the spuds for tea. My gut swirled with a mixture of nervous excitement and trepidation. What would I say if someone spoke to me, what should I wear? Maybe it was easier not to go at all . . . Pulling on every ounce of confidence I possessed, I had my roots touched up, still determined to be blonde! And I put on an extra coat of lippy and off I went, making Simeon promise not to leave my side.

Nipping off to the loo during dinner, I stared in the mirror, studying my voluminous, bum-covering frock and trying to summon courage, feeling like a behemoth among the slender pint-sized beauties that seemed to surround me. I was wondering whether it might be possible to leave without returning to the table where I felt on view, wanting to run home and hide, but not only was my husband waiting for me at the table, I was a long, long way from home.

I turned to see a woman in her mid-sixties, washing her hands in the sink next to me who said, 'You look beautiful!' She winked and then swept out, as if I might have imagined the whole exchange.

Her words buoyed me up, filled me with confidence and bolstered my flagging self-esteem. *She* was fabulous! Flawless! A stunningly, stunningly beautiful woman made only more beautiful by showing me the kindness and character that lurked inside her wrapping – and who I happened to know was once Miss World and *she* had said that to *me* . . . I shan't ever forget her kindness, her heartfelt gesture of support. It was the most wonderful example of how kinship and understanding bolstered me in ways she could only have guessed at.

Yet still, to see such hostile messages pop up, was also the first time I'd had my weight and my face so openly addressed. Was that how people thought of me? Did it matter how many bestselling books I had or how much my family loved me, if that was who I was – '*a fat b*tch with a moustache?*' It makes my heart skip to even write that.

I found that my brain readily opened a gateway for imposter syndrome to take root, helped it find a door. Jeez, I practically took its coat while ushering it inside, before making it a cup of tea! Allowing the most negative, dangerous and destructive thoughts to wheedle their way into my head and take up residence. *Who do you think you are, Mandy? You thought wool rhymed with school! You're an idiot! You don't deserve success! You don't deserve anything!*

I felt all my negative thoughts about my appearance and my size and my averageness rush at me. Who *did* I think I was, publishing books and going on telly when my family had toiled long and hard for far less? How was that fair? And that teacher who had laughed at me, she knew what she was talking about, just like the woman who had called me an ugly duckling . . . Maybe I shouldn't write another book, maybe it was better I go and find a different kind of job, and I should probably stay inside and not go to parties or premieres or launch events because then I won't have to worry about what to wear, and it will deny any keyboard cowards the chance to call me a fat c*nt.

It all got a little bit too much.

It was as if I didn't believe I had the right to be slim, pretty, successful or even happy.

It started to affect how I thought about my face – my ageing face – the one I knew deep down it was best to accept and not tamper with, but what if I could fix it and turn back the clock? *Should*

I fix it and turn back the clock? And actually, wasn't winding the clock back on my face a whole lot easier than trying to shift the pounds of fat on my body? Yes, it was, much, much easier . . . and it was a path I walked for a short while with disastrous consequences.

'Shut the f*ck up and go back to the pies.'

Chapter Thirteen

'KEEP YOUNG AND BEAUTIFUL IF YOU WANT TO BE LOVED . . .'

I celebrated my forty-eighth birthday in our 'new' house, where we had lived for two years, and the novelty of staying put had not waned. Ben was studying in Liverpool. Josh was at university reading Biology, and while his A levels had not quite gone to plan and with a diagnosis of depression to deal with, he was, thankfully on campus living the life we had told him awaited; finally he seemed to be on track. I could not have been more delighted and so very proud of both our boys and the men they were fast growing into. My life was simple: supper each night with Simeon, cups of coffee with my mum and dad, writing like a whirling dervish each and every day, trips abroad to promote books, and all the while sales of my stories hitting the dizzy heights in territories all over the world. With books fourteen, *The Food of Love*, and fifteen, *The Idea of You*, out, my literary star continued to rise.

The Food of Love was a particularly hard book for me to write. It's the story of what happens to one family when their youngest daughter, who is anorexic, teeters on the brink of self-destruction while the disease and debate over how they as a family should treat it threatens to tear the loving family apart. Her dad is angry, frustrated, shouting, 'For the love of God she just needs to eat something!' Her mum, however, recognises that it is a complex and devastating mental illness that is more about control and emotional issues than the calories consumed, although this is of course how it presents itself.

While researching the book and speaking to sufferers and their families, the parallels I found between anorexia and overeating surprised me. Not the end result of course, that of being obese or emaciated, although some would argue that there is some equivalence in illness and mortality. I know it sounds ridiculous, but it had never fully occurred to me that undereating and overeating were two sides of the same coin, both denoting an unhealthy, toxic relationship with food.

Certainly, the effects of malnourishment are similar. I recognised many of the emotional responses to living with anorexia and some of the physical compulsions too, as ones I established in my youth when I would eat so very little and revel in the success of it. The feelings of shame and self-loathing were also the same, as was the absolute preoccupation with food, the obsession with eating, and the emotional toll of the skewed relationship with food on both the sufferer and those around them. There was also similarity in pressure from peers, loved ones and society to conform to the 'norm' and of course the terrible spiral that sufferers of both become locked into, aware that they are damaging themselves mentally and physically, but more often than not ill-equipped to break the cycle.

One aspect of anorexia that particularly struck a chord with me, as someone who was now overeating, was the ritual around food. By this I mean the whole end-to-end experience of secretly buying, diarising and plotting how and what would be eaten, and the 'high' it was possible to experience when doing just this. Also similar was the disposing and hiding of food, the secret eating or not eating, and the bodily function and weight obsessions. The mindset, internal dialogue, permissions, justifications and twisted logic around eating habits and the attitude towards food were also strikingly similar.

I knew that until I managed to overhaul my eating habits and break the mental shackles, I was going to remain hitched to a food-toxic lifestyle whether I was eating too little or too much. One of the main differences, in my experience, is that someone anorexic is seen as poorly, in need of help, support and kindness and is even feted in some communities and groups (think high fashion and Hollywood), whereas someone who has distorted their body in the other direction, who has an equally unhealthy relationship with food that is obsessive and out of control, well, those people are often the object of ridicule or disgust.

Both, however, are rooted in an unhealthy food obsession. And it was an obsession that had started to spill over into every single aspect of my life. There was not one facet of my existence that wasn't hampered, reined in, restricted or made uncomfortable because of my weight. I felt compelled to write the story to try to better understand why and how I was punishing my body. I guess I was looking for answers.

My books sold in more territories globally, were translated into dozens of languages and continued to sell in the millions. To see a foreign edition cover pop out of packaging made my heart sing! Very often from countries I hadn't visited and had no idea of their language or custom and yet there it was, my book for people to read, connecting me to women like me.

With no sign of slowing, I kept dipping into those filing cabinets and pulling out ideas that I could weave into novels, and inevitably one sad rainy day, my little word processor gave up the ghost. I kept it of course. It was replaced with the smallest laptop computer I could find. Simeon laughed and tried to tempt me with wide fancy screens, neon keyboards, desktop doodahs and all kinds of widgety wonders that would make my writing life easier, apparently. A screen for research, a screen for writing, a screen for flippin' God knows what. I, however, a creature of habit, wanted none of it.

What I found hard to explain is that these little machines are my instrument. I hit the keys with the rhythm and commitment of a musician; I don't have to *think* about the note or what note comes next, I just play! And the words flow from my mind, via my fingertips, which glide speedily over the keys with the lightest touch and appear on the screen in one swift movement. The thought of someone giving me a different instrument that might not sound the same, feel the same, might not fit me and my style of working in the same way felt like too big a risk. Anyone who has ever seen a musician pick up their first guitar and run their fingers over the frets like they are greeting an old lover will know exactly what I mean. Sitting here in this moment, I'm tip-tapping on a wonky little laptop resting on my knees. It has bashed edges, loose keys and a screen that is eleven inches, it's a bit battered, but it's what I know!

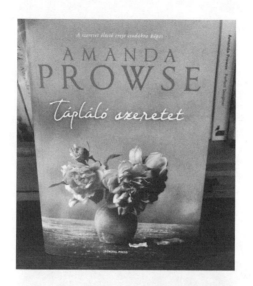

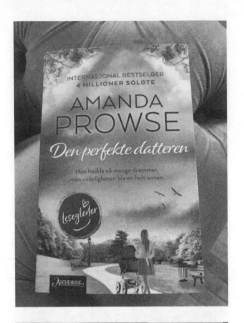

Dutch edition of Will You Remember Me?, *Hungarian edition of* The Food of Love, *German edition of* To Love and Be Loved, *Czech edition of* What Have I Done?, *French edition of* A Mother's Story, *Norwegian edition of* Perfect Daughter, *Polish edition of* Christmas for One, *Hungarian edition of* Christmas for One.

I continued to smile and laugh my way through interviews and on screen, but there were days when my appearance, coupled with waves of self-doubt, threatened to pull me under. Having avoided scales since moving into our new home, I could tell by the way I looked and felt that I had gained yet more pounds. If previously I had experienced frustration by the fluctuation in my weight and a desire to be slimmer, fitter, now I felt the beginnings of physical revulsion. I actively started to hate my body, and this was a whole new ball of wax.

I began to avoid physical contact with Simeon, which was immensely saddening for us. The topic sat between us, a spiky barrier to the relaxed atmosphere we had so enjoyed when first in our new house. It was devastating for us both. So nervous was I of the subject being raised, I spoke to him less, saving any important snippets of conversation until we were in a crowd or the kids were around, figuring a delicate personal matter would not be raised in company and was therefore safe. I would also go to bed at a different time and be snoring by the time he came up the stairs. Both aspects of my behaviour that were cowardly on my part.

I didn't look at myself in the mirror. Throughout my younger life in the times when my weight was within a healthy range, to lose poundage I would simply cut down on food, calm down my consumption and within weeks, days even, it was possible to achieve a goal that meant I could slip into a new frock, fit some fancyish lingerie or not have to hide inside a kaftan on a beach. But as I ate more and more, got heavier and heavier, this was no longer an option, there was no quick fix. I'd lost sight of how I used to look and feel when I quite liked myself. I can only liken it to trying to find a single snowdrop blooming inside a dense forest – you might know it's there and be able to recall its beauty, its fragrance, its delicate nature, but being able to locate it, handle it, admire it, well, that was something else entirely. I was trapped inside a distorted body that I no longer recognised as my own and no longer wanted to look at. This was entirely different from not wanting to look at (or anyone else to look at) my mishmash of scars, a part of my body that I could hide inside pants and jeans, this was about not wanting to look at any part of my body and not wanting anyone else to look at *any* part of my body.

Now, don't get the wrong idea, this is not where I talk about how *bad* it is to be fat and I'm certainly not advocating everyone strive for skinny as though it's nirvana.

It is not!

I for one will never be a skinny girl. I have lost weight but will always have a certain solidity about me that is as much about genetics as it is my food choices. And I am definitely not suggesting that all thin people are walking around with perfect lives. I also know that being overweight or obese does not necessarily mean unhappy or unhealthy. For some it is a very content state in which to live. I am sure we have all met very unhappy slim people and very happy large ones! Plus, I am of the firm belief that what is right for you, is right for you.

It *really* is that simple.

If you are large/fat/overweight/skinny/slim/athletic – or whatever word you want to apply – and are happy with your body then I envy you, because whether your body is rounded, thin, somewhere in between or regularly fluctuating between the two, but you are HAPPY and HEALTHY, meaning you are in a good place mentally and nothing about your food choices and food consumption is causing you bodily harm – then you are a bloody winner because that has always, always been the goal. So, do I believe you can be older, overweight, happy and healthy? Absolutely! Yes, I do. One hundred per cent. So, as I nudged my fifties, at my heaviest, was I fat, happy and healthy? No, I was not. I was the exact opposite of happy. I was very, very miserable.

At my heaviest, family and friends *still* kept telling me that I looked pretty, people who loved me would bolster me with damaging platitudes that meant I could overlook the reality of my situation and the toll it was taking on my health.

'You look fine – you have nothing to worry about.'

'But I don't feel fine, I feel ill . . .'

'Oh, Mandy, you're not fat! Not *that* fat! No way!'

'Actually I am.'

'You're a lovely person!'

'Thank you for saying something so kind, but it won't matter how lovely I am if I don't address my weight and health . . .'

'We love you just the way you are!'

But the fact was, *I* did not love me just the way I was. I was celebrating this incredible global success and yet I was dying inside. I was the only one who truly knew what lurked behind the floaty linen top and the oversized costume jewellery and I really was '*that fat*'. Again, this is a perfect example of people not wanting to hurt my feelings. And families, friends and loved ones of overweight people all over the country replicate this, deciding that it's best not to say anything . . . How crazy is this? Can you imagine if I or someone you loved was walking on a crumbling cliff edge and you were watching, would you shout out, 'Hey, come back from the edge! Come here now! The ground's not solid, I don't want you to fall! I don't want you get hurt!' or would you think, 'I don't want to embarrass them or mention the fact that they look like they might be heading for danger, so I won't say anything! In fact, I will distract them. Hey! The sky is blue today, isn't it lovely? Oh, the crumbling cliff edge? What crumbling cliff edge?'

In fact, being told not to worry by friends, family and colleagues was a common theme for me. Sweet Jesus, I had so much to worry about that it was laughable. But rather than tackle my worries, I sought solace in the biscuit barrel, the bread bin and the dimly lit interior of the fridge where cheese and leftovers lurked. It became a terrible habit, eating and eating and eating until, very often, I had to force myself to eat. Can you imagine? Putting another piece of cheese or slice of pie into your mouth even though you were full right up and even felt sick – but I had to finish them so that there was then no temptation to eat them. Because if they were gone, I couldn't eat them . . . I know it doesn't make any sense. And my rationale for all this gorging? There was none! It was as if I was stuck on a conveyor belt of gorging and sleeping and I didn't know how to stop it or jump off even if I had wanted to. And trust me I wanted to. No, correction, I *had* to. There was no rationale at all.

A lot of morbidly obese people who have courageously opened up to me, have admitted that they lie either to themselves or others about the reasons for their weight – I know I did. And the reason they lie and the reason I lied is because of the blanket of shame and disgust society wants to throw over us, which is stifling, cruel and unfair. I personally felt pushed into the metaphorical corner and confronted, not only by the predictable rhetoric the media trotted out on obesity, but also by those who told me it was fine to be obese! That I should be happy fat! How I envied those women who exposed their rounded tums and jiggly thighs, how I loved the bikini-clad, plus-sized girls who stared challengingly into the lens as if to say, 'what?', and how I longed to feel their level of self-assuredness and confidence, but I did not, and I could not, no matter how hard I tried. I didn't just dislike my morbidly obese body, I hated it. I was never able to get past the thought that I was really a slim girl, trapped inside the blubber.

I started to decline offers to appear on programmes or attend literary events, didn't want to be seen, which only ladled guilt onto my already collapsing self-esteem. Every time I met a new person – and walking into rooms of new people to give book talks or hold a book event meant this happened a lot – I would scan people's eyes and try to detect their initial reactions to me based on nothing more than my size.

I could instantly draw up a fat scale of everyone in the room and then position myself on it. Was I the fattest in the room? The biggest? I became very good at spotting micro gestures that were a good indicator of other people's reactions to me. Some people, women in particular, if they were slim, might touch their own pointed chin while looking at my rounded jowls and large women would sit up straighter and smile wider – as if recognising that this was an accepting environment. *'Look at her, she's big too and she's the guest speaker. I don't need to hide right now.'* And while I understood,

I wanted to announce that I didn't feel I belonged in either camp. I was certainly not slim and confident, but neither was I obese and proud.

I started to make jokes in my talks and interviews about my weight as a shitty pre-emptive strike and to show that I was aware of my size. I laughed heartily at my jokes, as if I didn't care – I thought it was comical, accepting even, but hindsight has taught me that I did care and that it was far from funny. It wasn't only denigrating but was harmful, reinforcing a low opinion of myself, presenting it to the world as fact, and it couldn't help but negatively affect my self-worth. And when your self-worth is reduced, so is your confidence and your mood and that touches every single aspect of your life.

I was stuck. Literally, I felt trapped between the two worlds: a slim, judgmental person stuck inside the obese body I detested. It was a very unpleasant and damaging way to live. And the crazy thing, the *craziest* thing, is that in every other aspect of my life I don't follow the herd. I couldn't care less if I am doing what people expect of me and I carve my own path. I gave up sensible, stable jobs to write full time and everyone, bar a very small handful of people close to me, told me I was nuts!

'Everyone thinks they can write a book!'
'No one will publish it and then what will you do?'
'You're in your forties, you have responsibilities!'
'Do you know how the world of publishing works?'
'It's a pipedream and a waste of your time!'

I have just completed my thirtieth novel and have sold millions of books all over the world, translated into dozens of languages – and this is not a brag, but merely me trying to let you know that I am the kind of person who sets out on a journey and won't rest until I get to my destination, regardless of the naysayers.

And yet when it came to my weight? It was a very different story and one I could not seem to write a happy ending for, not for the longest time. Yes, I am proud of my attitude and my work ethic and of my success. So why, why could I not apply the same logic and work plan to my diet and fitness? Why was I so defeated? So weakened? And so very, very saddened by it. It felt like the one situation in my life that was beyond me. My clothes were reduced to a couple of items which, like when I was pregnant and sporting that space hopper, I would wash, dry and wear on an endless loop. Jeans and a loose-fitting grey kimono. I wore it to sleep in, I wore it on TV, I wore it for photographs.

A couple of days of giving up or cutting down on certain foods or even fasting made no immediate difference to the way I looked and felt. I had gone way beyond that. It was the difference between mopping up a drip with a paper towel and trying to mop up a pond. It needed a lot more work, effort and tools. The volumes involved were so great that it required an entirely different approach and plan, not that I realised this for the longest time. With a reluctance to get on the scales I was still flying blind, unaware of exactly what I was dealing with, exactly how much I needed to lose. And again, this is not about being fat and fat being bad, it's about how I felt about myself. Had I been obese and happy, there would not have been an issue. Simeon read the room and took his lead from me and didn't mention my weight. It was as if we both tiptoed around the topic, too afraid of what a conversation like that might look and feel like.

It wasn't only my body that was beyond recognition, but I also began to think more about my own ageing face. Like most of us I guess, I'd never overly considered what it would feel like to see the last of my girlish attributes replaced by a face that had started to resemble an older person. It wasn't that I minded so much but it was more of an adjustment to the fact that the rose of my youth was wilting, and the petals starting to crisp and brown. I have role models like my mother who see ageing as the start of a positive chapter. I know she is simply thankful to still 'be', having come perilously close to losing her life, but also in her seventies, admits that some worries and preoccupations can be shelved, not least of all trying to attain and maintain beauty. It's almost as if in the great beauty race, she is happy to fall back and enjoy the view at a more leisurely pace. This is in stark contrast to friends of mine who have raged against the decline of their looks, haring to the front, elbows out to maintain a lead in the beauty stakes that has been hard fought for and won over the years.

With my fluctuating weight and less than perfect face, I became overly aware of the images of youthful perfection being beamed into my phone every second of every day via the pages of the magazines and the newspapers I idly scrolled or devoured with my morning cuppa. The women featured were more often than not surgically enhanced, airbrushed or filtered to within a pixel – meaning the picture I stared at was about as far from the reality as is possible. And I should know, I have once or twice featured in such publications and had to do a double take as my double chin shrunk, my skin blemishes faded, and my eyes were a whole lot clearer and greener. Did I moan? Did I heck as like! I looked fabulous! But when I sat back and really thought about it, it felt a lot like cheating.

And that made me feel uncomfortable. I was telling my readers in my books via the stories of ordinary women I chose to tell, and when interviewed, that I was a woman like them, just any other mum/wife/daughter you might meet in the supermarket or at the bus stop. Yet there I was in newspapers and magazines or on social media, paying no heed to the fact that the proffered image of beauty or youth was simply not attainable without trickery, surgery or a couple of rolls of gaffer tape and an expensive lighting rig.

I began to ask myself what I could do to preserve what 'prettiness' I had left and again came to the conclusion that compared to trying to lose over a third of my body weight, fixing the face might mean a much quicker win. With my fifties fast approaching, I started to think seriously for the first time about getting some kind of cosmetic intervention; after all, I had worked with enough beauties who told me how they maintained their 'youthful visage' and 'taut complexion', and they looked like goddesses – so why not? And would it be such a bad thing if I ended up actually liking my face again? Could a lift to my looks erase the sadness I saw every time I glimpsed my reflection?

Towards the end of 2016 and still desperate to raise my beauty game, I was working quite a lot in TV and doing my best to swallow my self-consciousness.

I threw myself into the concept of 'bought beauty' wholeheartedly and sincerely: telling myself that what I was doing was no different from putting on lashings of mascara and getting my roots touched up to restore my 'blonde' and look the best I could on camera. Besides, everyone around me was doing it and so what was the harm? Maybe I would feel better about myself if I followed the examples of the women I was surrounded by and went with the flow. I figured that as I was unlikely to fix my weight issues quickly and satisfactorily before I hit the TV sofas for various interviews, there was another way that I could join the pack, fit in and most importantly, look much, much better than I currently did. It could, in fact, be the answer to my prayers, an instant hit of confidence that might once again have me physically reaching for the husband I loved. I hoped so. I missed him and I know he missed me.

I'd been up close to many women who filled their cheeks with plumping fillers, smoothed their brows with Botox and other toxins, had enhanced their pout with trout-mimicking procedures and who had resorted to cosmetic surgery in an attempt to hold back the sands of time: facelifts, neck lifts, eye lifts, tummy tucks, liver spot abrasion, you name it! Women who stuck hair extensions on their head, had fake boobies put inside their chests, changed the shape of their bum, lash extensions on their eyelashes, sucked fat from their bodies with liposuction and glued dazzling veneers onto their ageing or less than perfect gnashers. It felt like a lot of effort. But was it worth it?

Cosmetic surgery was, I knew, not for me, no way. I've gone under the knife enough to last me a lifetime and know how horrible the entire process was each and every time, not to mention the toll it took on me mentally and my ugly scars. However, fillers, Botox, extensions and all other manner of stick-on and injected frippery, why not? What could possibly be the harm?

I flirted the idea with Simeon, who said the thought repulsed him and he was worried that I might look 'different', and he didn't want that, pointing out several celebrities who had overly stuffed cheeks or had 'Joker' mouth alterations. Neither did I to be honest! Having spent time with people who were unable to show varying degrees of emotion, as nearly every part of their face was frozen, was not something I wanted to emulate. And I saw it a lot, beautiful women who once the filler had set and the Botox had done its job, could no longer raise their eyebrows, wrinkle their noses, or twist their lips in all the ways that are comical, expressive and interesting and were literally reduced to widening their eyes and showing their teeth to express joy, happiness or interest and narrowing their eyes and closing their mouths for sadness, distress or pity. I think what makes a face the most beautiful is the myriad of natural and personal indicators, tells and quirks that make a face unique, and all are based on movement. It also felt, in my inexpert opinion, that the more surgery and/or procedures they had, the less 'beautiful' they became – as if they lost their original reference points, strayed too far from their baseline and were making improvements on their 'altered' face, until very little of what made them beautiful to begin with remained. And it seems to me that the more procedures you have the more you *need*, meaning that the initial subtle tweaks become far more obvious and therefore more obviously altering. There is also something else troubling me – if your face can't move to tell a story, all those non-verbal cues that we pick up on, letting us know when someone is sad, happy, angry, shy, if Botox, fillers and facelifts reduce that, does it also reduce our ability to interact and connect with each other? I'll get back to you on that one.

I began to study the faces of various television personalities and 'slebs' and realised that many of them had a similar look – clearly, they had been smoothed and injected with the same stuff in the same places until some looked remarkably similar, sporting a homogenised, smoother, doll-like visage. All I wanted was improvement and enhancement not alteration, was that even possible?

Armed with my concerns, questions and I must admit no small amount of excitement at how I might be able to 'rejuvenate' my flagging face, as the adverts promised, and against my husband's better judgement, I headed off to a doctor, an 'aesthetic practitioner', who treated a friend of a friend of a friend. A big clue should have been the face of said 'aesthetic practitioner', whose age was indeterminate, but whose face looked pulled, smooth, wrinkle-free, yes, but – how can I phrase it without sounding mean – a bit odd.

'I don't want to look like I've had anything done. Just want to look a bit fresher, younger.'

'That is what *everyone* says to me.' They laughed. This I know because I heard the chuckle sound – even their eyes were wide and fixed.

My friends, whom I had quizzed endlessly over what to expect, all told me it was no more than a little scratch in your face here and there, nothing much really. But as I sat back in the fancy leather chair and the needles went in – I thought it bloody hurt! But then I am a bit of a wuss. I had Botox in three areas: my forehead and either side of my mouth, which I was told would lift my 'marionette lines' and make my mouth more youthful. Marvellous. Didn't know I had marionette lines, but when I *did* know I was jolly glad to have them removed. I then had some filler put into my already plump cheeks.

'Already you look so much better!' my aesthetic practitioner trilled and handed me a small mirror.

I must admit I didn't think I looked *that* much different, which was good, exactly what I had asked for, phew! The bill came to a little under a thousand pounds. It was a huge sum of money and more than I had paid for my first car. I left the clinic feeling a strange mixture of excitement and revulsion. What had I done? Was it worth it? Could anyone tell? Did I look fabulous or hilarious? How could I justify spending that sum of money that would at various times in my life have been enough to radically change my circumstances?

I was, however, excited to look fresher and younger, thinking it would take attention from the size of my bum, but also concerned at how easily I had capitulated. Still, I carried the question, *why* was it a problem? Why couldn't we just *embrace* ageing? And yet I was on shaky ground because these might have been the words I had always spouted, but how could I now that I had a face stuffed full of toxins and fillers?

I was a traitor.

And it didn't feel good.

Arriving home, I avoided Simeon's eye line as he studied me from all angles. It was like I had done something dirty and illicit and had been caught out.

'You don't look that much different' was his summary and I was as glad as he was relieved.

An hour or two later, however, it was a different story. I noticed bruises appearing around my mouth, bad bruises, but this was nothing compared to the sensation a couple of days later when I felt a heaviness in my brow – that's the only way to describe it – a heaviness like someone had put concrete into my forehead. I didn't like it – and spent the afternoon Googling all similar experiences, reading that it was quite normal. Well, it might have been quite normal for them, but it wasn't for me. My brow also dropped. The exact opposite of what I had hoped for, so much so that my eyelashes were under my brow. It was devastating and there was no one to blame but myself. I looked odd and ugly, worse than before, and I had handed over a thousand pounds for the privilege.

Simeon could see I was upset, but I avoided confiding in him just how much. How could I when he had told me it was a crackers thing to do in the first place? I called the 'Dr' who had injected my face who said it was most unusual and offered me a skin treatment 'with a laser that might . . .' I stopped them mid flow. They had done enough. I didn't think there was anything that had happened to my face that zapping with a bloody laser could improve.

But I wasn't angry with them, I was angry with me.

Hair, Botox and fillers as a disguise . . . Fake face, fake hair, fake smile . . . and still in my grey kimono.

Stage two in my 'get fabulous quick' scheme meant hair extensions. Now, I have always had thick, curly hair, which I have been dyeing blonde for decades, but for some reason I decided that long and straighter hair was the way forward. I figured it might be slimming, as if long straight hair, which was less bouffy, might make me look longer and straighter. I was also now keen that the hair might distract from my odd-shaped cheeks and face.

The hairdresser was incredible and skilful. Using real hair – I have just shivered at the thought of this, now knowing where much of this hair comes from and how it is procured. It's an often-exploitative industry with poverty-stricken women selling their hair to agents who tour villages in India, China and Eastern Europe. They sell their hair out of necessity and it's not uncommon for women in poor households to be forced to sell their hair. Embarrassingly uninformed about the exploitation in the global, billion-dollar human hair business, I was more concerned with the silky feel of it and its glorious shine. I couldn't wait to have it clamped and glued to my head, even if there was something vaguely revolting about the thought of someone else's locks going onto my scalp.

I sat in the chair of the salon for eight hours straight while the hairdresser deftly and painstakingly glued thin clumps of it onto my own hair with something resembling a craft glue gun. The gluey bonds were fixed to my hair, and I walked out of the salon with a numb arse and a mane of mermaid waves all the way down my back. It was incredible! When I was little my mum always kept my hair short and I often used to walk around with a pair of tights on my head, making out to have long hair, swishing them this way and that. This felt similar: exciting, glamorous and temporary.

When I got home from the salon, Simeon stared at me and I could see in his expression that he didn't want to derail my happiness or delight, but at the same time was slightly unnerved that I had gone out that morning with my usual curly mop and returned at teatime with the luscious long locks that used to belong to another human being.

'What do you think? Do you like it?' I did a twirl. My glorious mane settled about my shoulders.

His answer spoke volumes. It was what he always said when feeling extra cautious, wary of doing or saying the wrong thing, looking for my lead.

'What do *you* think, Mandy?' he fished.

'I love it!' and I did.

'Well, that's brilliant then.' He sounded a little sarcastic and it hurt me. I was trying to do things to help my crumbling self-confidence and I really wanted him to be on board.

Now, even when feeling my most undesirable, Simeon and I have always enjoyed close contact, even if it didn't lead to anything more physical. Never more so than of an evening when we like to huddle together on the sofa, either we are both working or we gather around a laptop screen to catch a movie or we read books or watch my beloved *MasterChef*. He always sits with his arm around my shoulders and runs his fingers through my hair. I like the closeness of him and the little ritual that can make even a really crap day feel better, a small reminder that he is present and we are a couple, facing the world together, no matter what.

On the day I came back from the salon, he came and sat next to me and I nestled in, huddling close. He reached up and touched my head and recoiled almost violently, removing his hand as quickly as it had made contact.

'Urgh!' The noise he made will stay with me.

'What's wrong?' I felt more than a little embarrassed.

'It's like . . .' I watched his nose wrinkle and his mouth twist (no Botox on this soldier). 'It's like touching someone else's hair and I can't run my fingers over your scalp because of all these gluey knotty lumps, it's . . .'

252

'It's what? Spit it out!'

'It's revolting! It's not you.'

Needless to say, my enthusiasm for my new flowing locks quickly waned. I felt stupid, sick and stupid that I had thought I could look like a glamourpuss, and everything would be better, whereas I might have just succeeded in making myself feel worse and in the process losing the precious connection I shared with the man I loved. It was galling. I studied the extensions in the mirror before bedtime and noticed that if I put my weighty hair up or flipped a part on the side, you could see the little attachments and the way the extensions were gathered in an unnatural even row.

But the worst was yet to come. One of my greatest pleasures in life is and always has been working a healthy, citrus-scented dollop of shampoo into a creamy lather and scrubbing at my scalp with my fingertips. That zingy, clean fresh feeling of newly washed hair and a clean head is incomparable.

It was a shock to discover that with hair extensions, I couldn't do that. Firstly, I was told not to wash them for a while to let them settle and then to do so with the utmost care – furiously scrubbing at my scalp was not possible. The bonds were like lumps and my real hair was tethered to them. My hair felt dirty and my scalp itchy. And the thought of this being how I might live for months on end without the ability to feel that tingly just scoured clean was not something I was willing to sacrifice. Not only could I not properly wash my scalp, but the thought of swishing hair about my face and having it rest on my shoulders, hair that had once been on someone else's head, having grown up through their follicles, out of their skin . . . the thought of it still makes me gag. There was no question: in the face of Simeon's reaction and the way I felt and looked, the hair extensions had to go! In fact, it all had to go! I didn't like it! Any of it! I wanted my old face and hair back.

My long 'D' curl eyelashes stuck onto my own either dropped out, taking my own eyelashes with them, or twisted and wrapped around each other as they grew, looking like a knotty mess. My upper eyelids were inflamed and all I wanted to do was wash my skin and rub my eyes, but it was impossible with the synthetic spider legs bonded to my own lashes with blobs of cement-like glue. My gel nails made it almost impossible to type quickly or do up buttons and every time I picked my nose or scratched an itch, I was in danger of giving myself a nasty injury. My teeth, while now dazzlingly white, felt somehow tender, overly sensitive, and Botox meant I could no longer pull the many and varied expressions that defined my face and gave me my character. The filler sat like two sausages playing hide-and-seek under the skin on my cheekbones and I hated it. What did I hate? All of it! Every synthetic, enhanced, syringed, smoothed, pulled, glued and bleached millimetre of the face that stared back at me.

I might have looked a little younger, a little smoother, but I didn't look like me, in fact, any elements of beauty I might have possessed were erased by these enhancements. To have gone to all that effort and not like the results left me reeling and had the opposite effect to boosting my self-esteem. I remember sitting on the loo and weeping with my head in my hands, just weeping that I been suckered into the whole circus. Not for the first time in my life I felt very stupid.

Filler and Botox free with my own hair.

Me with filler, Botox and hair extensions on the set of I'm A Celebrity, Australia.

With TV work commitments in the following month, and time running out for me to get the extensions taken out, I decided to keep the hair and face for that period and get everything removed as soon as I was able. I was off to Australia for a small involvement in the *I'm A Celebrity Get Me Out of Here* series, and so back I went to the country I had been to three times for book tours and events, a country I absolutely love.

It was hot! I was sweating more than usual, this due to the predictable heat of the Antipodean summer, the fat on my body and the ton of thick hair that I had voluntarily glued to my own head. With every passing day, I hated more and more the way the extensions felt, and couldn't wait to get them removed. Just to be clear, I loved the way they looked! My luscious Rapunzelesque tresses were things of wonder, but what was the point of being Rapunzel if my prince didn't want to touch them let alone kiss me, and my scalp smelled of sweat? Having made the decision to get them removed as soon as I was able when back in Blighty, Simeon laughed when I told him over the phone.

'I love you. I love you just the way you are,' he said.

And I believed him. I couldn't wait to get home. Our conversations were conciliatory, healing, and I was glad. I had missed him.

Lots of photographs and video footage was taken of me in Australia, and I would stare at it, hardly recognising myself with the hair extensions, eyelash extensions, gel nails, whitened teeth, Botox and those great big dollops of filler. I looked quite unlike me. Did I look beautiful? No, I don't think I did, but I was definitely smoother and more rounded. The issue was: I didn't look like *me*. But worse than that, I didn't *feel* like me either. This paid-for transformation did not have the desired effect – that of topping up my failing confidence until I brimmed with the stuff. Quite the opposite: it made me feel like a hybrid, a chubby imitation of the glamorous women I had so admired in the media.

My thoughts, however, were about to be channelled in a different direction altogether.

◆ ◆ ◆

It was early in the day, and we had just finished filming; I was on a bus when Simeon called. I could tell by the tone of his voice that something was up. He was hesitant, and he told me that Joshy, our lovely son, my baby Josiah, our youngest boy, had tried to take his own life.

I shan't ever forget it.

I shan't ever get used to writing it or saying it.

I shan't ever understand it, not properly.

The reason Joshy is still here is down to a whole lot of luck.

I couldn't take a full breath. I couldn't think straight. The words scrambled and I felt a pain in my heart and head that was familiar yet different. It was the *worst* pain and with it the most overwhelming sense of helplessness and guilt. Why was I on the other side of the world when my family needed me, when my boy needed me? And what could I have done, *should* I have done, to prevent this happening at all? I'd been preoccupied with writing books, hair bloody extensions and how fat I was while Joshy was falling apart, unravelling . . . What had I missed?

Simeon assured me Josh was safe, at home and safe. He had brought him back from university and was watching over him.

I counted every minute, every second, with a smile on my face, doing what I needed to do to get through the next couple of days, while every fibre of my being screamed that I needed to be home.

Josh reached a point of crisis that was in some ways the pinnacle of his battle with severe depression. We have written our story in the book, *The Boy Between*, which looks at what happens when depression comes to live in a family like ours. I thought mental illness was what happened to other people. Turns out we are other people.

Numbed, I returned to the UK, and having sat with Josh for a couple of days in the quiet reverence of sorrow that wrapped us, I took a few hours out, leaving Simeon at home with our boy, while I asked the hairdresser who had spent eight hours putting my hair extensions in to take them all out. The mass of fake hair and what it represented was made all the more grotesque in the face of what was going on with Josh, all so irrelevant in the great scheme of things. I sat in the salon chair not four weeks since they had been put in and in a mere five hours, they were removed, one by one with painstaking care and skill. More than a handful of my own hair came away with the extensions and in other places my hair snapped off completely. And I had no one to blame but myself. The hairdresser kept shaking his head, as if quite unable to understand the waste of all that work, all that time, all that money . . .

Not that I gave a shit: Joshy had come very close to taking his own life. *My son, my miracle baby, Joshy had come close to taking his life . . . I nearly lost him.* And it was knowledge I carried like a stake through the heart.

I was a walking automaton, keeping our son's rapidly declining mental health to myself with the firm and naive belief that it was a case of least said, soonest mended. I had no idea what the next few years would bring, the battle we would fight daily. And I'm glad I didn't because if I thought things were tough then . . . well, our journey with Josh was only just beginning.

Sitting in that salon chair, I received twice-hourly texts from Simeon telling me all was well, and I felt my heart breaking, knowing then as I do now, that I would give up every penny, every book, every word written, every spare bloody bedroom, everything, everything I have worked for, if it meant a single peaceful night for Josh.

Joshy is still here.

And that is everything.

It is everything.

I am thankful for every day I get with him, every sunrise with him on the planet and every chance I get to tell him how lucky I am to be his mum. He is the baby that was not meant to be. We cheated nature, Joshy and I. I shouldn't have been able to carry a baby with my dodgy pelvis and all those little ones I lost . . . and yet I got Josh and Josh got me and if the universe thinks I will give him up easily, it can bloody well think again.

Joshy.

Chapter Fourteen

'FROM THE OUTSIDE LOOKING IN . . .'

It's hard for me to describe my life in the couple of years following Josh's collapse, but it's fair to say that I fell apart on the inside while presenting a happy, got-it-together exterior. On the outside I had it all, my books were flying up the charts in the UK, Australia, New Zealand, South Africa, Europe and elsewhere. I'd travelled on book tours to Norway, a country which stole a piece of my heart and holds it fast. PR and publicity came my way, with articles in nearly all major newspapers and magazines. And Simeon was safe at home. Ben was happy. Mum was physically and mentally the best I could remember. My brother Paul and his wonderful wife Stevie had given us our beautiful nephew Arlo. Dad had successfully come through the other side of triple heart bypass surgery. Financially we were secure. Time to sit back, put my feet up, breathe a sigh of relief and enjoy the fruits of our labours . . .

Ha! If only.

It was like living on a knife edge. Every text Josh didn't respond to, every call that went unanswered, every lack of reply when I called up the stairs to say I was home, and my heart would hammer in my chest . . . *Has he . . . ? What if . . . Oh God, help me . . .* I had never fully understood the term 'living on your nerves', but I did after this. My insides seemed shredded. My gut felt watery with all my worries and all my fears sloshing around inside. I could only sleep when Josh slept, only relax when he was having a 'good' or 'good enough' day.

For anyone who also has mental illness in their house, you will know what I mean when I say, it is a dark thing that has tendrils in every crevice between the bricks, it sits in the tiny gaps in the stairs and it gurgles up the plug hole. It's insidious and exhausting and that is for those of us who do not suffer – I can only imagine what it must be like for people like my son who are the sufferers.

When Josh was suffering or having a 'bad' day, I felt a gnaw in my stomach of something that felt a lot like hunger and I would hit the carbs, eating usually at night when there was no chance of working off all those extra calories. I almost convinced myself that I could plug the leaking sadness by filling all the holes inside me with cheese on toast or a bag of crisps. But of course, I couldn't. I could only make the situation worse by stuffing my face until I didn't recognise the bloated face that stared back at me.

Simeon and I went from feeling slightly estranged by our lack of intimacy to a tightknit team, as if an emergency of this nature made us forget everything else and snap into shape as a dynamic duo, knowing it was only by being united, together, that we would all pull through. He stepped up to the plate for Josh and for Ben and me, and I will never forget his calmness, his practical suggestions to keep the house running, keep Josh out of harm's way and keep my feet on the ground, but most of all I will never forget his kindness.

Dealing with depression at this level was new to both of us and while I had a tendency to cry myself into a fretful sleep at the unrelenting horror of it all, he quietly figured out how we were all going to get through. My reaction to Josh's illness was to find a solution. I had an urgent and desperate need to fix him, fix him, fix him, but, eventually, we figured that we just needed to let Josh 'be'. It really was as simple as providing a nest, making him feel secure, unhurried and taking it day by day, understanding that all we could do was love him. That's pretty much still how we live. And right now, Joshy is in a good place. Come on, you know the score by now, touch wood, salt over shoulder . . .

Book sixteen, *The Art of Hiding*, book seventeen, *Anna*, book eighteen, *Theo*, book nineteen, *How to Fall in Love Again – Kitty's Story*, were all out and punching high in the charts, much to my joy. Writing was still my happy place but it was also my escape. If the real world felt a little too much, I could slip away to somewhere else entirely, just for a little while.

Now, sometimes a perfect storm whips up to enable a situation, good or bad, to thrive, and very often it is a perfect storm that you would find hard to fabricate or plan or avoid. This was certainly the case when my first book caught the attention of my agent and the imagination of my readers.

It was also the case when things for me went from bad to worse to the very worst in terms of my weight and I became morbidly obese. Of course, this wasn't a sudden thing. It didn't happen overnight, but it did, however, take me by surprise.

I was working hard, head down, writing and riding life's bumpy roller coaster. And I can't deny that with all the curve balls that kept being hurled in my direction, hitting me squarely in the solar plexus and knocking the wind from me, it often felt more like sitting in a U-bend than on a roller coaster. And there I stayed, waiting to see what was going to drop onto my head and shoulders next.

And so preoccupied was I dealing with day-to-day life that my eating, my size and my weight were relegated on my worry list. A good thing, right? Well, kind of. And don't get me wrong, they were still a worry, but they lurked somewhere between fighting to stop my son from taking his own life, writing like a crazy thing to meet my self-imposed deadlines, spending several days at a time in a recording studio voicing all of my own audio books (did I mention that – that I have recorded nearly all of my own audios, which when you are writing as many as me is one hell of a commitment), mourning my beloved grandparents, trying to pick apart my loss when it came to my miscarriages and generally trying to keep all those plates spinning with a big smile on my face in case someone needed a photograph.

Audiobook recording in a London studio.

I thought I had to keep a stiff upper lip, to contain that ball of sadness in my gut and to set a good example to those who relied on me. My belief was that if I fell apart then everyone and everything might follow, and the resulting slippery mess of tears and a jumble of softened people lying in a heap without the strength or inclination to carry on would be more than any of us could cope with.

In my late forties, the worry over my son sat like a boulder in my gut, which I hauled around – it was growing bigger, as if made up of small bits of everyone I had ever lost, whether it be the babies who left me too soon or people I'd loved and who'd got to live long and happy, happy lives.

I also learned that grief is not solely the preserve of mourning the dead. There was the grief I felt for people I'd lost who had not died but had simply left me. The lovers who had broken my heart, the friends I'd drifted apart from and those people who for a million different reasons you have lost closeness with. Each human connection severed or severely weakened had the same effect on my heart – it tore it a little, and over time that meant collective emotional damage that I don't think ever fully heals. Again, I did my very best to fill the empty void of grief and sadness with food, trying to dull the ache, heal the rip, plug it with carbohydrate, fat and sugar.

Among the chaos of my thoughts, living surrounded by a million small smouldering fires that might need extinguishing at any time of the day and night, I was getting fatter. I gave in to my food cravings, supported by an unhealthy addiction to food. Food filled all the hollow sadness inside me. It soaked up all those watery feelings that had been sloshing around in my stomach for the longest time. My deep, deep sadness and lack of self-esteem encouraged each morsel I shoved in my mouth and justified each craving that rippled through my stomach as if I were in starvation mode, panicked almost about when I might get my next calorie fix.

It's hard for me to write about, hard for me to think about, but this book is about ripping off the Band-Aid, unmuting the difficult words and talking without the veil of shame or deceit that often prevents such discussion. I think it's vital, in fact, for a woman like me. For women like us.

Not yet fifty and having yearned for and then cursed my fertile years, I went into menopause. Yaaay! My crappy womb was the gift that just kept on giving!

Menopause wasn't something I'd overly considered. Like jowls, mild incontinence and forgetting what I had gone upstairs for, the ending of my periods was just another consequence of ageing that lurked in my future. I was, I must admit, a little surprised by the timing of it, thinking I had years before I had to worry myself with 'the change' as it was affectionately known in my nan's house. Menopause was for *old* people, wasn't it? And was I old? Was I heck as like! I am now fifty-four and am *still* not old. My mum is seventy-something and informs me that she is not old either and she is right. 'Old' is most definitely a state of mind to which I refuse to succumb.

So, what did I know of menopause? Very little as it turns out. I had heard my nan and Aunty Kit whispering about it under their breath. Both women, in an almost relentless, lifelong competition for who was the sickest/had the most ailments/was closest to death's door, had asked for hysterectomies in their forties so that all that business was done and dusted. And a surgeon skilfully obliged.

Sitting in the car on the way back from the consultation when my menopause was confirmed, I felt a little desolate at the thought. Not so much because that was the end of my hopes of having a baby. I had already let that dream float away and had almost made peace with it, but more because I didn't want my body to go through yet another metamorphosis. The many articles I scoured that assured me menopause need not be disruptive, painful or life-changing gave me faith that I would probably just sail through it . . . the bloody liars!

Now, I don't want to be a scaremonger and would like to point out that many, many women go through the '*change of life*', as it's often so delightfully called, without a hiccup; these women we call the very lucky ones. One such woman, as I might have hinted, is my own mother, whose periods ended in her late fifties, and she didn't notice until she realised one day that it had been a while since she had reached for the tampon box secreted at the bottom of the airing cupboard. Please note she was a tampon user, no blue sanitary belt with unwieldy plastic anchors for her! She *thinks*, in retrospect that she might have gained a couple of pounds at the end of her periods and her eyebrows possibly thinned a little, but that was all. Her exact words were, 'It was a picnic really!' Well, good for you, Annie!

I was comforted by the fact and convinced by the anecdotes that my experience would probably be similar to my mother's. In anticipation, I binned my hot-water bottle, threw out the Nurofen, discarded my tampon stash and barely gave the coming event a second thought. I, however, was not so lucky. I'm struggling now to think of the right adjectives to use when describing what happened to my body and mind during menopause, a mind that was already, frankly frazzled, but I will try. Here goes:

~~I was . . .~~
~~It felt . . .~~
~~I was a little . . .~~
~~It seemed that . . .~~ no, no I can't sugarcoat it.

I WENT FUCKING BAT SHIT CRAZY! I lost the plot! My head exploded! My body went berserk, my hormones haywire and I wanted to (depending on the time of the day or night) either:

Kill someone
Eat

Sob into a cushion
Eat
Drink gin
Eat
Move house and not tell anyone where I had gone
Eat
Get a divorce
Eat
Cling to my husband like he was the only rock in a stormy sea
Eat
Put my head under the duvet and stay there. Permanently
Eat

Full menopause came at me hard and grabbed me by the throat. It pulled the rug from under me and knocked me for six. If my mum's menopause had been a toe dip in a sultry bath, mine was more like water boarding under an icy tap. Suffice to say it was about as far from a 'picnic' as it's possible to imagine. Unless it's a picnic where the host hoovers up every available biscuit, pie, slice of bread and square of chocolate with an insatiable appetite. And then cries on the couch with self-loathing while giving off enough heat to melt a polar icecap. Yes, that kind of picnic I can totally relate to.

I joke, but the truth was it felt like I was losing my mind. It was a fearful time when dark thoughts threatened to overtake the good ones and I mistrusted nearly every thought I had, as huge holes developed in my memory, as well as my already fragile confidence: *Have I turned the tap off? Did I get milk? Am I supposed to be somewhere? Does Simeon really love me? Is it my fault Josh is depressed? Am I a good enough writer? How can I go out in public looking like this?*

I gained weight. *No shit, Sherlock!* And then I gained more weight. The menopause certainly seemed to affect where the fat gathered on my body. It sprung in new pockets, clinging to my stomach whereas before it used to sit on my hips, bum and boobs.

My arms got fat. My face was bloated. I sprouted hair on my face. It was a new low for me and one where I felt I was too far gone in terms of fatness to action a quick result or improvement and it really changed things.

I had completely lost my way. I was used to feeling concerned over carrying extra weight but previously could, with a bit of hair primping, clever dressing and a slick of lippy, convince myself and others that I was still a functioning member of society and one with a certain flare . . . but in the first years of menopause, all this changed. Not only was I physically unrecognisable, but I lost my way mentally. I wasn't sure how I was supposed to live like this and was at a loss as to what on earth I could do about it. I read much on the topic, and articles about weight gain and hormone fluctuations really resonated with me.

I learned that this 'change' was certainly responsible for my ever-lowering mood. The extra timber I was carrying did nothing to help with my internal thermometer, which had broken. I write this flippantly, but it was in fact, alongside my weight gain and mood swings, one of the hardest aspects to navigate. Hot flashes/flushes were mere words to me and if I had to hazard a guess, I thought it might mean the slight warming of your skin, akin to stepping out in the sun or cosying up in front of a radiator. That was until I woke up in the middle of the night and wondered if someone had doused me with water or maybe a pipe had burst above. My nightie was damp, my hair stuck to my head, my skin slippery with a slick of sweat and my breath coming in short bursts as I lay on a soggy sheet. What in Sweet Mother of Betsy was going on? I figured I must be sick, fluey or poisoned! This was not normal!

Now, Simeon and I have, as a couple, weathered loss, grief, hardship, and have helped our youngest in his mental-health battles, and for those of you who have been here since the beginning this is not news, but we have never, ever come as close to divorcing as we did over the temperature of our bedroom. Who would have thunk it that we came close to throwing in the towel on the grounds of 'irreconcilable thermostat differences'?

My body has always operated within the normal range, from chilly to toasty, hovering somewhere in the middle. A cold night or chilly morning was nothing an extra jersey or pair of thick socks couldn't cure, and similarly in the balmy summer months I'd shrug off my thermal vest and reach for floaty linen. But this was very different. Essentially, I lived with two temperature settings: 'deep ice arctic freeze' or 'the fires of Hades' – there was no in-between. Regardless of the temperature outside, I either had all the windows open and sat in my cotton muumuu watching *Corrie*, fanning myself with a rolled-up copy of the *TV Times* or the house was like a furnace with me under a duvet, wearing my PJs, a pair of the kids' old rugby socks and a balaclava, clutching a hot-water bottle with as much determination as Kate Winslet clung to that bloody door. It was like living in a slapstick comedy, with me opening the windows and my husband slamming them shut, me whacking up the thermostat and him turning it down. And my fluctuation between the two could occur hourly, barely enough time for the boiler to crank up the heat before I was shutting it down again.

It was lonely and it was miserable. It was almost impossible for me to explain what I was going through, as I didn't fully understand it myself. Of course, our friction wasn't solely about the temperature of our room, but it was certainly how we released all that pent-up angst and frustration at the situation we found ourselves in. HOW CAN WE STOP JOSH LEAVING US? This is what I screamed with every action, every sigh, every tear. My menopause hardly made me the best housemate, let alone life partner.

The kids avoided me: Josh in his room living his horizontal life and Ben choosing to stay out or in his student digs. Simeon might have once mentioned one Sunday afternoon over a quiet cuppa that life was a little tough for him . . . living with a wife who was so very unpredictable. He was right: I was either raging, crying, eating or sitting in an ice bath. He also confessed that he was struggling with the fact that our bedroom was either freezing or boiling. I calmly put my cup down and looked him in the eye.

'I know it's tough for you, darling,' I began, 'having to pop on an extra jersey while I sob uncontrollably, gain weight, sprout whiskers, can't remember my *own* name, let alone anyone else's. And with a new and unrelenting melancholy closing its jaws around my brain and spirit. And this on top of the fact that I can't sleep – not ever – and I'm exhausted. I'm anxious, full of self-doubt, beating myself up over Josh, who I fear might not be here tomorrow and, guess what, my ovaries have stopped working! What's the point of my sodding womb? It has always let me down! Oh, what's that now? Sex? You want *sex*? While my body is falling apart? I'm on the edge of reason and my mind is wired, you want *sex*? For the love of God! Just fuck off!'

I can't say it was my proudest moment. But it did make us laugh, which quickly for me turned to tears, and it put a puncture in the balloon of tension that had filled the room, bringing a moment of sweet relief.

It wasn't only my body that went into hibernation mode, but my brain turned to mush and my mood was . . . erratic. Case in point above, when laughing turned to tears and tears could turn to rage and that in turn would invite more tears, which would send me scurrying to the biscuit barrel. And worryingly, my sharp wit and incisive interior monologue that keep me amused on most days, basically turned into the mental equivalent of armpit farts. I went on a promotional book tour and sat next to a suited and booted gent, and, as ever, I thought it polite to strike up a conversation. It went like this:

Me: 'Afternoon. Where are you heading today?'

Him: 'Er . . . Sydney, via Hong Kong.'

Me: 'No way!'

I jumped up in my seat, gesturing excitedly to Simeon. What were the chances! It was so far away! 'So are we!' I marvelled.

The man stared at me before commenting, 'I guessed as much because we are on the same plane . . .'

This, folks, was a fine example of my menopausal brain. He then reclined his chair into bed mode and slept all the way . . . or at least pretended to. I'm pretty sure I saw him reach out a hand from under his snuggle blanket and grab a bag or two of pretzels as the steward waltzed past with a loaded tray. I don't blame him. I wanted to avoid me too. I wanted to hide away under a snuggle blanket until the unpredictable and raging sea on which I bobbed was no more than calm waters.

I went to see my GP, who offered me HRT. I had heard of it but didn't really know what it was. So, I hit the internet, reading the scary and opposing arguments for *taking* hormone replacement therapy and *avoiding* it, drawn by diverse headlines, some claiming it was the holy grail while others quoted hair-raising data about the dangers, pitfalls and why it was to be avoided at all costs. There was about the same level of differing opinion among my friends and peers; some women were all for it, saying it had restored their life, libido and sanity, while others chose more organic means to get through, adapting their diet and taking herbal supplements.

Talk about confused! The volume of information in all its forms: conflicting, scary, alarmist, comforting, encouraging and hopeful left me in a state of utter confusion. Cancer had already knocked at my door twice; did I really want to go down the HRT route? Could I afford to risk it? I have always been averse to taking tablets and medication of any kind. And I am not talking about things like insulin, chemotherapy or any other situation when medicine is *needed* and necessary, but I am talking about the popping of ibuprofen and the swallowing of paracetamol to 'take the edge off' and the habitual reaching for painkillers for the most minor of ailments, taking them for everything from a light headache to a stubbed toe. Similarly, with antibiotics, I've only taken them once or twice in my life, believing, rightly or wrongly, that if I took them regularly, then if and when I really needed them their effect might be diminished. And so, the idea of adopting a daily drug regimen was not something I felt comfortable with.

I decided to go cold turkey and adopted a natural approach to menopause, figuring that millions of women since the dawn of periods had come out of the other side and I did, slowly, too slowly! It took a full five years before the last of my symptoms disappeared, my mood steadied, and I felt ready to face the world again. If I had to go through it again, I would, now I am better informed, go down the HRT route – no question.

I liken the whole episode in my life to climbing a mountain and daily thinking I was going to reach the peak only to find myself on a ledge on a bend and with another painful ascent ahead of me. This was the case, month in, month out, until July 2018 when I felt . . . different.

I was at the top of menopause mountain. Standing quietly, I got to look out over the landscape of my fertile years, littered with sanitary products, contraception, hours of stomach cramps, babies, lost babies, warm baths, bloated tums, pregnant tums! All of it threaded through with my life's blood. A red trail that led me to that point – and I realised that I had endured. I had survived.

The word menopause must rank as one of the most feared in the English language. It's whispered behind closed doors to trusted companions, preferably medically trained, and is for many the start of futile attempts to recapture lost youth in a quest to prove that just because the old ovaries have packed up – I am still raring to go! Thanks to its end-of-life imagery and the terror women display in admitting they're in its grip, it has more in common with a virulent disease than the mere resetting of our biological clock. I can joke, but menopause certainly changed me. It made me introverted, it robbed me of my sparkle in many ways, but in all honesty, the Mandy that has emerged from the cocoon of change is stronger, sharper and sparklier than my younger self and I am thankful for that.

But it didn't happen overnight, no sirree, there were a couple of hurdles I had to clamber over first, a couple of walls that needed breaking down. One was getting my emotional well-being back on track and quieting that voice of self-sabotage that had dogged me for most of my life, and the other was dealing with my food obsession, because as I was about to hit fifty, my weight had hit a staggering 20 stone or 280 lb . . . This is the first time I have admitted this, ever. But coming clean about my size, my weight, my overeating was a very important first step in what turned out to be a life-changing part of my journey . . .

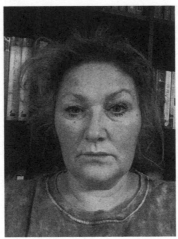

I think this picture sums up my menopause. Bloated, broken and exhausted.

Chapter Fifteen

'The Walrus Roll'

Hitting fifty felt like a milestone of sorts and certainly everyone around me seemed very keen to celebrate my half-century. There were sparkly glasses with '50' on them to wear, gifts to unwrap and Simeon bought me a wok. Do not adjust your reading, that's correct, he bought me a wok. For my fiftieth. If ever I'd needed a reminder of how far we had slipped into the comfortable married zone it was this wok! The first of my birthdays we spent together he bought me Chanel perfume. Although in honesty I hate Chanel perfume so maybe I should have been more grateful for the wok. Mum whipped up a couple of quiches and there might have been a balloon or two, but as ever, the whole exercise was coated with a thin veneer of reluctance on my part because of how I looked. The thought of celebrating gave me palpitations.

Book twenty, *The Coordinates of Loss*, and book twenty-one, *The Girl in The Corner*, came out and my sales continued to rise and rise. This was and is incredible for me to consider. I always write my book for one woman. I picture her on her sofa reading and I talk to her directly, so the fact that there were millions of other readers like her was and is mind-blowing! My brother

Simon, an estate agent in Gloucestershire, called me discreetly from his phone the other day to tell me he was in someone's house and he'd seen my books on their bookshelves. He was amazed, proud. 'They don't know you,' he marvelled, 'and they've got your books!' and I understood.

On the advice of my best friend who told me that in order for the whole family to feel grounded and to build a solid base, I needed to put down roots in my 'forever home', I became an online house snooper. When not watching *MasterChef* at the end of a long day, I could be found scouring Rightmove with my nose inches from the screen, wondering what kind of house I wanted and what kind of house we as a family would suit best.

Still, I knew that a fancy gated mansion with all mod cons was not for me, but the consensus from Simeon and our now full-grown boys was that we could do with more space. We had certainly outgrown our little house that had served us well for the last few years and I must admit I hankered for a spare bedroom so that friends and family could, without too much disruption, come and stay. And maybe my own special place to write might be nice. One thing was for sure, whether it had two bedrooms or a dozen spare, a window box or a few acres, I wanted it to feel like the houses I had visited in my childhood. The warm kitchens and welcoming small rooms of Roedean Avenue, Lonsdale Avenue, Rosedale Road and Charlotte Gardens, where to walk in felt like coming home and love bounced off the walls and landed in puddles on the scrubbed linoleum.

It still makes me laugh, but this city girl fell in love with a big old stone farmhouse in a small farming hamlet on the outskirts of Bristol – at its highest point, looking over the River Severn towards Wales. Knee deep in pigs, cows, sheep and mud, I am in heaven. It's a house that was always beyond my dreams, with space and a couple of lovely little rooms with just the right amount of cosy and a library – my very own library, yes, one of those libraries that is opulent and subtly lit with leather-topped desks, wing-backed chairs and floor-to-ceiling glass-fronted wooden cabinets. I sit in it a lot; it's my happy place. Although in fairness, my happy place is anywhere with my laptop inches from my face, lost to my latest novel. Simeon says I write everywhere and that I write all the time and that I've spent most of our married life conversing with him over the top of my screen. This I absolutely refute!

Josh, I knew, could only benefit from having somewhere to roam, and freeing him from the small room that had been his prison for a year or so seemed like a positive thing. I remembered very well our family's rural life in North Yorkshire. It had felt a lot like freedom, and this was something that stayed with me, an association no matter how deeply buried that a rural, quiet life was one that was good for my health, both mental and physical, and so why would it be any different for our boy? A place with some outside space would also mean we could finally get the dogs, plural, we had promised the boys when they were young. You didn't think they'd let me forget, did you?

I actually believe the house found us. Other than my online snooping, we weren't actively looking, but had it in the back of our minds that if something caught our eye, we'd take the leap. Nothing did. Until Christmas time and we were taking the back roads through rural lanes on the outskirts of Bristol, one grey-skied, muddy-floored day, when we stumbled across a farm for sale. It was not too far from Thornbury – you remember Thornbury? The place I decided not to get too attached to, figuring there was little point in building friendships or getting to know the landscape, as I could bet my bottom dollar I wouldn't be there that long . . . yes, that Thornbury.

The house looked gloomy, a little unloved, dark and in shadow. I felt an instant and powerful connection to it. By sheer coincidence we found out it was on the market with a friend of ours who had set up his own estate agency in Bristol. We went to look at it the very next day. Simeon warned me not to be too eager, not to be overexcited and if I liked it to go gently to allow for negotiations. After all, it had been on the market for some time, and it didn't feel like there was a rush of people queuing up to buy it.

It was a rainy day when we parked on the driveway flanked by full and ancient oak, walnut and cedar trees. I looked up at the grey facade and felt a surge of something that felt a lot like joy. We walked through the back door into the cold, empty garden room, which had a double-height ceiling and a flagstone floor, and I could see it . . . I could see it with furniture in lamplight, I could see a Christmas tree, I could see our boys and family running through the rooms, I could see me in it until I was old!

'We'll take it! Full asking price. We'll take it!' I beamed.

'But you haven't seen the rest of it!' Our friend exchanged a nervous look with Simeon, who was shaking his head.

'I don't need to. It's my home.' I knew it. I felt it. And I was right.

We moved in some months later and I woke in wonder that this house was ours. We've been here a few years now and I still feel that way and at the back of my mind I half expect someone to tap me on the shoulder and say, 'get out!' as if I shouldn't be here at all. Two French Bulldogs arrived to make our family complete and to take over completely! Much to my amusement and wishing beyond wish that my nan was here to share the joke, there is a big old fancy swimming pool with Roman steps, and it sparkles blue and clear when the sun hits it, littering the surface with its diamonds. I wish with all my heart that she could have seen it, although I know she'd think it was all too much to take on. '*All that cleaning . . .*' I can hear her voice.

So, there it was, this ruddy great hole in the ground with sun loungers around the edge and brightly placed cushions sitting on them just like in an upscale hotel. Lovely and inviting on the warmest of days, and oh you know how I love to swim! But because of the size of my arse, I felt I couldn't get in the bloody thing. Have you ever heard anything so ridiculous? All those years of hankering for a pool, dreaming of a pool and there it lay, awaiting the splash and splash of someone who was not so ashamed of their body they could enjoy it at their leisure. I would stare at it longingly from the upper windows on hot days, but couldn't get in, overly fearful that someone might see a ripple of white thigh beneath the surface or my bingo wings working hard to propel me through the water. It was madness! I'd be the one ferrying drinks in the heat, blowing up the inflatables and working the barbecue – anything rather than get my kit off and dive in.

I *have* been in the pool a handful of times – having devised a foolproof way of getting into the water without being seen. I execute the move when I am home alone, and I call it the walrus roll. It involves wearing a swimming costume under a voluminous kaftan and moving a sun lounger to the very edge of the water. I position myself on it as if I'm settling down for a good old read, classic in hand, and then when and if confident that no one else is around – I chuck the book and roll sideways, landing with an almighty splosh in the drink! It's marvellous. No need to walk falteringly around the edge, hiding behind oversized plant pots and trees – one quick twist to the side like a lolloping whiskered mammal and in I go.

The issue, as I was to discover one balmy summer day during our first summer here, was how to get out of the pool without being seen. Now, as anyone who has ever swum in a kaftan or any kind of clothing can attest (I can't be the only one who had to put on pyjamas and jump into the public baths to attain some swimming badge or other circa 1986?), material that might ordinarily be floaty and forgiving can, when wet, become cloying and sticks to every lump, bump, roll and bulge – putting you even more on display. I wasn't too worried, figuring I could simply run up the steps and back under the bath towel, rolled on the end of the lounger, and from which I could form a little towelling tepee for such a purpose.

What I hadn't banked on, however, was the arrival of guests. My friends, neighbours and family know they are always, always welcome, no need for an invite, the kettle is always on, there's always a cake in a tin and a plumped cushion poised on a sofa awaits the feel of their bottom. So, yes, having perfected the walrus roll, I was one day, mid length, paddling away at my leisure and revelling in the utter bliss of the moment, this was what life was about, when I looked up to see some friends standing there in shorts and tees with towels rolled under their arms. Their obvious and express intention was to have a quick, cooling dip. What the hell was I supposed to do now?

I felt my heart quicken, mortified and panic-stricken. I couldn't run up the steps in my clinging kaftan. Rolling back onto the sun lounger in the same way I had rolled off it was scientifically impossible. The trouble was, I was starting to go a little pruney and I needed a wee.

'Hey!' I waved as discreetly as I was able. 'Why don't you guys go and get changed and dive in?' I had a plan, that as soon as they had turned their backs or nipped into the pool house to step into their cossies, I could scoot to the steps as fast as my chunky little legs would carry me and then run up the steps, to hide inside my towel tepee on the end of my lounger. My wee would just have to wait – easier said than done at my age.

'No need!' my friend beamed. 'We've got our swimmers on underneath!' And with that they peeled off their shorts and tees and jumped in. They got out several times, had a cold drink, sunbathed a little, swam a bit more . . .

One hour and forty minutes, people. You want to know how long I can hold in a full bladder while simultaneously hiding under water that felt to be rapidly cooling against my skin? That's how long – ONE HOUR AND FORTY BLOODY MINUTES! When they announced they were going to 'chip off!' I swear I nearly cried. And having explained how I *would* come and see them off, but I was keen to do a few more lengths I took a breath and let go of the side. As I heard the side gate close, I hauled my water-logged body from its watery prison and flung myself on the warm sandstone slabs at the side of the pool. Simeon found me there some time later, immobile and panting, a lot like an actual walrus and one just as keen for fish, although I wanted mine served with chips.

Me in water-logged kaftan, post walrus roll.

It was funny in hindsight, but was one moment of reckoning, although there were to be others. Is that what I was reduced to? Hiding in the water, unable to enjoy my friends' company, excruciatingly aware of my flesh?

I was sinking fast, despite living in the most incredible surroundings, hiding away and beating myself up over my choices and lack of control. Life as a morbidly obese person in a thin-obsessed world was not easy. I've decided to be completely candid in sharing my experiences; not only do I think this is the way to best further the dialogue and promote understanding, and, goodness knows, greater understanding and kindness is needed, but also, I want everyone who is still living this way to know that they are not alone and that you can make the changes necessary to live a different kind of life, *if* you want to.

It got to the point where I always, always preferred to stay in, to remain cloaked within the comfort of my own home rather than go outside. There was nothing, no event on the planet I would rather have attended than to sit curled on my sofa. I have said no to invites to dinner, drinks, cinema, parties, premieres, theatre shows, concerts, holidays, boat trips, you name it, all because I couldn't stand the idea of slipping into a black velvet sack while everyone else in attendance would be in something pretty.

And as my career rocketed and attending these events was almost considered part of my job, particularly by PR companies who had worked hard to secure an invitation or get me in the door, I knew I was letting people down. It didn't feel good. Friends too could barely conceal their frustration when they called with the most amazing news: they had tickets for such and such and could I make it? No. No I couldn't, sadly, because the thought would make me heave with nerves before I had even checked my diary. I didn't want to be judged and it *wasn't* living. A life where you have to say no to everything that others might find wonderful made me think about how I existed and what it must be like to be married to someone who lived that way. I deserved better and I know Simeon did.

Parties became my very worst thing. And this makes me immeasurably sad as I love company, love meeting new people and listening to the tales of their lives. And without these elements to my life, I felt lonely and isolated. But the thought of going to a party? The build-up of anticipation, the dread of having to attend, based on no more than my size; this would start the moment the invite landed in my letterbox. Very often I would put the date in the diary and think to myself 'well, that's six weeks away' or whatever, 'I can lose quite a bit of weight in that time.' And I might even start to diet – saying no to a morning biscuit and swapping toast and butter for muesli – but as the invitation got pushed to the back of my mind, so did the intention to lose weight and I would resume normal service of eating anything and everything that I happened upon, like some monster who could crunch through an entire bread bin or larder.

On one particular occasion, although there were many, I got ready for the birthday barbecue of a friend and neighbour. I told myself it was a small affair in her garden, a simple supper, a slice of birthday cake, chat to the people around you, a quick 'thank you for a lovely evening' and home. Boom. Simeon looked smart in a white shirt and jeans. I took my time on my make-up and hair, had bought a fancy bouquet and a lovely candle as a thank you to the host on her birthday. I sat on the bed, applied my scent, grabbed my little woven clutch bag and was ready to jump in the car, but one final glance in the bedroom mirror before I walked down the stairs and I felt my gut fold with anxiety and disgust. I slipped off my shoes, wiped off my make-up and crawled under the duvet in my summer dress, absolutely unable to leave the house, so very ashamed of my appearance. Simeon came up to find me and was lost for words.

'But . . . But . . .' I could see him trying to find the right thing to say and heard the uncertainty in his voice, unsure as to whether he should persuade me to come along, go alone or climb under the duvet and hold me. I understood his confusion; I didn't know the correct thing to do or say either. He climbed in with me and held me until I fell asleep. And I woke feeling the full smack of horror that I had let my friend down in this way.

It was only a few months later that Simeon, now a Lieutenant Colonel in the army, had been invited to a very fancy-pants dinner that required me to wear a smart frock to partner well with his formal mess dress, medals proudly displayed and all the pomp that goes with it for a formal military dinner. I've always wanted to support him, I love him and I'm incredibly proud, and yet as the date loomed for the event, I felt nothing but utter despair as I shopped for a dress. I tried shovelling my body into Spanx and not breathing as I shoehorned myself into oversized velvet shifts with the obligatory bit of sparkle around the neckline, as if that might lift the outfit or at the very least detract from the fact that I was wearing a shapeless garment that hung from me like a duvet cover.

Comparison to others is I know the route to madness and instils an even lower sense of self-worth, but it was almost impossible not to at events like these when everyone was dressed up and me, the overweight one, stuck out like a sore thumb, wearing black again and going double with the red lipstick in the vain hope that people might only look at my red lips and not my big arse. I remember crying while I curled my hair and got dressed, I cried all the way to the venue and I cried in the loo during the dinner, blotting beneath my eyes and practising my smile before I went into the room where people were keen to talk to me about my books, which was so lovely of them.

I thought about the lady who had told me I was beautiful at an event so many years ago when I nervously stared in a mirror, but this only drew mental comparison between how I looked then and the size that I had become. It didn't help. I sidled back into my seat and Simeon winked at me, proud of my staying power, knowing it was torturous for me and I hated that he had to check on me in this way. How could he fully have fun when wondering constantly if I was going to bolt?

My anxiety was no doubt added to by the fact that on one previous occasion, a woman flirted with and practically propositioned my husband – a slim, attractive confident woman who acted as if I wasn't there or, worse, was of so little consequence it didn't matter to her that I was. As if she must be able to scoop up that nice chunk of soldier because his wife was a fatty and therefore no competition. I noticed it and felt my insides turn to ice. Simeon acted as if he hadn't heard or was unaware of her flirtations, holding my hand tightly, trying to reassure me – which was not and should not have been his job, but I can't deny it made me feel so much better. Her behaviour was in stark contrast to how I was treated when I was slim. Things like that never happened, as if being overweight and then being obese, took me out of the running. Her behaviour only added to that feeling of not wanting to be seen which has dogged me for all of my obese years.

This was never more so than when it came to shopping. I absolutely hated shopping and at my largest, bought clothes exclusively online where the embarrassment and shame factor of having to reject items sized 24+ as I couldn't get into them was only marginally less traumatic than having to do so in a store.

My mum loves clothes and loves to shop for clothes. She has always been a savvy dresser, buying one or two expensive items a season that last for years. Sometimes if we were out for a stroll – she often accompanied me to work events in London – I had to venture into shops with her. Maybe it was my tainted view of the world or maybe I was hyper-sensitive, but I would see the sales assistants purse their lips, the rise of an eyebrow and on one occasion an actual nudge between them, as they eyed me lumbering into their store. The relief when they realised it was my gorgeous mum who was shopping for their wares and not me was palpable. And trust me the only person who did not want me to darken the door of their fancy store more than them, was me. I found the whole exercise excruciating and would find myself being extra polite to the point of obsequiousness, finding a chair and sitting quietly until we could leave, trying to make myself small, as if apologising for my size, my intrusion, nay my very existence! It was at those times that I wish I had the confidence of my body positive sisters who might just have eyeballed the spiky assistant and told them to go fuck themselves! How I wish . . .

When forced to buy new clothes, I always chose items that were neutral in colour like grey, oatmeal and black. The tops were always either voluminous or block-shaped and always, always long enough to cover my bum and thighs, while wide enough to not cling to my bust or arms. These soft, shapeless garments I would accessorise with large necklaces and jewellery that drew the eye. And on the bottom half I would wear jeans. I was always, always in jeans no matter the occasion or weather. A regular day meant jeans and a sweatshirt. A lunch meant jeans and a shirt or blouse. Dinner or something more formal: jeans and a floaty top or one with sequins. They were like my safety blanket, the material thick enough to hold me in and the seams sturdy enough to contain any movement. Whether they were flattering, too long, too short, the right colour, ethically made never came into it. I was merely glad to have something to cover me up and contain me.

I used to think if anyone were to delve into my wardrobe, they would have wondered how many people shared it! I had clothes in there that were a size 10, clothes that used to fit me and I kept, determined to get into them again one day; I never let go of the idea that there was a thinner me trapped inside. This very thought made me feel conflicted. It certainly held me back from ever accepting and making peace with my bigger size, and yet it was also quite possibly the light at the end of a miserable tunnel of existence towards which I slowly climbed. And there were clothes sized 14 to 26. If I put on weight, I bought bigger clothes and if I lost a bit of weight, I hid them in a dark corner of the wardrobe, almost as if I knew I'd need them again at some point.

And the irony is I didn't even like my clothes, any of them! They were all merely garments to cover up my body. The only thing they had in common was that the very instant I got them home or received them through the post, I would cut out every single label identifying their size – just in case someone might peep inside and see that I was wearing a size 26 – like they couldn't see that without the aid of a tiny label hidden inside. There was no joy in clothes for me at all. How could there be when I was staring at shapeless panels that were meant to disguise and not accentuate, to drape and not cling, all worn in the vain hope that they would create an illusion that I was not morbidly obese or that I was not there at all, an invisibility cloak of my own making?

There were many aspects of being obese that I hated, but by far the hardest aspect for me was getting washed and dressed each morning for the day ahead and then getting washed and dressed for bedtime. This was for several reasons. First it was a time of quiet contemplation when I had no choice but to focus on my oversized body in the shower or bath when for the rest of the day, I could often distract myself *from* myself by talking, working, cleaning, reading, writing . . . but if the job in hand is washing that body and drying that body it was fairly hard, impossible even, not to think about that body. I hated the way the springy fat-laden flesh felt beneath my palm and could remember with such clarity what it felt like to run my hand over my hip and feel the curve of a slightly jutting hipbone that it could make me weep. And frequently did.

My boobs were vast, heavy and painful – I wore a 48GG bra. My huge breasts distorted my silhouette at every angle. I missed the days when I could wear a vest, a T-shirt or a jumper without two mountains jutting out so far that I could not see my stomach or feet. Clothes hung from them like an awning and dropped down, conveniently masking the wide bulge beneath my bra strap that met my stomach, but also meaning that my shape was vast – exaggerated – and yes, it's true that when dressed I couldn't see my feet and when naked, I couldn't see my scarred bikini area and therefore neither could I groom my intimate area; how could I when I couldn't even see it? It would have been like pin the tail on the donkey but a lot, lot more painful.

My underwear was vast, with slack elastic, greyed through lack of care, worn thin in places from having to work hard. To clamber into big, big knickers and hurl my huge chest into a bra that could double as hammocks for a couple of small mammals every day was mortifying. I never got used to it. Shoehorning the chevrons of flesh that hung down my back into a drab garment was a daily task that sickened and saddened me. And after going through this distressing rigmarole, was it any wonder that it was hard to greet the new dawn feeling perky? I can only liken it to trying to roll a too small swimming costume onto a wet body in a confined space – you know how it sticks and pinches and it takes a while to wrestle it into place while your muscles groan and spasm and you hold your breath and frustration builds? Well, it was like that every morning and each night. It was the very worst way to start any day and it kind of set the mood.

Even a good day, one where I was doing fun things or loving my life, was tainted by that feeling of my flesh rubbing against the cheap fabric of whatever I had slung on that morning. And at bedtime I got to repeat the whole darn fiasco. I like to shower in the morning and have a bath before bed each night. Lying in the bath, I would watch the water slip over the undulations of my stomach and thighs with a sense of shame before climbing into leggings or pyjama bottoms with a long nightdress over the top for good measure. I mean, God forbid an inch of flesh might be revealed as I wriggled around in my sleep! In the winter I would add bed socks to this fine ensemble. My husband said I was one of the only people he knew that could be woken in the middle of the night and be ready to go skiing! He was right and we laughed. But it was far, far from funny. It of course had a detrimental effect on our relationship, every time I recoiled in horror if he so much as tried to hold my hand.

Now, it might be psychological, but it's weird how when I most hated the way I looked, it seemed like there were mirrors everywhere. And for years I had avoided mirrors. I didn't look at myself in shop windows and didn't have a full-length mirror at home. This meant for the longest time I carried a picture in my head that was unrealistic and outdated. In my head, with the right clothes and make-up on, I didn't look that bad. I imagined myself a few stone lighter than I was, and this fact alone was a contributor to my denial about my truly obese state. I never watched myself on TV and hated, hated, hated nearly every photograph I ever saw of myself. Lots of my lovely book readers or TV watchers would snap photographs of me and put them all over social media, and it is absolutely lovely that people wanted to say hello and get a picture and I had no choice but to capitulate. The images that showed up online were often horrific and unflattering and probably very representative of how I looked and how I moved – but I preferred to live with the more subtle, slimmer version of myself in my head and this was hard for me to see.

No unflattering photograph or video of me wobbling across a floor, however, was needed when I found it hard to climb two flights of stairs and avoided sitting on a floor, knowing it would be too hard for me to get up. It's a sad fact that there are hardly any photographs of me with the people I love. Nearly all the photos I have were taken in a working situation where I had no choice but to smile for the camera. You remember that smile? The tight-lipped wonky one that hides my teeth. This photo situation is something I hope to redress in the future: what a ridiculous state of affairs that I might have a thousand pictures of me with complete strangers but none of me with my family.

I loathed the sight of myself, the feel of myself and hated even more my weakness at not addressing my weight issues with more conviction, so much so that my preoccupation allowed fault lines to form, running through my character and allowing envy to snake into my thoughts. Even having to admit this fills me with shame. What a horrible thing. I have never been that person, I've always, always been happy for other people's good fortune, cheering friends, family and strangers alike on from the sidelines in every win. Yet I began to look at women who had cracked the code (were not overeating), women who had discipline (were not overeating) and women who did not carry such huge amounts of weight on their body (women who were not overeating), and my yearning to be like them and look like them verged on being a dark and destructive force. Comparison, I have learned, is the killer of happiness and confidence. Of course, it wasn't really about envy, but was just another way that I allowed my voice of self-sabotage to be heard. I didn't dislike these slim confident women; I just desperately, desperately wanted to be like them.

The way people treated me when I was morbidly obese was very different from how they treated me when I was slim. This could simply be me projecting my own insecurities and negative introspection in social situations, but my belief that others either sneered at me or ignored me is backed up in any number of other accounts from overweight people and their own lived experience. And I can totally relate to this, the way eyes glance over you while travelling from point a to point b, wanting to have a look but not *look* at you. Being ignored in a queue, overlooked when trying to order a coffee or at a bar, discriminated against on grounds of weight, heckled and humiliated . . . the examples are too numerous. Each one taking a sharp scythe to whatever ropes of self-esteem kept me grounded.

There are some plus-sized trail blazers, some of whom I've met and interviewed who make a point of flaunting their size and their weight in a challenging, positive way that confidently confronts those who want to stare, jeer, judge, and I applaud them, admire their stance and their chutzpah and indeed their beauty! And yes, I *can* see beauty in them no matter that they have rejected the construct of slim as beautiful. I mean, whose right is it to define beauty?

When I first saw the Tess Holliday cover shots for *Cosmopolitan*, I have to admit, I felt conflicted. First, I thought she looked sensational! I also loved how bigger, fatter women were finally, finally being represented, but a part of me did not want that level of obesity to be 'normalised'. I didn't want kids and teens to experience what I had in a world geared up for fat shaming and didn't want their health to suffer as a result of piling on the pounds. And just to clarify, I am not decrying fat, and hailing skinny, I'm not suggesting that we all strive for model-like perfection, no way! But I am talking about the likely complications that come with *morbid obesity*. But isn't that the dichotomy? Building confidence while not encouraging any lifestyle that is unhealthy or damaging, fat or thin? I wonder if I had Tess's confidence would I have felt so negative about my body? Probably not. Definitely not.

I became a sneaky eater. I'd eat on a par with my family, chatting over dinner, as I passed on potatoes and pudding, and stuck to healthy vegetables, but then while clearing the table and doing the dishes after supper – I would gorge on leftover Yorkshire puddings, spoonfuls of stuffing and cold roast spuds like they were going out of fashion, consuming far more when having to do so stealthily than if I had simply taken a modest portion of each during dinner and not denied myself and shifted the mild 'want' to a hard stab of craving. A craving I had created through the psychological impact of denial. And worse, far worse.

It was a Saturday night, winter 2019, and Simeon and I ordered a Chinese takeaway, which was a rare treat in our house. We were excited, it was an occasion. The moment he jumped in the car to go and collect it, I ran into the kitchen, and it was like a stomach-churning treasure hunt, I rummaged through the shelves in the larder with urgency, alone for the first time that day and able to gorge.

I ate a box of chocolate cupcakes, a whole box, six large cakes that eaten individually would leave you with a sickening sugar rush and a mouth filled with cloying chocolate, but I wasn't done. I then ate a family-sized bag of crisps and then two smaller bags of crisps and a handful of biscuits.

He arrived home with a smile and laid out our rice and noodle dishes slathered in sticky sweet and sour sauce, and I scoffed the lot, even though it was quite hard to get it down. I wanted to go to bed – to cry, to rub my sore stomach, to close my eyes and make out I was somewhere else, someone else . . . I wanted to wish the night away, which I had to endure with an aching gut, a salt-swamped body, nasty breath, a coated tongue, uncomfortable gas and heaviness to my limbs. I can't even begin to tell you how my spirit was shredded, my mood desperate. It was the worst kind of self-disgust. Cleaning my teeth, I looked in the mirror and uttered the words cued up on my tongue, 'Greedy, greedy cow, what is the matter with you?'

My wall was complete.

I felt beaten.

This was almost my lowest point.

Me during my gorge and be damned phase. Weighing 134 kg. It was a miserable, miserable way to live.

My food intake and obsession were wildly out of control. I planned my day, my week, my life around eating as much as I could and ramming it down my throat as quickly as possible. It didn't matter what it was: breakfast cereal, bread, cheese or chocolate. It wasn't about taste or desire or even what I had a fancy for, very often it was whatever was within reach or what lurked in the cupboards. Sometimes it wasn't even things I liked. I didn't enjoy eating it. I didn't *want* it most of the time, but I couldn't stop.

I fell into bed each night full of disgust, but at the same time looking forward to waking up so I could go back to the kitchen and start over. A new day . . . new food to be eaten. I would let myself picture and plan my food intake for the next day, and took comfort from knowing that my cupboards and bread bin were full and that I had a ready supply of butter in the fridge to slather on my many slices of toast. I would very often plan my day around the food I would eat and the snacks I would gather. This gorging on food was closely related to:

My mental state – the lower my mood, which the menopause did its level best to keep low, the more I ate.

My worry level – the more acute, as days and nights were spent in a mental spin over Joshy, the more I ate.

And the scale of my self-disgust – which was at its most extreme as I overate and ate some more, fuelling greater self-disgust, the more I ate.

I never disclosed my weight even to those close to me, banning scales from my bathroom and doing my best to avoid medical intervention at all costs for any ailment for fear of the doctor asking to weigh me. This I have learned is quite a common trait for those who do not feel they are the 'ideal' body shape. And it is a perfect example of how my obesity was like a tree trunk with every branch and root of my life growing from it – bound to it, dwarfed by it, a dark symbiosis with no hope of independence.

Vast food orders were placed online. This delivery of groceries was perfect for a secret eater like me. I didn't have to face the person on the checkout who would handle my vast haul of grub, which I would grab the moment it had been bleeped and shove as quickly as I could back into my trolley, trying to hide the junk. Neither did I have to see the other shoppers glimpse into my trolley. I was sure they would take in the family-sized packets of crisps, the fresh bread, the cheese, the chocolate and then take one look at my frame and think, 'Ah well, that makes sense . . .'

When I *did* go out to shop for food, driving to the supermarket would give me a feeling of great anticipation and I'd plan in my head the things I might like to eat, before loading up the bags with all a family required for the week, including foods I *never* ever ate openly at home, like crisps, chocolate bars, cakes and sandwiches, but then I would put some of these illicit foods on the seat of my car and eat it in the car park or on the way home, again gorging until I did not want to eat any more, but I did, continuing until it was all gone.

The car was a private haven for my overconsumption, where I was not disturbed or observed. Sitting in the car, shoving cakes or sandwiches in my mouth. I would then cram any litter from my ill-gotten spoils into the glove box until I could dispose of it discreetly. And I would drive home as if it had never happened, as if I had not consumed a day's worth of calories in a few minutes sitting in a dimly lit car park on the other side of town and hoping that no one I knew saw me. Arriving home, I'd stash certain foods out of the eyes and reach of other family members. It was mine and mine alone.

And this is going to sound bizarre, but sometimes, if there were certain foods in the house, like cake, iced buns, fresh bread or cheese, I could hardly sleep knowing they were in the kitchen and so I would often devour them before bedtime so I didn't have to worry about them or obsess over them because they would be gone. I told you . . . bizarre. This confession makes me feel sick with disgust. It was a dark, damaging way to live, cloaked in guilt that I was doing so in secret, thinking I was fooling those around me when in reality the only person I was fooling was myself. And it really was as desperate as it sounds.

In the spirit of opening up the conversation around food addiction and how it affected my mental health, I've decided to give you a glimpse into a day in the life of my 280-lb/20+-stone self.

6 a.m. Wake up and sit on the edge of the bed for a moment, admire the beautiful airy room that I sleep in, with its expensive drapes, muted tones and antique pine wardrobes, the stained-glass windows of the ensuite and the views out over farmland, and feel like I don't deserve to be here. This is a pretty room for pretty girls, not someone like me. It is in fact wasted on someone like me, someone as ugly as me.

I wait for the sick and dizzy feeling to pass then stand up, faltering on knees that ache. I rub beneath my bra, which I always sleep in; otherwise, my boobs slip under my arms and lie next to me on the mattress. I rub until it hurts, trying to relieve the chafe of the elastic against my skin. Walking slowly past my husband's side of the bed, I pull my nightdress down over my leggings to ensure no roll of fat or hint of cellulite is on display. I nearly cry as I picture the woman he fell in love with, the slim me, a disguised me and yet look what he has ended up with. I fight to control the mental anguish that floods me with worry that he might up and leave because of how I now look, and how I have become, like I trapped him.

I walk slowly across the room and hope the floorboards don't give way. I know it's unlikely, ridiculous even, but it's a six-hundred-year-old farmhouse and I wonder how the joists and timber cope with a weight like mine hovering on them. I head along the corridors and down the wooden stairs, feeling the treads flex and creak beneath me, then head straight to the downstairs loo – the one furthest from everyone else. And as unpleasant as it is to mention, I can't even detail how foul that first visit every day is and how predictable. As if my body tries each morning to rid itself of the fats and toxic processed junk I have crammed into my gut late into the previous night. Sitting on the loo with my stomach resting on my thighs, I feel sick and ill as I pass what my body is able to process. It isn't surprising, not really, I mean the old adage 'shit in shit out' very much applies. I then sit on the sofa and write for an hour with a cup of coffee, escaping into whichever world I am creating, a world where I don't have to think about my size.

7.30 a.m. Breakfast in the spacious kitchen with the sunlight streaming in, the Aga warm, the coffee machine purring – I feel ravenous – unsurprising as I am never full, never. My stomach has stretched, and I can and often do, eat for most of the day. For breakfast, I eat three thickly cut slices of toast with butter and peanut butter or marmalade; I get these down my throat very quickly and feel a little better because I have eaten and simultaneously a little disgusted that I have yet again started my day on the wrong track. I then go back to the sofa to sit and write until midmorning.

10.30 a.m. A large cup of black coffee with four or five shortbread biscuits or similar then back to the sofa to work. The sugar hits my bloodstream and I feel content, warm and happy. It takes all my willpower not to go back and finish the whole packet; some days I do exactly this. I crumple the packet as small as it will go and hide it in the bin, ashamed but happy to have the biscuits inside me, plus if they are gone, I won't be tempted to eat them, because I can't.

12. p.m. An early lunch of cheese on toast or a toasted cheese sandwich with pickle or cream of tomato soup with another three slices of thickly buttered toast. I try to eat alone while Simeon is

at work and the kids are in the studio or outside. I often make out it's the first time I've eaten that day. Lying to my family, lying to myself. This makes me feel worthless.

3 p.m. A cup of tea and more biscuits or toast or any snack I might find lurking in the fridge like half a cheese and onion pasty, cold roast potatoes, some chocolate, leftover pasta, anything I can get my hands on, as if afraid that once everyone gathers in the kitchen or arrives home, I won't be able to eat what I like, as they will be watching, judging, and the thought makes me almost panic and I eat something else. I write but will often cry at how messed up my intake is, how I am already thinking of when I can eat again. Back to writing.

4. p.m. A nap. A nap between writing to let my food settle, allow my body to process the calories it has consumed and to recharge my batteries. I come to, have another coffee and write until dinner.

7 p.m. Dinner. Again, I make out I haven't eaten since lunch, such deceit makes me feel like shit. Spicy fried rice with sticky teriyaki salmon or fish and chips and mushy peas or vegetable korma with naan bread, a couple of onion bhajis and pilau rice. And for pudding, some chocolate or a slice of cake.

11 p.m. Before I go to bed and if no one else is around I have a quick snack of cheese (Brie) and crackers (butter puff), a couple of packets of crisps or handfuls of peanuts or crisps. I climb into bed, pulling my nightdress over my legs to hide, hide, hide my body and, conscious of how much space I am taking up on the mattress, set alarm for 6 a.m., when I will wake, sit on the edge of the bed and do the whole thing again. Another day of either guzzling food or feeling 'starving' and all with a tingle of shame and disgust that prickles my skin.

Horrible to read, isn't it?

And trust me, it was even worse to live.

Writing it down and putting it out there for you to read and imagine is a big deal, it makes me feel incredibly vulnerable, but I also think that it's part of the honest and open narrative required around food addiction, because that's what I am describing, and I hope that by me 'coming clean' it might encourage the conversation among others.

I began to look at the slim women I knew, the slim men I knew, watching their choices in restaurants, the way they stood in a lift, what they put in their shopping trolleys in the supermarket and the way they interacted with their partners. Why couldn't I be like that? Eat like that? Stand like that? Act like that? And the only point of difference that was obvious to me was that they were slim, and I was not. That was it. I never took into account my successes, my career, my personality, my achievements, obstacles I had overcome, challenges of life or any positive attributes – it was all about fat versus thin. My horizon was reduced to this very narrow and unhelpful metric. It is of course never that simple. Were they happy? Addicted? Ill? None of these things entered my mind; it was all about the size of their waist. I envied not only their bodies but their apparent self-control and it was a state I was desperate to attain.

I hated to see other severely overweight people eating in public. What a terrible, terrible thing to say, I know it is, but it's the truth. Of course, at the heart of this is that I could not bear to see *myself* eating. I would see them as a mirror, knowing that was how I looked too, and the idea of so very publicly admitting to my over-eating was something I would never and could never have done (she says, now writing a book about it – quite possibly the most public way to put your innermost feelings out there). I might, if pushed, eat salad in public, or munch an apple. Who was I trying to kid? Wearing size 24 jeans and the baggiest of baggy shirts, I would sip water and nibble kale when all I really wanted was a milkshake and fries. Farcical. And yet being seen to 'try' or heralded as 'making an effort to ditch the pounds' was important to me. But I wasn't fooling anyone.

My general health, apart from the obvious implications and fears that I have already touched upon, suffered as a direct result of being overweight. I was frequently breathless after the smallest exertion, my joints creaked in resistance at having to support my moving bulk and my energy levels were through the floor. Yet going to visit the doctor, as someone who was morbidly obese, was a thing I absolutely dreaded and avoided at all costs. I was anxious about sitting face-to-face with a professional who was going to pull up a chart or show me on a diagram how overweight I was or tell me that I needed to lose weight – I already knew it and so to be reminded would only feel like pressure and judgement. Of course I can now see that this was far more about how I felt about myself than the reality of a medic simply doing their job. And I should also say that nearly all the interactions I have had with my GP and others in a medical situation have been kind, understanding, and they were clearly aware of my obvious anxiety. But no matter, for me the dread was very real.

I'm embarrassed to admit that I put off having smear tests, mammograms, check-ups and other standard medical tests that can and do save millions of lives and millions of pounds through early detection, treatment and advice for a whole host of diseases. Yet I stupidly, ignorantly and resolutely refused to visit my GP because I was too ashamed of my size. The shame manifested itself with two main concerns: firstly that I might be weighed – I can't tell you how even writing that down as someone who has their weight more under control makes my throat feel dry and my heart race. I was *petrified* of getting onto scales and having my true weight confirmed. Second, the idea that I might have to take my clothes off and let a stranger see my flesh. Good lord above, I had spent the best part of a decade trying to hide my flab from my husband and those who loved me, how on earth was I going to show it to a complete stranger? All utterly ridiculous I know, it's not as if they haven't seen it all before, but the horror for them having to put their hand on my obese form was more than I could contemplate. I also at some level felt like I was done with medical interventions – the thought of my earlier surgeries to fix my pelvis, and all the interventions for my miscarriages and tumours had beaten me. I did not and still don't like the thought of going near a hospital.

It seems that I am not alone. There are numerous articles detailing obese people's experiences with doctors that are negative, not all of course, but many medical professionals can't see beyond the fat, and can we blame them when they spend time and resources treating something that is so contentious? Part of the problem, I think, is a reluctance to look beyond a fat person's weight. I guess the hotly discussed debate is not dissimilar to the discussions over whether smokers should be given assistance for lung disease and alcoholics treatment for their livers.

Unsurprisingly, when I was morbidly obese I was always too hot. Again, I imagined a slim person inside me trying and failing to shrug off a fat suit, layers and layers of white lard before you got to my muscles, organs and bones – no wonder I was hot. It was like being permanently wrapped in a close-fitting parka – one of the ones with a fur lining and a hood lined with fur too. I felt claustrophobic and restless, suffocating in my own skin. I also sweated a lot, which brought me no end of embarrassment.

At my heaviest, I wasn't only sweating excessively, but I slept a lot. You know how sometimes after an enormous Christmas or celebratory lunch, all you want to do is nestle into the nearest chair or sofa, preferably with a blanket thrown over you, snoring and farting until someone puts out the call for trifle? Well, that was how I felt every day. This apparently is one of the key methods that Sumo wrestlers employ to add to their bulk, they eat and then sleep immediately, ensuring the food is laid down as fat and not too much is expelled as energy. Again, it was part of the damaging cycle of overeating. To eat to excess made me feel this way physically and yet the very best thing I could have done was to go for a long walk or swim: any kind of exercise. Instead, I curled up like a dormouse and 'recovered' before trundling back to the fridge. It was as if my body needed to shut down to regroup and so every afternoon, if possible, I would close my eyes for at least half an hour and fall into the deepest sleep.

It soon became apparent though that my afternoon nap was not sufficient for me to function and on a typical day of writing at home, I would also nap in the morning and sometimes in the middle of the day too. I guess it was unsurprising, as anyone who has ever carried something very heavy for a long period of time can attest; it is exhausting, and so with nine or ten extra stone hanging off my bones I was no different. I was always tired. I woke up yawning each morning and went to bed yawning each night. My movements were lumbering, my walk ambling, not only because of the awkwardness of moving with a very large frame, but because a deep fatigue meant every action was a little laboured.

There have been moments in the last few years when I felt a brief acceptance of my size that was both liberating and terrifying in equal measure. Like the time I laughed and laughed when friends visited, and I forgot to be overly aware and anxious about my size for just a minute or two and it was lovely. Or meeting other friends in a restaurant where I felt I was in an adequate disguising outfit that gave me the smallest amount of confidence. Liberating because I glimpsed what life would be like if I was accepting or actually loving of my large body, and I can't deny it was a nicer way to spend my days and so much better for my mental health. I walked straighter and ordered food in a clear and confident voice and gone was the feeling of inferiority that had dogged me for years.

And yet it was also terrifying. I was terrified that acceptance of my obesity meant that I was never going to find a way to 'fix' it.

I've looked at my old pictures and felt disgusted, some here in this very book for you to see too. Not that I would remove them from circulation and I've never Photoshopped or adjusted any pictures of me no matter how unflattering, as I believe that this is part of the problem towards our attitude to body shape and beauty – yet another way that we are less than honest and open about fat – encouraging others to chase the unattainable, while unable to accept our own flaws – I think that's a road that if we start to travel leads to no good place.

I knew I was very fat when people stopped being able to use the word 'fat' to me – in the *Fawlty Towers* manner of 'Don't mention the war!' It made me think about why. In front of me, the topic was taboo. It would be like saying to a man with one arm, oh look, that person has got an arm missing, can you imagine? Consciousness of their similar state would prevent it, and this was exactly the same.

And I understand why. People's preconceptions about being overweight are bolstered and supported by advertising. The situation is better than it was, with the occasional plus size or slightly rounded model to show clothes, but essentially severely overweight people are largely ignored or made the object of ridicule, reinforcing the idea that no one wants to see fat on TV or online when shopping. And I understand this too in part – advertising is all about selling 'perfection'. Sparkling homes with shiny-haired parents, well-behaved kids and immaculately plumped cushions to sell everything from vacuum cleaners to laundry soap – we know homes aren't really like that, don't we? And to sell a car, the couple are always ridiculously good-looking, hard-working executives in well-paid roles, and come the weekend they shove a surfboard on the back seat, tousle their damp, lustrous locks and take to the sea at a pleasant, deserted cove. No doubt before watching the sunset from the bonnet of said vehicle and having lots of fabulous sex before packing up and travelling home in time for *Antiques Roadshow* on Sunday night.

We know that's not how people live, right? And so, I *get* that flogging fashion, make-up, perfume, is no different. They are selling the ideal, the unattainable, perfection – but what does that do to the confidence of overweight people who are bombarded with these images day and night either on screen or in magazines and movies? Well, I can't speak for them all, but I can say that for me it made me feel 'less than'. Less than sexy. Less than attractive. Less than wanted. Less than normal. Less than capable. Less than valid. Less than everyone who was not severely overweight.

Newspapers too – especially the tabloids – no matter the topic being written about, countless are the descriptions of women as having 'an enviable flat stomach', 'sculpted washboard abs', 'perfect bikini body', 'curvy frame', or my particular favourite in one single headline, referring to a member of the TOWIE reality show: displaying her 'eye-popping cleavage, taut stomach and VERY perky posterior!' Sweet lord above! Is it any wonder we are body conscious when the media insists on carving up the whole and approving or commenting on particular parts of the body? This kind of reporting only feeds the obsession with size and weight and the idea that there is a right way and a wrong way to look.

I find it mystifying that it's not only keyboard warriors whose go-to insult is the size of my arse, but people in real life too! Now, I will admit that there have been times when I have maybe drifted a little in my lane or been going too slowly for the likes of the man in the Honda CRV on the A38, heck, I have even taken more than three attempts to manoeuvre my car into a space while parallel parking. Annoying misdemeanours, yes, but hardly hanging offences. And yet those around me who have given in to the road rage simmering inside them have all factored my weight into their insults or observations.

'You stupid, fat cow!'

'Look where you are going, fat ****.'

And this again is so completely unrelated to my less than perfect driving and just another indicator of how much fatness is hated. These comments hurt and linger in my thoughts long after the knobhead shouting them has probably forgotten the incident. Weirdly, despite my love of swearing in the car, I have never felt the need to lose my cool quite so viciously in a vehicle, and if I did, I highly doubt I would yell anything along the lines of:

'Oi! Missus! Yes, you there with the eye-popping cleavage, taut stomach and VERY perky posterior! What the f*ck do you think you're doing?'

Because for the life of me, I don't see how their weight, body shape and driving ability or lack of, are in any way related! In all seriousness, I think it's a direct response to the observation that overweight people are considered lazy, stupid, incapable or all three. I know that when I was slimmer, people I worked with, socially or even complete strangers would say:

'Have you lost weight? You look fantastic!'

'You look so much slimmer. How have you done it?'

'Ooh lucky you, you've lost weight!'

'Have you had to get a new wardrobe?'

'I could snap you! Look at you, you are shrinking!'

And yes, it is nice and kind even that they noticed, took an interest and felt strongly enough to comment. Arguably I wish they could have been as vocal and supportive about my weight gain, helping me fathom my addiction and offering advice. Not that I was unaware, of course I wasn't, but is it just me that finds it odd that we as a society feel so comfortable in commenting and openly judging people's 'thinness', celebrating it even! Whereas 'fatness' is taboo. Can you imagine if the above narrative was directed at people who had gained weight? There would be absolute outrage!

'Hey, you look really chubby today!'

'Have you gained weight? Your face looks rounder.'

'I expect you have had to go up a clothes size since I last saw you?'

'From the back you look massive!'

'Did you want to gain weight? Do you want to talk about it?'

But why *don't* we have these conversations? It's either okay to talk about body size/shape and the amount of fat on it or it isn't. And if it wasn't so taboo it wouldn't feel so shameful.

Now, just to be clear, I am advocating *neither*. I am not calling for parity in the bullying, discrimination or shaming stakes, absolutely not! I hate it and want it all to stop! It is completely unacceptable to body shame any body type – the triggers and pain that comments like these can cause are dangerous and I have already detailed how I have been on the receiving end of some hurtful remarks and insults that have stayed with me. BUT I feel it is ludicrous that fat is demonised and the insults, scrutiny and snickering comedy around fatness only serve to legitimise this. Why are we so fixated on size? Why can't we simply look at health for all sizes? It's that word again: balance.

Let's take it a step further: have you noticed how if you mention someone's weight loss or thinness they will often reply with 'Thank you!', assuming it to be the compliment it is nearly always intended as, and yet try the same with commenting on weight gain – the 'thanks' would be limited to a very small group of people in specific circumstances and the majority would be hurt, upset, angry, embarrassed. I would like to live in a world where we didn't need to comment on body shape at all – where we could all just BE!

And now the really hard bit for me.

Here are a few pictures that are not easy for me to show you, not easy to put out there for public consumption and scrutiny, but here's the thing: I write a lot about the importance of being transparent about my weight and struggle and this is very much part of that. The constant barrage of filtered images that fill up our Instagram feed, the digitally altered posts of perfection on social media and in magazines, they aren't real! And they help build the mirage and set a beauty standard that is unattainable and is damaging for all of us who have no hope of achieving it without great lighting, a team of experts and a bank of fancy filters. It's dishonest, and it's not enough to casually throw in a hashtag to make it look as if no effort has been taken – it needs to stop, all of it. We need more honesty, more transparency, less filtering, truth in our pictures. Better for our own mental health, better for everyone's mental health. And so here goes. This is me. Unfiltered. Unedited. Morbidly obese. At my worst.

These pictures have been sitting in my phone for the longest while and many is the time I have gone to delete them, didn't want to see the reminder and didn't want anyone else to see the reminder. But to delete them would feel like a cover-up. And if things are going to change, I need *not* to cover up, but to reveal, expose and discuss so that I can really, really move forward. I've talked generically and openly in earlier chapters about what it was like to live in my morbidly obese body, often with tongue-in-cheek humour or fey commentary that really belies the health implications of it for me. But these pictures are the reality. They are me.

Chapter Sixteen

'BIG FAT ROCK BOTTOM'

When Simeon and I first got married, with one eight-year-old boy each and a lack of funds, we used to sit on the sofa and talk about how lovely it would be if we could afford to take our brand-new family of four on a fancy holiday – and by fancy I mean somewhere sunny, a warm sea to swim in and an ice cream every afternoon before a walk up the prom of an evening. We worked hard and our fantasies involved two weeks off work and taking the kids to play in the sand somewhere. When the boys were older, we then discussed going away on our own. Years later, funds did allow, but it would have been hard to take a holiday and leave Josh at home to his own devices, not when he was in the tightest grip of depression. Neither of us would have been able to go away and relax, unsure of how Josh was faring, and it felt safer, easier to be close to him, on call if you like.

Then came the point when Josh was in a good place, both boys were home and able to look after the pups, and with book twenty-three, *The Light in The Hallway*, book twenty-four, *The Day She Came Back* and book twenty-five, *The Boy Between*, out, it felt like the perfect time for that getaway, maybe even the honeymoon we never had . . .

And yet we didn't. Why? Because of the size of my body.

I spent my life cowering emotionally behind the wall I had built in my mind, a shield that stopped me facing all that lay on the other side, and if any uncomfortable thoughts or memories dared to float over the top, I batted them away with a chunk of French stick. This was my uncomfortable truth. A holiday was my worst nightmare. Why would I want to hit a beach or go out in public somewhere very hot when I would be in jeans and a big top, sweating and uncomfortable, while everyone else frolicked in a swimming costume? I didn't think performing the walrus roll while clad in a voluminous kaftan would cut it in a busy hotel pool.

Sitting in front of the fire on a winter's night a couple of years ago, Simeon was online looking at holidays and my heart raced at the prospect. He'd stare at beaches and say, 'How do you fancy a week here? You could write? We could swim . . .' But rather than join in the planning and take an interest, I pointed out how busy my calendar was, how the boys and dogs needed me at home, and besides, I didn't want to cancel the milk delivery. Plus, I'd made plans with my parents, wasn't feeling a hundred per cent, didn't like the look of the resort . . . and a million other ~~reasons~~ excuses, as to why it would be almost impossible for us to go anywhere anytime soon.

His face dropped and it was another reminder that my body issues didn't only affect me. The real reason was a lot harder for me to admit and a lot more tragic: the prospect of having to put on a swimming costume or a T-shirt or shorts, to go into the sea or a pool and let any part of my body be seen in public. Summertime at home was hard enough and I coped with any heatwave by sticking to my jeans, often quite literally, and by swapping jumpers and sweatshirts for floaty chiffon-type tops that allowed a good waft of breeze and by trading my boots for flip-flops. A holiday though at a resort or a beach would have been a lot harder for me to manage. The anxiety induced at the thought of people seeing my dimpled thighs, rounded stomach and wobbly arms was similar to the dream where you find yourself naked in the middle of Tesco while running around trying to find the mint sauce. Just me? I can laugh but I've actually spilled a river of tears at the thought of what I was denying myself, denying my husband and denying us as a couple. Wonderful experiences that would bring us closer and give us a much-needed break, all missed.

'You can't keep hiding, Mandy.'

He closed the laptop and turned to face me. I made to stand up, eager to escape, not wanting the exchange, and about to voice my sudden need for a glass of water, but he pulled me back down and I knew I wasn't going to be able to avoid the conversation. Not this time. I was fifty-two and we had been through so much as a couple, and yet in that moment, I could barely look him in the eye.

Simeon confided that each time he saw me shuffle off to stick my head into the fridge, it left him feeling defeated, scared and impotent, unable to voice his fears for all the reasons we have touched upon. You see, it isn't only in wider society that words like fat, overweight and obese make us all feel a little uncomfortable, but in our home too.

This was the first time he had talked openly with me about my weight, and it was like he'd discovered I was involved in some nefarious activity. I was mortified, felt exposed and so uncomfortable at the prospect of the conversation which felt inevitable. It was part of the same process and initiative of honesty needed to move *us*, as a couple, forward if we had any hope of recapturing our physical closeness and our loving contact that was, at best, sporadic. We were great friends and had weathered many a storm, but this was a hurricane that had been looming for the longest time. It battered the door and rattled our windows. And I was scared.

We sat on the sofa, facing each other, and in a voice that warbled with nerves, I told him of the guilt I felt at being obese and that it wasn't solely staked in my appearance and lack of physical ability.

'I feel very much like I tricked you, or if not tricked you then let you down badly.' It was the hardest thing to say.

'But that's not the case,' he told me. 'I love you unconditionally. That's what this is.'

I so wanted to believe him. His words were calming, but I was in a state of high agitation. 'I don't want you to leave me,' I blurted.

'Leave you?' He screwed his face up.

'For someone slim.' Admitting to the underlying fear that he might walk was huge for me, but I also felt some small amount of relief at being able to voice words I'd carried for the longest time.

It was his turn to laugh. 'Mand, if I was going to walk, it would have been when we were at breaking point over our baby.' He paused and I know we both thought about that dark day and the desolate, lonely days that followed. 'Or when things with Josh got tough, or when you made me sleep in an ice cave because you were too bloody hot!'

I smiled and he took my hand. 'I didn't leave then, and I won't leave now or in the future. That's not how this works. I love you. I don't want anyone else; I love *you*.'

I cried quietly with relief, knowing that this was the foundation I could build from. It was lovely to hear, and we sat quietly for a while, letting the words land. Neither of us moved, as if we knew there was more talking to be done. The thought almost paralysed me with anxiety.

Despite his reassurances, however, I couldn't help but wonder what it had been like for my man, who has lived with me as a slim woman, a fat woman and a very fat woman. I needed to face up to the reality of how Simeon felt about the situation, to deal with the truth of how I lived, if nothing else to break the cycle of constantly and unsuccessfully trying to hide my body from him, either by wearing voluminous muumuus in the summer, twenty various layers in the winter or by wrapping myself in a blanket on the sofa of an evening. What did I think? That I might fool him into thinking I had the body of Elle Macpherson and it was actually the many layers I wore that made me look large? Or that it was the drape of my comfort blanket that made me look fat? Actually, yes, it was something very close to that and of course it fooled no one, especially not the man who knows me back to front and inside out.

We got a cup of tea – as everyone knows, any conversation is made ten times easier when you are holding a cup of tea, this I learned at the feet of my great-nan. The lighting was kept low, just the way I like it, only lamplight in fact, again allowing me to hide inside the softened shadows cast over the walls and furniture. We sat on opposite ends of the sofa and spoke honestly, asking each other questions that were tough to hear and even tougher to respond to. The air felt weighted, crackling with nerves, which was odd; this man was my husband! But this was new ground, new and scary ground.

'You must find me less attractive now I look like this,' I whispered, half hoping he might not hear, so I wouldn't have to hear his response. To voice it took all my strength, my heart hammering in my chest.

He took his time; his nerves were palpable, aware that this was a big deal for both of us, a crossroads if you like.

'Yes, a little, but mainly because of how it's changed you, your shyness, secrecy. Your reluctance to try . . . anything!'

It was all of my worst fears come true, to hear how his attraction for me had waned a little, although I am sure he meant a lot.

His words were like arrows that landed in my breast. I wanted, no, needed, this honesty, but that didn't mean it was any easier to hear.

He kept reaching for my free hand, knowing this would calm me, anchor me. 'But I mean it, I love you unconditionally. We're on this journey together. Your weight is only a small part of that, but, yes, I found you more attractive when you weren't like this.'

I cried – of course I did – self-pitying tears to think of the years we had lost with this barrier between us. And then came the killer blow.

'My biggest worry though, Mand, is not how you look, but that you might not make fifty-five. I think we could lose you.'

It was staggering to hear, and I wasn't expecting it. He believed if I didn't change my dietary habits, I might not be here in a couple of years.

It was the biggest thump in the chest, a reminder of how my weight impacted every area of my life, which in turn impacted everyone else's. I didn't confess to the fact that I *already* regularly woke up with a tight band of pain across my chest, my mind running riot as I lay in bed with a racing heart, chest pains and sweating profusely. Was this chronic indigestion, panic attack or full-blown heart disease? It scared me, and after his comments, I began to picture what it might be like for my husband, my kids and my family to find me dead or to watch me die and to do so with the knowledge that I had effectively, if not directly, caused then contributed to the situation with my food addiction.

It made me look at how I grieved for those I have loved and lost, some of them passing away from old age or similar, and I questioned how I would feel if I looked back and tried to imagine what the grieving process would look like if I felt they had had even the smallest choice in leaving the world. That there were definitely things they *could* have done, behaviours they *could* have changed to possibly live longer. I would have felt angry, let down and abandoned and I did not want those I loved to look at me in that way.

I had to change.

I had to find a way to change.

I sobbed then, letting his words sink in. His worry was real and there was nothing I could say or do to deny it, he was right. And I knew it.

He held me until I calmed, and we talked softly about what attracted him to me when we first met. My sense of humour, our brilliant connection, the way we could chat until dawn and laugh until sunset . . . yes, all of that, but also my body positivity. We were physical and confident with each other.

It was hard and heartbreakingly sad to compare this to the person I had become, sitting there swathed in a blanket with the lights turned low, as we talked about those early days. He confessed to feeling sad for all we as a couple missed out on: holidays, sitting in the sunshine, intimacy, and not *only* intimacy, although yes, that too, but if he held me, I would shrug him off or run away or go and grab a long bath. I could never relax, more worried about him seeing my dimply bottom than having fun. And the size of me meant swinging from a chandelier was out of the question. It would have to be a bloody huge chandelier and very well anchored into the ceiling.

The truth is, the thought of my husband's hand on my flesh went from being something desirable that I craved to something I dreaded, and this had been the case for a year or two. How very sad is that for us both?

Not only did I find it very hard to feel sexy when I hated the body I was encased in, but also being severely overweight came with some unpleasant physical aspects like snoring and sweating more. Physically I took up a lot of space and that bothered me. It was embarrassing to be occupying two thirds of the sofa, hogging the

316

duvet, commandeering the majority of the mattress. Having been single for so long before Simeon and I became a couple, I remembered the way it felt to have this big man sit alongside me or climb into my 4' 6" bed. It felt like a huge and exciting invasion and yet also comforting, as if he might protect me (not that I asked for or needed protection) but it was like for the first time since becoming a mum, I could sleep without one ear cocked, nestling into his strong arms, like sharing the nightshift with someone else. And I liked it. Yet now I felt like a huge thing, an encumbrance, a gargantuan presence rather than something to be protected. And this on top of the fact that I was dressed like a hockey goalie about to hit the ice.

Simeon thought it was because I did not want to be touched by him, as though it was something about him, but it was never, ever that. This confession from him broke my heart. I explained that it was only because I pictured his fingers pushing into the cushion of fat that not only reduced the impact of his touch for me, but the visualisation of it made me feel sick – who would want to touch my blubber? It made me shiver with revulsion to touch it, let alone someone else.

'Can you imagine the impact of losing you, Mandy? On us and your parents?' His voice broke and it brought me back to the present.

I began to think about my future cut short and all that would mean, including the effect this would have on my family, on Josh, who was finally on an even keel and was experiencing more good days than bad. And what I might miss out on, being there to help my parents as they aged, or my family and friends in whatever crisis lurked around life's next corner. And the joyous things too, like holding the wedding reception we never got to have, the many familiar milestones and markers in our sons' lives and, dare I say it, grandchildren. All wonderful pockets of joy on the horizon if I let myself stick around for them . . .

One of the hardest parts of the conversation was when Simeon pointed out that he had always considered me to be smart, and yet had sat by while I made bad decisions every time I fed myself with something fattening or to excess. There was nothing smart about that.

He was composed. 'But I understand it's more than just eating, it's about filling something up inside you.'

And it was. I sobbed then, great huge gulping tears that clogged my nose and throat. The man I loved, whom I thought I was fooling with my secret eating, so clearly expressing the simple fact that I ate to fill up all the holes inside me, to plug my sadness. I reached for *his* hand, thinking that if he got it, then maybe there was a chance I could get it too – figure it out, find the way to break free from this devastating cycle that, we both admitted, might kill me.

'I don't know how to stop eating. How do I do it, Simeon?' I wanted him to do what I had found impossible: give me the answers.

'I'm not sure. But I know you'll do it at your own pace, and in a way that works for you, go gently. And I will support you, we all will.'

I nodded, feeling a certain lightness to my spirit, relief almost. His clear suggestion made it feel that there might be a solution. That I wasn't a lost cause and that I could, if I wanted to, turn things around and live well beyond my mid-fifties.

This conversation was the start of the change in my life.

I understood that I could have been addicted to cocaine, nicotine, white wine spritzers, gambling, painkillers, crack or any other number of substances that reel us in and hold us fast in their grip, but my addiction was to food. I was addicted to food. Using it to numb all that swirled in my busy head. And my relationship with it was toxic.

Much of what he said resonated with me. We switched off the lamps, climbed the stairs and went to bed. We lay on the mattress holding hands like we always used to, as hope danced above us in the night air. It felt like the start of a new dawn, and I was happier than I'd been in a long time.

◆ ◆ ◆

I spent the next week or so thinking about the course of action I needed to take, what was going to work for me. Simeon and I were newly reconnected, we spoke more, hung out together more and laughed more – it felt a lot like relief on both our parts. Having him as a sounding board made all the difference, it gave me confidence to discuss my weight and what I might want to do about it, instead of creeping around like a shadow, hoping it all might go away. It reaffirmed something I had forgotten: that self-isolation and intro-spection are rarely the way to solve a problem.

I called a weight loss group that met in a local village hall and spoke to a lovely lady who told me about the course and how I only had to turn up, pay my subscription, get weighed and with the support of the group and by following a calorie-controlled diet, achieve my goal. She told me of some of the incredible successes: 'Three-stone losses, four, five . . . all amazing . . .'

I liked her.

'Can I take your name?' she asked.

'Amanda, Amanda Prowse.'

'Oh!' she laughed, 'I was going to ask if you were the author. I love her books. I've got them all on my Kindle. You're not *her*, are you?'

I agreed to go along but knew I wouldn't. I wanted to be anon-ymous when I took this most important step on my weight-loss journey. I never went. She was right, the bubbly lady on the phone, I was not *her*, not at that moment. I didn't feel like me at all.

Deciding group weight loss probably wasn't for me, I bought a book about fasting and read about how if I didn't eat, I would lose weight, which, despite not being medically trained, I had kind of already figured out. It was chock-full of recipes involving courgettes.

It occurred to me then that Simeon was right; I needed to understand why I ate before I could figure out how to stop eating. It wasn't enough to simply attack the next diet with vigour while dreaming of chips. I thought about the last summer when I decided to give up crisps and take up swimming. I was on my way . . . yet again . . . Woohoo! Here we go! With all the usual rhetoric and fanfare, this was going to be IT!

However, as soon as the sun began to retreat behind the clouds, the rusting barbecue was relegated to the garage and frost lay sparkling on the ground, I was back to hiding inside an oversized woolly pully, yanking it over my bum when I stood up, and back to snaffling cake like it was fresh air. My swimming costume and kaftan were consigned to the dress-up box along with my Halloween witch's hat and my stick-on moustache collection.

I'd had enough of this life, recognising that if I wanted to change the way I looked and felt, I needed to change the way I thought and behaved, not only where my weight was concerned, but also about how I viewed myself and the many mental obstacles I had created to stop me living my best life. It was about quieting that voice of self-sabotage that had been whispering in my ear for far too long.

Easy, right?

It was obvious that I didn't eat because I was hungry, and I didn't eat because I particularly liked food. I ate because of what was going on inside my head.

Now, I'm a firm believer that sometimes the universe sends you a little sign, something that can help put you on the right path or help a thought grow or water a seed that might have already taken root in your mind. Stumbling across our forever home, for example. And such a thing happened to me only the very next weekend.

It was the summer of 2020, and I broke my ankle in a shameful and embarrassing fashion. There was a slightly uneven patch of lawn at the back of the house where a few digs, grassy potholes and tufted mounds lived. Never one for perfect uniformity, preferring the look and feel of a more cottage-style garden, this lumpy terrain never bothered me. That was until I headed back inside at dusk from a trip to the compost bin. My toes seemed to catch on a mound of grass, and I heard a crack as I went over on my ankle.

I lay there in the twilight – looking like an upturned beetle. The sharp pain told me I had damaged myself and yet it wasn't easy for me, even without such an injury, to get up off the ground. It was a low point, embarrassing, painful and a reminder of why I needed to do something about my weight. For the love of God, I couldn't get up!

I stayed there for ten minutes or so until Josh discovered me with the words, 'What *are* you doing, Mum?' It was a good question: what was I doing? *Lying on the ground with a snapped bloody ankle in the dark, like a little insect that couldn't right itself, wondering how I was going to get up and all because I couldn't stop putting biscuits in my mouth!* What the bloody hell *was* I doing? I was so embarrassed to be found by Josh like this. It was an incident that seemed to underline the very thing that Simeon and I had discussed: the impact of my weight on my life.

Josh helped me up and dragged my sorry arse off to A&E. My anxiety was through the roof. I'd done my level best to avoid hospitals and yet there I was. The triage team were as ever stretched to capacity, harassed, running back and forth across the waiting room with notes and clipboards in their hands. They were doing their very best in an over-pressured, trying environment. There were many people filling the rows of chairs, waiting for X-rays or to be seen by a medic. I was in an NHS hospital, taking up a chair, taking up time and resources. I was placing an even greater burden on NHS resources, not only in A&E but in every area, and I felt terrible.

Josh sat in the waiting room while I spoke quietly to the medic who dealt with me, avoiding eye contact, swamped with guilt.

I left the hospital with my leg in an unwieldy cast. I was quiet, reflective and decided to have a frank discussion with a friend of mine who has worked as a doctor in the NHS for three decades. Having avoided doctors for the longest time, it was facing my fear issue head on.

I called him up and explained how the more weight I gained, the more I fell over, damaging my wrists, fingers, several watches, a plant pot and my pride. I worried that there might be something wrong with my brain and balance, thought it was my clumsiness going into overdrive, but it turned out it was just that darned science thing again: the fatter I got, the bigger my body in ratio to my legs, plus it's harder to see your feet and the floor, like when you are pregnant and that big bump stops you seeing anything below sea level for a good few months, and therefore, quite obviously, the more likely you are to misstep, not see an object/obstacle, but also it is harder to keep your balance.

I asked my doctor friend how much my ankle break could be attributed to all that extra weight. I wanted to know, wanted to hold the fact in my mind as a motivator that would help kick off my lifestyle change. He took his time, as if he wanted to speak freely, but erred on the side of caution and said, 'Let's put it this way, Mandy. The extra weight doesn't help. Doesn't help at all.'

'So, you'd advise me to lose weight?' I asked the obvious question, keen to add his voice to the plan that was already taking shape in my mind.

'It's a delicate conversation about a multi-faceted, complex issue, but yes, lose weight. I can say right now that I don't think there is a medical ailment you might have or a joint in your body that is *helped* by the carrying of that much excess weight.'

Thought so.

It was quite unplanned when with Ben away and my leg in plaster, we sat as a family around the kitchen table for supper. Simeon spoke openly about our discussion in front of Josh, saying how he feared for my health if I didn't change my diet and reduce my consumption. Josh and I when trying to get to grips with his depression had some very difficult conversations, but ultimately conversations that did, I believe, contribute massively to his improved mental health. This conversation around my weight was no different.

Josh, in his usual blunt way, quite unable to sugar-coat anything, had something to say, as if once we had opened the door on the topic, all the words could come tumbling out – words to the effect that for someone who worked as hard as I did, it seemed like a shame not to enjoy the fruits of my success, held back by my weight. He also pointed out, almost in confirmation of what I was thinking, that he too felt I was heading for an early death and that he found it really, really galling that I would choose toast and biscuits over staying around to see him and any potential grandchildren that might come my way.

It was a hard chat to have and hurtful to hear, but, ultimately, another of the catalysts towards me taking control of the situation and facing my obesity head on. The biggest blow was when he reminded me of his battle to stay on the planet whereas I too was killing myself, just doing it slowly and with less fanfare.

He was right. Of course he was right. What would his life look like without me in it at his times of need? And what would my life have been like without all those strong elderly women, my aunts, my nans, what if they had died before I had the chance to know and love them? I sat at the table for a while with my ruddy leg in a cast and decided enough was enough.

I went upstairs to howl alone on my bed, crying until my eyes were swollen, my nose runny and my face blotched.

But it was time I stopped crying.

I'd cried a lot over the last couple of years and it was getting me nowhere.

And time I started doing.

Action! That was how I effected change.

I hopped out of bed and clunked down the stairs, hobbling into the room where Simeon now sat alone.

'I am going to do this, Simeon. It might not be quick, I might fall down a couple of times, but I'm going to do it!'

He smiled at me in the same way he smiled when we first met, as if he couldn't believe his luck, as if he was proud. It was like I finally understood what I needed to do: it was time for me to face the truth that no matter how strong my good intention or desire to lose weight, the fact was if wishing and thinking about it was all it took, I'd have slipped into my boob tube and skinny jeans and hit the catwalk of life years ago! What was required now was action and commitment.

It doesn't take a smarty pants to understand how difficult it is for sufferers and their families when the addiction and obsession *is* food. It is one of the things every animal needs to survive and yet when food is your enemy, your drug, your fear, your pleasure and your craving it is also very hard to arrive mentally at a place where food is also your cure. You can't avoid it, take a break from it or swear never to be tempted by it again. You can't go to a place where food is forbidden or discouraged, you can't make a pact never to partake, in fact the opposite is true; there is no opportunity for putting the thing that is toxic to you out of harm's way.

Imagine being an alcoholic or someone suffering from drug addiction, and their cure was to only have a little bit of heroin or a small sip of vodka? The very foundation of sobriety is abstinence, indeed many reformed addicts count their sobriety in days, marking each one, quite rightly, as a success if they have gone without, and I understand this motivation. But for food addicts? This is not possible. We have no choice but to have a little bit of our heroin, a sip of the vodka, because without our drug of choice, we literally die.

With this realisation, I figured that if I was going to combat my food addiction and rid myself of the obsession, I had to do it mentally because, like it or not, food was going to be ever present. In every kitchen cupboard, inside every fridge, at every mealtime (duh!), in every meeting, every shop, every gathering, in every advert, every social event . . .

So what was I going to do? The answer was quite simple: die or change. These for me were the only two options. And in the spirit of openness, I should confess that I absolutely felt the attraction of anorexia. I am ashamed to admit this, as I know the devastation the insidious condition can cause and yet I'd be lying if I did not say the thought of simply avoiding food altogether felt like a possibility. To *not* eat at all felt at the time like an easier option than having to avoid certain foods or restrict myself by just taking a little bit. But of course this is utter nonsense, only swapping one very, very bad habit for another.

I started to look at my values. I've never hankered after diamonds, designer handbags, flash cars or designer clobber and have never truly been able to understand why others did – what was it about the acquisition of stuff that validated people? My childhood and family background had taught me that the one thing that did not make you happy was stuff. I had never been that kind of person, preferring old things, second-hand things, upcycled and recycled things, and this was before I chose this lifestyle as a way to do my bit for our declining environment, but suddenly it seemed obvious to me; in this regard I had always run my own race.

So why was it that my weight and ageing seemed different from this? Why was I so desperate to be accepted, to be one of the herd? To conform? I had learned to set my own beauty standard and be confident in those choices. I knew I didn't need breast enhancement, or to have a surgically enhanced face, a taut chin or even lipo on my lumps. I had come to that conclusion when I tried to turn the clock back with Botox and fillers and hair extensions while my son's life hung in the balance, putting it all in perspective. I now needed to apply the same logic to my food consumption.

My heart lifted and my spirit soared when I realised I was looking at things the wrong way. It wasn't about trying to change my body; it was about changing the way I *thought* about my body. This was the start of my awakening, and this is what changed *everything* for me.

I went back to basics, trying to understand how eating, drinking and expelling waste is how we all function, so why does it matter so much if some people are leaner and some are fatter? It struck me as odd that in this golden age of diversity and acceptance, where inclusion and reminders to choose 'kindness' are flung out as often as I used to dip my hand in the bread bin, how was it that a layer of fat sitting beneath a person's skin could invoke such strong reactions and opinions? And yet, trust me, the difference in attitude to those who are slim and assumed 'fit' and those who are fat and assumed 'unfit' is really staggering. And it massively affected how I viewed myself, but why? *Why* was I so keen to listen to the opinion of others on this but not in any other area of my life? It didn't make sense. Again, I reminded myself that in the circle of weight – there is but a narrow line where fat and thin meet – why, why oh why, do we have such different language, tolerances and socially acceptable standards for both groups? I figured that maybe I could not change the attitude of society, but I could change my own attitude. And this struck me as a very good place to start.

It was like giving myself permission to change. And for someone who has never battled with overeating, I can see that this concept might be hard to comprehend, comical even, that it has taken until my fifties for me to grasp this most basic of principles, and it bears repeating as it is core to successful weight loss:

I *can* change my relationship with food, and I *can* only eat what my body needs and no more!

But trust me when I tell you that it is one of the hardest battles I have ever undertaken.

So, I guess the big question is, HOW to rid myself of the obsession, how to overcome my addiction?

And the easy answer is *gently*.

Chapter Seventeen

'ALL CHANGE PLEASE! ALL CHANGE!'

So, here I am in my mid-fifties, with book twenty-six, *An Ordinary Life*, and book twenty-seven, *Waiting to Begin*, and by the time this goes to print, my twenty-eighth novel will be out, *To Love and Be Loved*. Turns out Mrs Blight was right, I couldn't write a book, but I might just write fifty or a hundred – who knows? My filing cabinets are still full to bursting with characters and plots rattling to be let out.

Lifestyle change for me started in earnest when I figured out that what Simeon had said was right, I needed to:

Do it in a way that worked for me. And I needed to go gently.

Pace was key. Not setting myself up for a fall when there was the chance I might fail to meet a self-imposed deadline. I ordered my thoughts. Having lived in a mental state of high panic over my weight, with thoughts racing over how to fix it for so long, the first thing I needed to do was breathe and slow down. Instead of rushing headlong into solution mode, doing a quick internet search to see which was the most popular diet and running with that as my latest quest, I took my time, figuring out how to go forward. And strangely my immediate goal was not to lose weight, but to calm down my thoughts, and to try and weaken the grip of addiction that drove my actions, my obsession with food.

My default setting had always been to believe the hype, especially with any get-thin-quick diet or any potion or pill that promised a flat tum and skinny bum with no effort at all. The dieting nirvana! And we all know how those ventures had ended. No, this time it had to be different. It was as much, if not more, about mindset as action. I had to own up to the sadness that lurked in my stomach and which I tried to smother with cheese. I knew that every time I felt sad or stressed I reached for food as if it were a comforter. I decided to treat my healing, my recovery if you like, as a project.

For want of knowing how else to start, the first thing I did was buy a notebook. As any fellow stationery lover knows, every good project, hobby, idea or distraction starts with the buying of a notebook!

It's my bible where I write words of inspiration, positive affirmations, recipes, observations, ideas, anything that might help me sort through my jumbled thoughts. The great 'how to stop a woman like me overeating and raise my self-esteem' project was a bit like building a jigsaw puzzle but doing so in the dark and without the printed box in front of me. I have to feel my way, see what fits and then lock behaviours and thoughts in, until what I have is a complete strategy, a roadmap, if you like, that I now keep in my mind. It guides me, it shapes my decision-making, it keeps me on track, and it has its very own filing cabinet.

My notebook has become a handy tool. There are no rules – what I write doesn't have to be structured or dated or even neat – it just has to be 'open' and 'honest', the exact words in fact that I have used throughout this book to help initiate the frank discussions around weight and beauty, and I believe that's how we move the debate, and in turn self-esteem, in the right direction.

By writing down my thoughts, it helped me be kinder to myself, steering my internal monologue so that I was less self-critical, using positive, caring, softer words and not berating myself if I was feeling low, which would have ordinarily sent me straight into the arms of a packet of biscuits.

And yes, I might have a bent nose, wrinkles, thinning lips and brows, and the hint of a tache, but again this phrase: why did it *matter*? Who was it important to if it wasn't important to me? Why had I let it become an issue?

As part of my going gently approach, I began to talk more kindly to myself, out loud too. I stopped telling myself I was a greedy cow and using negative, harmful words that stuck. Instead, I started to see myself as a flawed, imperfect human, just like every other who walked the planet.

This encouraging dialogue was bolstering and effective. I listened to the words and accepted them just as much as I had the negative ones – I chose positivity! Accepting that I was never going to be confident one hundred per cent of the time was huge. Knowing I wouldn't munch solely on kale and lentils, I would fail, fall off the wagon, and that was okay. It didn't have to mean the end of my health journey but was instead a chance to set the behaviour pattern of getting up, dusting myself down and continuing.

Understanding my mindset and how I had let my weight run away from me in the way it had would be crucial in helping make sure it didn't happen again. It was a fundamental part of breaking the cycle. Change is hard when habits, behaviours and the psychological reasons behind them are entrenched. But it was of course vital if I was going to alter both the way my body looked and the way I thought about my body. I was drawn to the old adage, if you always do what you've always done, then you'll always get what you've always got – right?

I might not have had all the answers, but it became clear that a lot, if not all, of my low self-esteem came from the dreadful and futile preoccupation that is comparison to others. It had been a preoccupation for much of my teen and adult life, watching the popular girls at school with their cool air and marvelling at their enigmatic qualities, staring at graceful women on the dance floor of nightclubs as I clodhopped around to the beat, and looking at the other mums at the school gates and noticing they were not chunky like me.

Speaking personally, this desire, nay pressure, to 'keep up' and to 'be a slender, groomed, wrinkle-free achiever' has done nothing to aid my mental health. It makes my anxiety rocket when I can't resist comparison between myself and those who seem to not only *have it all* but also *do it all* AND achieve both without a lock out of place, a smile on their face, a pert bottom and, with their left hand, manage to whip up an organic vegan tagine for the family, while recommending the perfect shade of Farrow & Ball paint to compliment dessert. (Not that there's anything wrong with a bit of Farrow & Ball – my home is an ode to Dead Salmon!) But that aside, is it any wonder my sense of inadequacy used to rise in direct proportion to each wrinkle and ounce I gained? Each of my efforts that failed? Each time I was too knackered to cook from scratch/go to the gym/shave my legs/socialise/have sex? And in the past when I have failed at these tasks, the tendency has been to rush into the arms of some salt and vinegar Pringles or a multipack of KitKats. This had to stop! And I began to question whether I am the only one who (much of the time) feels like life is a sticky pond of treacle through which I wade – praying that if and when I make it to the other side, the best I can hope for is that I've not lost a flip-flop en route?

Why did I compare myself? It did nothing to help me. And it wasn't as if I disliked these achieving, disciplined women, far from it, it was more about how I disliked something in myself. It was the worst kind of self-sabotage, the constant questioning in any public arena:

Am I the fattest person in this queue?

Am I the widest on this bus?

Oh God, I have the biggest boobs in the room!

This was the constant hammering on my head with a large mallet that I alone had crafted, until I sank further down and down, wanting, I suspect, to become flat and melt away into the ground unseen, like a puddle, but that of course didn't happen.

Understanding that I did this and how damaging it was, helped me come up with a way of combating it. Instead of looking at other women and other men and marvelling at how they looked, seemed, behaved, I decided instead to emulate them, to learn some of the attributes that meant they had their weight, at least, under control, but seeing their behaviours as a 'template' rather than a mirror in which I would compare unfavourably. I applied this particularly to women I knew and respected who did not battle with weight or their self-esteem, friends who ate slowly, ate small and often, friends who indulged in wine and pizza when they felt the need and who laughed as they walked all the way home, *guilt free*!

This strategy is a well-known business tactic and much has been written about copying the successful habits of the super-rich/system-thinkers/Olympians/entrepreneurs. Could part of cracking the code for me be as simple as emulating the habits of slim people? I figured I could give it a go, in the hope that it might help address that inner voice of self-sabotage that had constantly pulled me off track in the past.

Understanding that the people I wanted to emulate, people I thought might have it sussed and the slim ones who exuded confidence, were not actually super-powered was key. They failed too! They had good days and bad days with their diet, had days when they felt pants about some aspect of themselves physically and that was fine. Again, it's that flawed, imperfect human thing.

In this day and age, I am also acutely aware that sometimes those with the biggest smiles and loudest voices might just be hiding sadness or insecurities way beyond my own. We all wear masks, right? There are too many faces of the young and beautiful who have been lost to mental health battles, photographed beaming for the camera.

Only a couple of years ago I was at the BBC, standing in the green room waiting to go on the radio, feeling sick to my stomach, as if I wasn't worthy because, despite my success, I didn't feel like I deserved to be on the bill with other authors because they must be smart, and I must be, what? *Lucky?* This is a fine example of my own interior monologue belittling my commitment to write and the skill involved in crafting not one, but thirty-odd novels and the hours and hours spent sitting at my laptop, honing my craft and trying with every sentence to improve . . .

It was while I stood and tried to control my shaking limbs and fight the desire to throw up that I met a foreign author, a bestseller, and we chatted while waiting outside the studio. She asked me what I was working on and, a little awestruck, I rather vaguely mumbled the outline of my next book, concerned that she might in some way think I was taking any success for granted or worse that I might rank myself alongside someone like her! The thought alone was mortifying.

'Is it any good?' she asked.

'Erm . . .' I didn't know how to answer, how to strike the right balance between doing my characters justice, characters I had spent months with and had grown to love, while not appearing arrogant. 'Well, *I* love it. I love the lead character, her name is Victoria or Victory, she has two names really . . .' I began and waffled until I ran out of words. She listened and turned to me before disappearing inside the studio and said, 'I love how you talk about your book. I always think my last book is my only good one and the one about to come out is absolute crap!'

I could have kissed her.

The next part of my project fell into my lap almost by accident. I don't recall the exact day but remember the time of year; it was cold and wintry. Having been working on gaining control of my weight for a couple of weeks, I leant on the countertop, waiting for the kettle to boil and only half listening, when I caught the tail end of an interview on the radio and heard an athlete who was talking about the uncertainty of the Tokyo Olympics. He was asked how he stayed motivated, trained and got in the winning mindset, not knowing when his moment on the international stage would come, or if indeed it would come at all.

His answer, only heard as the kettle rattled to its crescendo and the gurgle of boiling water died down, was 'I don't think about that moment. I don't think about winning. I don't think about medals. I get up, I do what I've got to do every day and I trust the process and if I get it right, I win.'

I wish I knew who had said it; I wish I'd paid more attention. I drank my coffee with the words percolating in my thoughts. I ate breakfast, wrote for an hour or two, and still his calm tone and his method lingered in my mind, nudging all other thoughts out of the way. They were persistent. It was as I soaked in the bath before bedtime that I had a moment of clarity, an epiphany if you like: I was going to train for the next Olympics! No, of course I wasn't, but I *was* going to explore what 'trust the process' actually meant as I began to wonder if it might work as a strategy for me, enabling me to get my life on track. It seemed to fit with the 'go gently and calmly' philosophy I was trying to adopt. Maybe, just maybe, if I could trust the process that led me away from food obsession and concentrate on it every day, it might be the answer I was looking for.

It was a crucial part in a jigsaw that would see a whole new picture emerge, once I had figured out the rest, but it was an important piece. And not only was it a concept that would take on greater significance, more importantly, it was reaffirming that all I had to do was figure out what worked for me and that the wall I had built might be able to come down. I began to think it was *possible* for the wall to come down.

'*Trust the Process*' is, I researched, a slogan used by fans of the NBA's Philadelphia 76ers, but now in wide use. It's the idea that you do the small things without worrying so much about the bigger picture or even the goal, then before you know it you're making progress and can even win! Like taking a thousand small steps every day until one day you look up and you are at your desired destination, which for me was living a life where food didn't bookend my every waking thought and where I didn't turn to food as the cure for everything from stress, tiredness, headaches, regret, fatigue, you name it. I liked the concept and could relate to it.

After further thought, I managed to distil my project down to two main facets that needed investigation, understanding and overhauling.

WHAT I ATE.

WHY I ATE.

And one of the first things I did was to start reframing the way I looked at food, breaking it down to something as simple (and I needed to keep it simple!) as looking at what I put into my body every day. Simeon a soldier, Ben a qualified Army PT and Josh who was way ahead of me and has, as an aid to his depression, taken control of his diet and fitness with startling results – were all adamant that food was fuel and if I used it right, it would benefit my working body. I noted that they ate anything and everything (in moderation) and all are fit and healthy.

This really made me think. Throughout my life, I had always mentally divided food into two categories. GOOD food: salad, vegetables, thin soups, beans, legumes, nuts, fruit, pulses, stuff I didn't really fancy eating or know how to cook. And BAD food: all the man-made, processed, sugar- and fat-laden, sweet and or crunchy, chewy stuff that I loved to eat – from bread to biccies, from lardy cake to liquorice, crisps to crackling and everything in between! BAD. BAD. BAD. All of it! And putting it in my body made me feel BAD. It made me look BAD. And in my head it made me a BAD person. Or so I thought.

But of course, there is no such thing as GOOD or BAD food: there is only food, and what you choose and how much of it you put in your gob is what counts. This helped me enormously, understanding that it wasn't dynamite or cyanide, it was just food! And by rebranding all food as 'food' so that none of it was bad or disallowed or banned, helped me not to crave it. The theory being I could have it if I wanted to and the one thing that has rung true throughout my life is that if someone tells me I can't have it or I can't do it – then I almost want to prove that I can. When applying this to getting a book finished and published it is a positive trait, but when it comes to filling my stomach with whipped cream or pickled-onion-flavoured Monster Munch, not so much.

I think this constant defining of what was good food and bad food has been damaging my whole life. Another brick in that wall. It not only meant my sugar intake would spike and affect me physically, but I was filled with a lingering guilt that affected my whole mood and would make me hypersensitive to criticism and ultimately sent me in search of something to plug that gap, that feeling . . . more bad food! Put simply, I felt as if I wasn't worthy of praise or anything positive because I had shoved shit into my body;

336

it counteracted all and any achievements, even having a string of bestsellers.

I made a change in my mindset that if I 'messed up' on a diet and ate something I considered 'bad', that did not mean I had to self-flagellate with the consumption of more and more calories until I felt sick. It was about learning what a balanced diet meant and that moderation was key.

Part of this was getting into a routine that meant I took food when I needed it and not when I wanted it. Looking at everyone I knew who lived without the obsession that has dogged my life, I tried to mimic how they thought about food, how they acted around food and the choices they made.

And then something struck me: I didn't *need* to mimic them, quiz them, learn from them because I was already like that when it came to other aspects of my life. This wasn't something I had to *learn*; I already had this skill set somewhere! It had simply gone haywire when it came to eating. All I had to do was rewire and remember how I dealt with:

Showering – do it twice a day – enjoyable and refreshing, but when not in the shower I barely gave it a second thought

Drinking tea – a nice hiatus to a busy day, I like the ritual of choosing a cup, watching it brew while my thoughts swirl

Driving – necessary to get from A to B, pleasant to be on the open road with my music on, a safe place to swear

Sleeping – I LOVE my sleepy time! I look forward to it, prepare for it, am very good at it, enjoy it and get to do it for eight straight hours a night – lovely

Eating – THINK ABOUT IT EVERY SECOND OF EVERY DAY, PLAN IT, MISS IT, LONG FOR IT, WORRY ABOUT IT, PICTURE IT, OVERDO IT, FEEL GUILTY ABOUT IT, OBSESS ABOUT IT, WAKE UP AND REPEAT, WTAF?

So, there it was; all I had to do was relegate my eating to the way I thought about every other mundane aspect of my life. I needed to learn to eat to live not live to eat. It sounded easy . . . Ha! If it was so easy, Mandy, why hadn't you done it years ago? I needed to think very carefully about every aspect of my life and all the traits and habits that I utilised for all those tasks and chores that got me through the day and transfer them to the way I thought about food. I needed to help my brain remember what it felt like to live a life where food was not an obsession, or rather, I needed to help my brain *forget* that food was an obsession.

It's not only what I ate that had to change but *how* I ate – part of my new strategy is to consume one bite at a time. I figured quite early on in my journey that it was impossible for me to hold in my head the huge task that was required for me to get back to health: 3 stone, 4 stone, 5 stone, 6 stone (42 lb, 56 lb, 70 lb, 84 lb) to lose or more. When the scales were at best going to creep a little to the left on a weekly basis, how was I going to stay motivated? I needed to rethink how I tackled every day and put in place a plan for making a difference that would stop me from feeling overwhelmed by the task.

In the past, as you know, I had starved myself, often consuming nothing or very, very little, which fed the starvation/discomfort/give up/overeat/self-loathing cycle. But once I figured out that I didn't have to lose weight quickly or impressively or noticeably or publicly, as it wasn't as if I was doing this for anyone other than myself, it became obvious. I just needed to eat a bit less and then a bit less and then a bit less, training my stomach and my mind to consume a smaller amount, less than I needed and was expelling and therefore . . . I lost weight. A little at first, in fact a little every day, but just like with a loo roll, and yes, I am comparing myself to a loo roll, when the first sheet is taken it still looks plump and full, but one sheet a day and before you know it you are looking at a skinny tube that no one else in the house seems to know how to replace, but I digress.

My one-bite strategy meant literally thinking no further ahead than the next bite. TRUSTING THE PROCESS. It meant taking deep, slow breaths, calming my thoughts until they became centred and not mentally racing ahead or worrying about where I might be in a month, six months, a year. *How fast was I losing? How did I look? Could I see a difference? How much would I have lost by the time I had to go to that event? Work on that show?* It meant not thinking about the number I needed to reach on the scales, about going gently and not focusing on it. All I had to do was think about the next bite I was going to take. No more than that. And to make a good choice for every bite, mindfully. Every single time. Today is all that matters, not tomorrow or the day after that, just today, that's all there is.

Making good food choices some of the time, then most of the time, then all of the time became second nature. And it wasn't only about choosing to take a bite of something that would benefit my health rather than hinder it, but it was also about when I ate and how I ate. I made a conscious decision not to eat late at night but instead try to leave a minimum of twelve hours between my supper and my breakfast, allowing my digestive system to rest and my body to use up fat reserves while it waited for its next meal. This instead of scoffing snacks until bedtime, and never giving my system a chance to reset.

I used to eat very quickly, partly out of shame, partly greed and also to get the whole lot scoffed without being seen. Eating quickly didn't allow the food to be properly tasted or digested, how could it? My stomach must have thought it was at the end of a rubbish chute with grub constantly tumbling into it while it stretched and worked hard to break it down and keep up.

I began to eat slowly, mindfully, allowing my fullness to register, rather than eating so quickly my body was full to the brim before it had a chance to put up its hand and say, enough for now, thanks! My body responded well and responded quickly to these changes. I was less gassy, less bloated, more mentally agile and I slept better.

So, do I always make a good healthy choice for every single bite? NO! You can take me to any number of fancy-pants restaurants whose menus burst with things I've never heard of and I am too scared to ask about and I will carefully pick out veggies and salad and sometimes fish, but nothing, nothing tastes as good on a cold winter's night as a hot chip slathered in salt and vinegar nicked from someone else's chip bag, and I would choose that every time! But doing that on the odd occasion is not gorging on large fish and chips with curry sauce once or twice a week – and therefore I don't sweat it or berate myself and it certainly doesn't trigger a binge session because I have 'broken' my diet. Balance.

I also began weighing myself once a week. Yes! I jump on the scales! This is something I had to force myself to do in the beginning. I had feared scales and the number it would reveal for so much of my life, but that was the whole point. If I didn't address the number on the dial, didn't accept and make a note of my weight, how was I going to a) measure my success and b) get over the fear of doing so. It was time to pull on my big girl pants and face this sucker.

I stepped gingerly onto the scales before immediately hopping off again so that I could replace the batteries, as they were clearly faulty. I then moved them to various different floor surfaces in different rooms, testing them on linoleum, carpet, flagstones and even grass, but still I kept getting the same darn result! I wondered where the fault could lie if it wasn't the batteries, because there was no way I could weigh that much! But I did.

It wasn't a great feeling. In fact, it was a horrible feeling. To see the number ratchet up to a shade over 20 stone or 280 lb was mortifying, but it was also a moment to be proud. Not at the figure or how my out-of-control eating had reached this crescendo, but at the fact that I was facing it all, conquering my fear, stating my weight out loud right here to you, a stranger!

By weighing myself weekly it gives me a break point in the ongoing change in my lifestyle. I can feel my progress by the loosening of my clothes, the ease of mobility, the freeing up of my joints and the general improvement in just about every aspect of my health, but this weekly hop onto the scale is no bad thing as a means of keeping a physical record.

And as ridiculous as it sounds, it helps keep me on the right track. For the first time in as long as I can remember, it isn't about losing weight for anyone else, it isn't about achieving a particular number in a particular time frame, none of that pressure – it's about a simple ritual with the scales (every Monday morning in case you were interested) and it's something I do for me. Some Mondays I have lost a few pounds, on others a little less than one pound, and that's okay. And if on the odd week the figure stays stagnant or I even gain a little, that's fine too, because it's not about a small window of opportunity in which I have to succeed or fail, it's about a long-term strategy. A new way of life. I am in this for the long haul.

I also decided that if I was going to fully understand how and what to eat, I needed to know how to prepare food and, much to the joy of my family, I have learned to cook. This has been absolutely key for me. I used to dislike spending time in the kitchen and would instead reach for ready meals, takeaways, toast, snacks, jars of sauce or anything that was quick and easy to shove into the microwave or down our throats. These foods tended to be high in salt, fat and sugar and low on fibre and nutrition. *MasterChef* and the *Great British Menu* have always been my guilty pleasures on

TV, but now I watch as much to glean tips and copy recipes as I do for the enjoyment of watching. I realised I was a bad cook when the threat 'go to bed now and turn out the lights or tomorrow I will cook your tea!' was the only thing to get my kids up the stairs on time when they were little. 'Please, Mum! No! Don't do that!'

In the past, my enthusiasm to feed my family was never hampered by my lack of ability – and they bear witness to the unpalatable disasters that I am still reminded of on an almost weekly basis. These include:

Misreading a recipe for crushed spuds and adding two tablespoons of salt instead of teaspoons – who knew there was such a difference between tsp and tbsp? Not me, clearly. Anyhoo, the end result was a polite Simeon, newly coupled with me and not wanting to offend, vomiting violently after swallowing more salt than a drunk sailor who's fallen open-mouthed into the briny. I continue to apologise for trying to follow a recipe without my goggles on.

Proudly presenting my kids with chicken Kiev and chips – only for ten-year-old Josh, halfway through his supper to ask, 'Is my chicken supposed to be frozen in the middle?' I yanked that bird out of his gnashers quicker than you could holler salmonella! Thankfully no damage was done, other than leaving our youngest with a distinct dislike for chicken Kiev and a distinct suspicion of anything I have cooked since.

Trying to be different and put my twist on a trifle, I made one with grapefruit, lemon and lime, which was bitter, cheek-suckingly sour and provided the food bin with enough calories to keep it going through winter.

And no one in my family is keen to let me forget my fish pie – made by my teenage self with bone-filled kippers and very, very lumpy mash. And I remembered you were supposed to put an egg in it, but not that you had to boil it, cracking raw eggs over the crunchy pungent fish. The result was . . . I can't even go there, but it wasn't pretty.

That, however, is all in the past and things changed when I invested in a collection of second-hand cookbooks – some had never been used, others were well thumbed, but all opened up a world that I had hitherto been ignorant of. I was drawn by the stunning photography, a rainbow of food from cuisines all around the world and, even better, step-by-step instructions on how to cook rice, prep vegetables, sear meat, roast spuds, prepare a salad, knock up a soup, fry a noodle, produce a sauce or bake a cake – who knew? It was wonderful and made me wish I'd spent more time at my nan's hip, learning her skills. I pore over the cookbooks, running my fingers over the recipes, devouring the glorious images and learning what I can. And surprisingly, I've learned quite a lot. I feel excited at the prospect of preparing food from scratch instead of dreading it. Taking an interest in the food I buy, cook and eat has given me a much more holistic view and I don't think I will ever stop learning.

Now, I am never going to be the new Nigella, but I *can* cook! Or more accurately, I can cook enough that it means I don't need to reach for a packet. Cooking has given me confidence and has made all the difference in my food journey; it has helped me understand the value and nutrition of food and to respect it a little bit more. Me, cooking from scratch, who would have thought it? And while I confess my repertoire is not massive, it's growing daily! I like nothing more than preparing food with no more than a few ingredients and watching my family give me the thumbs up as they chow down, rather than the prodding of the protein sitting alongside a grey/cream/tinned slop and asking rather sheepishly, 'What *is* this, Mum?' that I used to get a lot. The more I understand food, what is in food, how and where it's grown, what certain foods do to your body and how they can affect everything from your skin to your mood, the better my diet becomes. I even own a pinny. My great-nan would be very proud, although her legendary stews are still something I can only aspire to. And my nan's apple pie? It'll take some years.

It wasn't a surprise for me to hear from a sportswoman how her diet was scientifically formulated for optimum performance when she was training – where food was bespoke fuel, with meals devised for her personally. Not that she didn't thoroughly enjoy the down days or holidays when she could eat what she wanted. I told her of my weight battles, and she spoke matter-of-factly. 'For me it's simple, and I know it's not easy for everyone, but as a rule, regardless of your exercise regimen, if you are consuming as little as an extra 50 calories a day over what your body requires – which over a month is about 1,500 and over a year 18,000, which is well over a week's worth of *extra* food, then you are going to gain weight, and to lose weight you reverse the sum. Energy in. Energy out.'

An extra week's worth of food? The thought made my head go cold. That was if you ate an extra 50 calories a day. I had been consuming so much more than that, *extra*. I felt sick. It was no surprise I had reached the state I had physically. It really made me think. The suggested daily calorie intake for the average woman is 2,000, and 2,500 for a man (although this has many variables and is open to debate). The extra 50 calories a day or whopping 18,000 calories a year, roughly equates to an extra 5 lb in weight – or roughly 2.3 kg – which if you did that for five years without burning it off, gives you an extra 25 lb or 11.5 kg and all from a mere extra 50 calories. So, what constitutes 50 calories? It may surprise you. Approximately:

Ten olives
Two marshmallows
One ginger nut biscuit

Nearly all of the above I've consumed by the handful in between meals or simply because I was hovering near the fridge. There are of course many, many varying factors affecting an individual's food consumption and their ability to burn calories and store or lose fat, but stay with me for the purpose of this example.

The capacity of the average-sized stomach in a healthy adult is about a litre. To understand by how much I was overeating, it helped massively for me to picture a litre bottle and think about it being full of . . . pasta . . . fruit . . . chocolate . . . whatever. I then imagined trying to cram more food into it – slices of thickly buttered toast, pizza, chips, a slack handful of biscuits – that bottle is groaning, fit to pop! Once I was able to make the visual connection between the size of my stomach and it being full with far, far less than I was stuffing into it every day, it made a huge difference to my mental association with the volume of food I was consuming.

I was beginning to understand the mechanics of weight loss and what I needed to address, but what about my addiction? Knowing these things and being able to act upon them are two very different things. Ask any reformed addict.

Okay, so in the spirit of honesty, I want to make a rare confession: on some days when I wake up full of the joys of spring and pop my jeans on with a shirt tucked in and a belt fastened at my waist, instead of being concerned with hiding my bum and thighs under a tent-like sweatshirt over stretchy leggings and have dragged a brush through my hair, eaten my porridge and am poised, ready for action . . . I have on occasion wished that I was still living the fat life.

Now, I know that's not what I *should* be suggesting or even confessing to, but, ye gods, you, dear reader, having read thus far even know about my toilet habits and the network of unsightly scars on my nether regions! What is a confession like this between friends? But it's true, there are some days when I am eating well and prancing around the place like a show pony who has just won a rosette, feeling very pleased with myself and liking the swish of my glossy mane and my not so jiggly legs and the fact that I can once again canter and am setting a good example to all . . . when I think how nice it would be, just for a day, to go back to the me who ate junk, fell into a food coma and slept. A bit like on Christmas Day.

The trouble was of course it was Christmas Day every day for me, but one without presents, tinsel, *Elf* on the telly and marginally fewer relatives clustered on the sofa snaffling through the Quality Street tin. And I think it's an important point that my desire to overeat and the way my addiction will prod me with a stick when my resistance is low means that I need to make effort to eat healthily and with balance every single day. Forever. It's not that the desire to overeat has disappeared entirely, I wish it had, but rather that I have put the genie in the bottle and have gaffer-taped the stopper in with a ring of superglue around the lid for good measure.

I have also changed what I eat, adopting a strategy to, as far as possible, eat things that are seasonally grown and very little that is processed. This, however, is a rule of thumb and not the law! As a consequence, eating wholesome, fresh things, I feel fuller for longer and without the sugar spike and subsequent low after eating chocolate, which I would try to combat with snacking. Simeon and the boys have benefitted too. They like the fact that I am cooking more and that meals are filling, and no one has to larder-dive to fill a hunger gap. My relaxed attitude to food has made all the difference to my thoughts surrounding it.

Something quite unexpected happened to me within a few short months of starting my new eating regimen. I began to view some of the food I had previously chosen to eat as unattractive. I used to crave butter and fried things and all manner of other highly calorific, but nutritionally vapid foods. But once I had made the switch to consuming wholesome, fresh food, I didn't want to put the empty calories into my body. And because what I was eating was nutritious and vitamin laden, packed with all the stuff my immune system, lymphatic system, digestive system, reproductive system and nervous system thrived on – my skin started to glow, my hair shone and even my eyesight improved! I shit you not!

And this boost to the way I looked and felt made me even more reluctant to reach for the family-sized packet of crisps late at night that had previously been my go-to. Instead, I reach for my husband, wanting to feel his skin next to mine, wanting us to reconnect in the way that had been missing for so long. Which, as a consequence has been pretty fantastic. We are closer, we are happier, and I like how he always kisses me good night and always makes me a cup of tea in the morning. This, I *know*, is real love. I began to fully understand the statement 'you are what you eat', and when I look in the mirror, I realise that what I'm now eating must be sexy and fabulous!

Part of the mental overhaul of my eating habits was accepting hunger: I could not stand to be hungry, who can? And this might sound like something obvious or even amusing, but accepting hunger is a fundamental part of my change in lifestyle and habit. No one likes to be hungry. Of course they don't. But when you've been an overeater for more years than you care to remember, hunger is something that is unfamiliar.

When I embarked on any new diet, which during my 'decade of diets' was done with regularity, the hunger, which would kick in fairly quickly, was almost more than I could stand. It would put me in a low mood, and I even felt waves of aggression when food was being denied to me, and my stomach growled, and my head ached, and my blood sugar was low. I felt resentful of anyone who was eating and missed the habit of eating. Grinding my teeth, my thoughts would go wild, obsessing even more, if that was possible, about what lurked in the kitchen cupboards.

Hunger is something I needed to get used to for two main reasons. First, as an obvious indicator that my body wants or needs sustenance, and this would, unsurprisingly, become the trigger for me to eat, rather than eating 'anyway', 'just in case' or because something was 'available' or simply 'within reach'. As a consummate failed dieter, I can tell you the hardest part of any diet was the hunger, and it was this uncomfortable sensation that caused me to give up and give in to that feeling. Making friends with my hunger and not dreading it was a huge step in beating overeating. I now eat when I am *hungry*. And it's a revelation. The first few days of any 'diet' were always the hardest. It wasn't only the gnawing hunger, but also my body crying out for the sugar and carbs that it had got used to.

Here's how I cracked it.

Still with the 'go at my own pace, go gently' philosophy at the fore of my mind, I knew it didn't work for me to go 'cold turkey' and jump from mega-portions to tiny ones in a twenty-four-hour period – simply announcing to my body, 'This is my latest fad! Get used to it, sucker!', as that was when the hunger and irritability kicked in for me. I'm not happy to admit that for me, this was just too hard. It felt like a battle I was not going to win.

This time it had to be different. I cut down my portion sizes, but also in those first few weeks, no food was off limits. This meant I did not have to deal with cravings or the irritable side effect of denial, but it did mean I got used to eating less of everything I *liked* to eat. I had one slice of toast instead of three, one packet of crisps instead of four and one bowl of sugary cereal instead of two; you get the idea.

Weeks three and four, still on reduced portion sizes, but still free eating, I made small changes, like swapping butter for sunflower spread, cutting out biscuits, and substituting whole milk for sugar-free almond milk.

Weeks five and six, still able to eat small amounts of anything I wanted, I changed what I ate for my main meals. Instead of fish fingers and chips, I made a big hearty vegetable soup with pearl barley and followed it up with a square of chocolate, not a bar. For breakfast I had porridge made with the almond milk and blueberries, instead of toast.

And after six weeks of this gentle phasing in, I was ready for my lifestyle change. My palate had changed a little, my stomach had shrunk a little and I was motivated, having lost another 10 lb, just by cutting down and cutting back and making the smallest of changes. It was a start and one where hunger had not lashed out and kicked me off course with its forceful foot.

Diets I had tried in the past made promises that I could drop X number of dress sizes in X number of weeks or that I could lose X pounds in X days. But not only are these promises hard to bring to fruition, when I failed, buckling under the self-imposed pressure to achieve in such a restricted time frame, my motivation to try again would be non-existent, my mood lower than it was when I started and my weight unchanged or, worse, heavier.

This gently and slowly approach works for me.

After the initial six-week phase, I made more drastic changes, deciding for the next month to cut out chocolate, sugar, processed food, cakes, white bread and takeaways. And for the first couple of days, I did feel a little hungrier, but here's the good news. It didn't last very long. On day three things took a dramatic turn when I wasn't aware of any roaring hunger, just the normal knowing it was time to eat 'reminders' that my body heralded – that's all it took to break my fear of hunger. And while the hunger might have been slightly uncomfortable, it was nothing compared to the surge that I would have felt before cutting back, cutting down and phasing my eating over the previous six weeks. And having been through the reducing of portions and the changing of food groups, it meant that when the hunger did come, I was not only in a better place to deal with it physically, but emotionally too; I had been 'on track' for six weeks, which in itself was some achievement.

I then set my sights on eating around 2,000 calories a day for a month and portioned my day's food intake into small meals that I could eat with regularity, and it really helped. For example, on one day I batch prepared a tasty sweet potato, lentil and quinoa salad, packed full of beets, onion, tomatoes, cucumber, walnuts, seeds and a zingy citrus dressing and divided it up into six portions. It made it easy to reach for something pre-prepped and it tasted great. On another day I made a fantastic spicy vegetable curry with couscous. A ripple of hunger might come over me, but it felt like I was always just about due another portion from the fridge. I found drinking water regularly and upping my fluid intake also helped fill me up and got me past it.

What came next after this month of calorie restriction and healthier eating, which for me was usually the point at which I abandoned my 'diet', was to structure my food intake so that I always knew what I had to eat the next day, and by carefully planning my meals, snacks and meal prep, it kept the temptation to fill a hunger gap with a biscuit or similar at bay. The secret for me was eating *enough* food. And this was where the question of whether all calories are equal came into the fore. Yes, I could have had one Mars bar but would have been hungry a short time later, but with the equivalent in bulgur wheat? I was fuller for longer. My stomach continued to shrink so I needed less food and after a month of eating this way, I adapted to the new routine and taste.

Very quickly, I noticed that sometimes there were spare portions of food in the fridge, as I hadn't been hungry and didn't want them. This was a revelation to me. After a further month of this controlled eating, I stopped counting calories. I didn't need to. I didn't *want* to. I had always been an intuitive eater – eating what I wanted when I wanted – and this was no different, but now what

I *wanted* was healthy, nutritious food that made me feel good! I do not count calories and I do not now restrict when I eat or what I eat BUT I only eat when I am hungry and I do my best to make a good choice. I am free from the shackles of dieting and more crucially I am not obsessed with food or food groups.

When I stopped counting calories and switched to 'free' eating, on one day, I chose to eat a bag of crisps and a slice of toast. The second week, I chose a slice of toast – but they didn't make me feel good. Now, I might have the odd brownie or some hummus or a couple of squares of dark chocolate but I really, really don't want to put things that are overly sugary or fatty into my body. I just don't want to do it! And that is something I never thought I would say or feel. And I have to say it feels bloody brilliant. I have more energy. I am happier. I feel more confident in my body and am free of the shame of being shackled to the fridge. And it's a positive cycle: the better I feel, the more confident I am, the more I want to experience, the more active I am. Heck, we've even booked a holiday!

My Simeon and me.

Chapter Eighteen

'New Mindset. New Habits. New Life'

I began to think about my female relatives who had raised and influenced me: smart, busy, strong, fierce women, who got on with life no matter what it threw at them. Their DNA runs through my blood. I am them. No one came to their rescue when poverty, the destruction of war and loss came knocking on their door. They might not have been book smart, but they figured out how to get through and keep the wheels of life turning and they did so with finesse. I am again thinking of my mum's great-aunt, the toilet attendant who went from wiping other people's shit from the toilet rim to wearing her beloved fancy coat and putting on lipstick. And I needed to harness their strength. This was the biggest awakening for me. Realisation that the life I live is in my hands and that if I really want change I can and indeed have to initiate it.

NO ONE ELSE IS GOING TO DO IT FOR ME.

There is no quick cure, no miracle pill, no instant jab, no gain without some small amount of pain or more accurately not pain, but effort. My job is to look after me and to be responsible for me. Sounds obvious, doesn't it? But for the longest time I thought my emotional and physical well-being was down to someone else: my teachers, my friends, my parents, my partner, the universe . . . you name it! As if I was ill-equipped for the task and wanted to hand over responsibility, return to that family bosom where someone was going to make the decisions and wrap me in a warm hug while something hearty simmered in the stock pot.

Yes, sometimes I wanted someone or something else to blame for my weight, because it felt easier – none of it was my fault, beyond my control, and if it was beyond my control then how could I be expected to fix it? But the truth is, despite the curve balls that knock the wind from my chest, the rug pulls that send me crashing to the floor and matters of the heart that leave me shredded with distress: I *am* master of my own destiny, and I need to take control.

Now, this doesn't mean I have to scale great heights or perform legendary acts in order to shine or reach my goal; it means sticking to something, seeing it through. Sometimes, the hardest and bravest thing we can do is remain upright when every fibre of our being is pulling us down. But always, always remember you can live your short, brilliant, glorious life in whatever way you see fit, as long as it works for you. If you are unhappy about a particular aspect of that life, be it weight, as it was in my case, or anything else, you have to *own* it, you have to *understand* it and then you have to figure out how to *change* it.

The buck stops with you.

And the buck stopped with me.

This realisation was empowering and scary in equal measure. It was the first step in self-reliance when it came to my physical and mental health, and that built resilience, which fuelled the confidence needed to absolutely commit to the journey I was about to undertake. It was the difference between being stranded somewhere in a vehicle with a flat tyre, no phone signal and with a growing sense of panic – and knowing how to get the spare tyre out of the trunk, or the puncture kit, and fixing it yourself. I walked taller. I felt quite proud of myself even though I was only just beginning, acquiring useful skills and knowledge, as well as directly addressing the issue of my weight.

I decided to employ a similar strategy that had helped me when I wanted to get my first book published and almost lost count of the number of people who told me it was an *'impossible task'* and that there was no point pursuing it: *'Don't you know how many people want to get a book published?'* and *'It will never happen!'* At that time, I thought about the pessimists, the doubters, the detractors, the ones who scoffed, scorned and mocked. I remembered that feeling in my gut of hopelessness in the face of their derision and I turned it into fuel. It required huge amounts of self-belief to push on in an industry about which I didn't have the first clue and in a swarming sea of competition, learning to ignore every rejection and keep going. It would have been very easy to go with the flow and not bother and this was no different.

As I took a step back and analysed what I ate, it was equally vital, if not more so, to understand my thought process around food, to look at the emotional factors that drove me to eat, to understand WHY I ATE. Ours is a crazy, fast-paced, ever-changing, and hair-pullingly frustrating, achingly beautiful world and did I mention it's fast? It's fast. And yet I realised that sometimes I don't want to live fast. I want to live slowly. Am I the only one who sometimes feels a little adrift? A little outside the inner circle? A little like I have just stepped off a merry-go-round and I'm looking at the crowds, trying to find the exit, and just when I get my bearings, someone shoves me back on and off we go again . . . and food had been my sedative. And when throughout my life, whether it was coping with surgery and isolation in my formative years, trying to support my son as a single mum, nursing my own mum, coping with loss or believing I could, despite all the odds stacked against me, get a book published, I'd always managed to figure out the answers with the help of those who loved me. This was no different. I thought about the advice I would give myself if I was sitting in front of myself and it was this:

'You *have* all the answers, Mandy. You need to unpack your jumbled thoughts, reorganise your emotional filing cabinets! Sort through what bothers you most and put it all back in an ordered way that means you aren't being held back, emotionally and physically, by the tangled net woven of addiction and negativity that has caught you fast.'

And *this* was the start of a huge emotional turnaround for me.

I decided to start with ordering my thoughts.

It's hard when you worry about or obsess over things, which I tend to do; breaking the cycle is not easy. Sometimes I felt I was worrying about so much, the varied topics sat like one amalgamated lump in my thoughts all jostling for position. My weight, my face, are the kids okay? Have I fed the dogs? Did I leave the iron on? Climate change, world peace, the global pandemic, my next book, is there milk in the fridge . . . Now I can see that the melting of the polar ice caps, worldwide disease and whether we had enough of the white stuff for our morning coffee should not be proportionate, but in my head, they were. This was not only tiring, but also made it hard to find a solution for anything – I was never going to be able to tick everything off on my mental 'to do' list if that list looked something like this:

Buy bread

Remove micro plastics from oceans

Post birthday card for Eadie

Try to source habitat for declining Koala population

You get the idea. And in the past when my thoughts felt too tangled, I sought solace, a break if you like, from the constant attempts to manage my worries, in the crunch and bite of food. I decided to apply process to this tangled-thought issue and started by making lists and drawing diagrams. It's almost as if by transferring the mental clutter onto a page I can let it go, like a mental 'to do' list that I write one day at a time. And if it isn't on the list, I actively do my utmost to stop worrying about it. It works. I even put things on the list and cross them through, a physical reminder that it is not on my list to worry about today!

As my brain fog began to clear, no doubt aided by the fact that my eating was slowly coming under control and what I was eating was more nutritious and therefore feeding my brain better, I understood that whatever path you tread, whether it's trying to learn to walk after painful surgery, trying to build a new family with two sometimes reluctant kids, trying to succeed in a relationship, trying to climb the career ladder, smash through that concrete ceiling or lose weight, there are always, always going to be boulders in the way. The trick to succeeding, I figured, is whether you turn back and give up, clamber over them or grab a bloody big drill and cut out a tunnel through which you can walk! I was motivated, determined, and I reached for my bloody big drill.

It's fair to say that I've found greater happiness and peace with age. Remember, I'm in my mid-fifties so these are not the sage words of a worldly, educated octogenarian, but I do think there's something about getting older that brings peace and perspective. Words, comments, failures, the opinions of others, the stresses of life, all things that had the ability to fell my thirty-year-old self and would send the sixteen-year-old me to bed with a hot-water bottle while my mum made me endless cups of tea, offered platitudes, and Simon Le Bon serenaded me from my tape recorder – well, now they barely register. Although, don't get me wrong, there are still some days when all I want is my mum to sit on the edge of my bed and stroke my hair from my forehead. How I loved those days . . .

when it felt like there was nothing a nap, a cuppa and a few kind words from her couldn't fix.

I do, however, have greater acceptance of the things I cannot change and deeper understanding that all my choices have consequences. BUT they are just that: *my choices*.

I've learned a bit about what I value, what I feel is important, and I cringe at my childhood thoughts, believing a spare bedroom or a pair of shoes that were not pork pies might make me happy. I now understand that taking time to figure out what my body needs is vital for my mental and physical health, listening to it and responding accordingly instead of stuffing my face.

If I feel a desire for food when I know I can't possibly be hungry, I step off the treadmill of my own making. These pauses in my day help reset my mind and help keep my food thoughts under control. I literally take a breather. I go outside, I sit quietly and *breathe* and if I can't go outside, I open a window and stick my head out! I understand that I am just like any other animal who needs certain things to thrive and I'm more tolerant of my failings; not berating myself and feeling down about my body, which ironically drove me into the arms of food.

This switch has been my saviour. I give myself permission to do more of the good things that make my day. And those good things vary day to day: it might be taking a warm bath, reading a good book, walking the dogs, spending time with friends, pauses that let me look up and stretch and keep me on track. They, instead of grub, are my reward.

I also now understand the power of talking openly to someone about my weight battles and food issues. It doesn't have to be a therapist or a professional, although that too can be useful. I find talking to a friend, family member, colleague, someone in an online forum – anyone in fact, who is a good ear, can make the biggest difference. I started talking (anonymously) on weight-loss threads and reading others' experiences and it helped. Hearing what others had been through and chatting about my own life has helped me understand that this is not a situation that is unique to me, and I am thankful for that. Knowing how common the issue is makes me feel less ashamed.

Speaking to some successful, athletic, beautiful women about body image I was comforted and interested in the language they used.

'If I'm having a crap day where I feel bad about myself . . .'

'You know those bloated days when you just can't be bothered . . .'

'I feel guilty if I have a blow out, might be alcohol or a massive dessert . . .'

'I am confident in my body, but I have really bad skin, cystic acne and when I get a flare-up, I don't want to go outside, don't want to see anyone . . .'

Their words, tone and demeanour were familiar and yet to look at them on the pages of magazines and to see their pearly-white gnashers on the TV screen – well, I thought they had it licked. Who knows what anyone does after the camera has clicked to capture the moment? Is it possible they too sink under the quilt with a bag of Quavers and a salad cream sandwich?

I reached the point where I had taken control of my eating habits and was losing weight, which seemed to boost every facet of my mental and physical health and I started to wonder if consuming junk food really was that toxic for me. I suppose what I was asking was, would it be okay for me to give in to my addiction once in a while? What would be the harm of having a day like I used to, stuffing my face with all the foods I used to crave, and so I decided to do just that.

I can't pretend the thought of it wasn't exciting, it was. On Boxing Day I'd been following my 'trust the process', 'one good bite at a time' philosophy for twelve weeks and it was incredible how much better I felt and how much weight I had lost – 24 lb. Simeon and the boys had gone skiing for the week; I was up to my neck in work and couldn't possibly get away. I was, however, very happily at home with my pups, a real fire and a book deadline to meet. It was now unusual for us to have so much junk in the house, but it was full of Christmas leftovers – the remnants of a cheese board, half a trifle, fresh bread, boxes of chocolates – and I decided to eat whatever I wanted.

I was shocked at how much my desires and tolerance for certain foods had changed in a little over three months. Prior to my lifestyle change I could have eaten pounds of cheese – buckets of the stuff, as long as it was popped on a cracker or a slice of bread and splattered with spicy chutney. I put some Brie on a cracker and ate it, surprised by how fatty it tasted and how it coated my tongue and teeth in an unpleasant way that I had not noticed before. I liked the taste but was also slightly repulsed by the texture. I ate another and did not want a third – this from a woman who regularly used to scoff a whole Brie over two days.

I switched to cake – cutting a slice from a rainbow cake with buttercream icing between each slice – it looked beautiful. I forked in a mouthful and quite liked the light sponge texture, having not eaten anything like it for quite a while, but it wasn't like food! It disappeared on my tongue without the need to chew and was overly sweet. After consuming nothing but vegetables, pulses, fruit, salad, legumes it felt like something fake that should not be ingested. I don't think the bright colours helped. It was an odd sensation. I again felt mildly repulsed by the thought of it, as if I was eating plastic or toy food. I set the cake aside and grabbed a handful of crisps.

Now, crisps had always been one of my go-to snacks. I loved everything about them: the mouth feel, the strong flavour and the crunch. I put two or three into my mouth and the crunch was wonderful! I really liked the texture and the strong flavour on my tongue. I had definitely missed it, but after one or two I felt like I had a mouthful of salt. I have not given up salt and indeed the use of various smoked salts, sea salt flakes, seaweed salt and flavoured salts has become a mainstay of my cookery. I have learnt that a simple roasted carrot or a panful of Brussels sprouts can be transformed with the stuff, but this feeling in my mouth, the synthetic taste, sharp and overwhelming, was unpleasant. I put the rest of the handful in the bin and then noticed the greasy sensation on my tongue. I could taste the oil the crisps had been cooked in and my imagination took over, picturing a vat of the stuff bubbling away, and again I felt quite sick. I never would have thought that, in such a short space of time, food that I craved, and food that had been my habit, would have the ability to repulse me in this way.

Okay, then I decided if I was going to indulge on this free day – what was the one thing I had missed more than any other? The answer came immediately: toast! I had over the last couple of months, collected piping hot fish and chips slathered in salt and vinegar for my family's supper that had sat on the front seat of my car as I drove home without so much as a nose twitch of temptation. I had watched the family devour pizza straight from the greasy-lidded boxes on movie nights – nope, no interest. Even the tins of Quality Street passed around at Christmas time had done nothing to tempt me away from my desire for health and well-being.

But there had been a handful of cold, wintry mornings and I suspect there always will be, when standing at the stove stirring my porridge, while my husband pulled thickly sliced toast from the toaster and covered it in butter and marmalade, I could have easily flung my oats into the sink and grabbed the buttery, carby goodness from his paws quicker than he could fend me off, and he's pretty quick!

And so, I made myself two slices of toast and buttered them before drizzling them with Marmite. I wish I could say it was revolting. I wish I could tell you I took a bite and grimaced at how I had misremembered the taste, the texture, the feeling . . . but alas! I cannot. Those two slices of toast were absolutely wonderful. Delicious and satisfying and moreish and I could have quite happily gone for another slice and another . . . but I didn't.

It taught me that I might always have a weakness for foods that aren't necessarily the best for me and that my overeating is always only ever one lapse away. But I didn't revert to type and demolish the loaf. Instead, I went to bed feeling more than a little smug and with a very full tum and knew that the next day I could start afresh and go back to the kind of foods that were the key to my dietary success and ultimately my body and health goals. And crucially I knew that if I wanted to have a couple of thickly sliced pieces of toast with Marmite I could! It didn't mean I had to have seven slices, as was my previous MO. It felt like a win.

The next day, I woke and felt . . . awful. Absolutely awful, and I remembered that this was how I had felt every single morning. My face was a little bloated, my mouth dry and my stomach a distended ball. I went to the bathroom and well, I'm not going to detail that, but trust me when I say I had forgotten the hell of not being able to leave the bathroom while my body dealt with diarrhoea and gas – a potent combination. And I was glad everyone was away, as the only people who would have suffered more than me were those who had to use the bathroom next. I walked slowly down the stairs and my joints felt stiff. I was exhausted, even though I had only just woken up, as if I had ingested something toxic or more accurately toxic for me. It felt like a hangover with headache, fuddled thoughts and all. I looked at the crusty loaf on the breadboard and knew that I did not want it. Did not want to put it in my system. It made me realise how far I had come and that this was how I used to live. Getting it right every day for the rest of my life might not be possible, but I was certain that the train of overindulgence and excess had left the station.

But it wasn't all about food.

The truth is that letting go is where I have found most happiness and possibly the most benefit in ordering my thoughts. Letting go of negativity, letting go of competition, letting go of fruitless, unreachable goals and self-imposed deadlines that only lead to disappointment, letting go of internal stress, letting go of guilt and regret of things over which I had no control. By letting go of these things I show myself kindness, which greatly helps me mentally. I've learned not to berate myself and carry around guilt and shame over things that WERE NOT MY FAULT.

I got in a van with a man who had planned to abuse me. He was an adult. I was a child. IT WAS NOT MY FAULT.

I could not hold on to all those babies, no matter how much I wanted to. It was a medical thing, a physical thing, and nothing I could have done would have changed the outcome. IT WAS NOT MY FAULT.

My mum stepped onto that crossing and even had I been with her, there is no guarantee I could have prevented it. IT WAS NOT MY FAULT.

My grandad got cancer and the doctor misdiagnosed him and I couldn't have prevented it. IT WAS NOT MY FAULT.

Joshy suffers with depression, an illness. He is ill. He believed for years that the world would be better off without him in it because he was ill. IT IS NOT MY FAULT.

And if none of these things are my fault then I can stop punishing myself by distorting my body and my face with the overconsumption of food. I can stop swallowing bread in the hope that it might prevent the sharp edges of guilt digging into my gut.

For me it's about looking at the world in a slightly different way. About reframing the things that held me back. About redefining those regrets and using them to empower my future that will help me grow! If I listen very carefully, I can hear my nan's voice in my ear:

'Bloody get on with it, girl, enough talking, more doing.'

And she's right.

◆ ◆ ◆

Part of owning my weight issue was not providing an environment that either enabled or normalised my weight gain. Throwing away the largest-size clothes was key to this. It was a big deal for me, as I always had a varied-size wardrobe for the days when I would be fatter, and this was really like giving myself permission to slip back into obesity. I mean, why not? I had the frocks. Throwing them away was a mental and physical declaration that I had decided never again. And it felt good!

With my image of myself so out of whack and unable to picture the amount of weight I needed to lose or how I might look post weight loss, I decided to find a physical representation of the excess weight that was hanging off my bones and sitting uncomfortably around my heart and other organs. According to every chart I put my statistics in, the result came out that I needed to lose almost half my body weight, approximately 10 stone or 140 lb.

It felt like such a huge amount that I wanted to doubt the suggestion, but it was correct. But to be honest, I was not holding that figure in my mind, as I had done before, allowing it to overwhelm me when the going got tough or, worse, feeling like it was such a huge amount it was almost too hard to begin. Instead, I decided again to own it but file it, and as long as day on day, week on week, month on month I was not giving in to the desire to gorge, that would be good enough and, by default, I figured the weight would start to come off. Trusting the process.

Still keen to find something that represented the amount I needed to lose, I thought about finding one of my friends or family that weighed roughly this and try to lift them or at least sit next to them. A scary yet vivid visual representation.

It was actually a trip to the vet that provided the perfect opportunity. No, I didn't lift the veterinary surgeon who treats our dogs – thought that might be a little weird – but I *was* staggered to find out that my lovely, healthy hounds weighed in at a combined 60 lb. This is obviously much less than I had to lose, but here's the thing. I couldn't lift them both at the same time. I had carried them all over the farm when they were tiny pups, loving the feel of their little furry bodies against my skin and their trusting submission in my arms, but as they had reached maturity and grown to their full size, I could no longer hold them both in my arms. They were too bulky, too heavy. And yet I had more than double that figure hanging off my bones. I looked at the dogs sleeping in their bed, sprawled, heavy and snoring, beautiful nonetheless, and I tried to imagine what having nearly five of them on me was doing to my heart, my joints, my frame.

Now, the old me would have crumpled at this terrible fact, rushing no doubt into the arms of cheese on toast, but not the new me. The new me made a decision to accept the fact, but not fret over how things were or even berate myself for how I had got there. I reminded myself of how much better I now felt, how much more confident and how my food intake was under control. Yes, I had a way to go, but I was on track. I put on some Abba, loudly, and I danced around the kitchen!

If letting go has been central to getting my health on track, then so has acceptance. I look in the mirror and I see saggy jowls, eye bags and so many wrinkles that close up my forehead and the side of my eyes look like an elephant's scrotum. I have excessive fat, tummy rolls, bingo wings, cellulite, podgy knees, stretch marks, droopy boobs, sun damage and a lattice of scars, which you, dear friend, know all about.

This is my body. My imperfect, ageing body. And it will remain imperfect for as long as I am blessed to walk the earth in it. I will continue to lose pounds for my health and well-being, but I'm not aiming for a number on the scales, I'm simply letting my body settle. My weight loss aids movement and bolsters my self-confidence, but I also remember that this body has served me well for over fifty years. It has battled disease, hosted numerous ideas both good and bad, taken me on a journey that has created a lifetime of memories, it has walked me around the planet, heck, it even grew me a child! Quite remarkable. I feel that every experience I have had, both good and bad, is etched on my face and imprinted on my skin. Smile lines earned by years of laughter, frown lines through years of thinking. I love the life I have led, and I love the life that lies ahead.

My view is unchanged that ageing is an absolute privilege and I have decided to grow old *gratefully*, happy to be that decaying lemon. I've stopped dyeing my hair, returning to mousy brown with the odd highlight that I thought for years made me look dull, and indeed it does! But who cares? Not me. I did some sums and worked out that since I started bleaching my hair, I've spent approximately 432 hours or 18 whole days sitting in a chair having the colour stripped from my locks and have spent close to £15,000. Yep, it's scary, isn't it? All that money and all those hours.

I struggle with the question why, oh, why are we so obsessed with keeping the years at bay? And don't you find it laughable that just like King Canute in his valiant but futile attempt at turning back the tide, it is a wish that can't be granted no matter how much money we throw at the 'problem'? And is it any wonder when it can sometimes feel that the world ceases to see you past the age of thirty and every other advert or spam email is telling you how to combat wrinkles? Dye those greys? Restore your failing eyesight or selling you fragranced pads to help absorb any leakages? All of which are the often-inevitable effects of growing old? It interests me that these are all lauded as 'cures' to the 'problems' of ageing, but why is ageing such a *problem*? Why can't we celebrate the success of it?

Ageing skin is not a problem to be solved, far from it; instead, I embrace it and recognise it as a sign of the gift of growing older. And how shallow is it that in the face of climatic catastrophe, war, famine, poverty, corruption and global disease we can be so preoccupied about our ageing faces? Easy to say, I know. But surely the biggest mistake women (and men!) make when it comes to wrinkles is thinking that they matter. I am now picturing wonderful women who never got the luxury of ageing; the wives, sisters, friends, aunts, cousins, lovers and mothers of us all who were robbed of life without so much as a wrinkle in sight . . . and so let's stop preying on women's insecurities and celebrate getting older!

This acceptance is the greatest thing I have learned. It is where I have found peace, accepting flaws in myself and others, accepting that the only life I have is the second in which I live it and most importantly, shit happens!

Not that I am a model of Zen living. There is no shining aura of positive energy around me. I'm not a yoga-addled, smiling oasis of calm. In fact, quite the opposite. I'm more of a running around like the proverbial headless feathered one, firing instructions into the ears of those I live with, worrying about deadlines, wondering what's in the larder that I can disguise as supper and still fretting over things as varied as the size of the cobwebs that lace my ceilings to world peace. However, if I'm this bad with acceptance and order as my byword, can you imagine what I was like before?

So, what have I actually accepted? Ageing, certainly, the actions of others over which I have no influence. All things I can't fix. All I have *not* achieved. Things that happened to me in the past, which I now cannot change and have harboured as regrets. How I look, how I think, how I feel – THIS IS ME!

With owning my size and my face, I have accepted that I will never have the legs of a supermodel, the brain of an Oxford don or the sharp wit of a court jester. I will never cook like these slick hob jockeys on TV who with no more than a squeeze of lime and a crack of black pepper can create glorious dishes that make your mouth water! I will never be lauded for my fashion sense, my domestic goddessery or my driving skills, which I practise while swearing. I doubt I'm a fantastic shag (apparently reminding your partner of gardening jobs or the fact that bin day is looming is a no no – who knew?) and even my pets sometimes look at me as if to say, 'Make more effort, love, call that a good ball throw?'

But it's okay. It is all okay because I have learned to accept what I can't do, as much as I accept there are things that I can. Write great stories. Make tea when it is most needed. Listen. Knowing when to ask for help and when to give it. Love like a giant – all these things I learned from the bold, brave, brassic and brilliant women who raised and influenced me.

Harder but just as necessary in my newfound regimen is quieting that voice of self-sabotage. Learning to do this has helped me in so many aspects of my life. That split second of fear and hesitation that used to hold me back, that voice of self-doubt that could knock me off course, I have silenced it – or more accurately, I have quieted it – and I go forward! Remaining calm, controlling any rising panic, answering the voice back and saying out loud, I'm not going to listen! I reject your idea and I want THIS! Just like making better food choices, I choose not to listen to the negative thoughts that swirl around in my head. I imagine a big fat eraser and I rub them out. In their place, I write new thoughts, good ones! Positive ones! And I only see and hear these instead.

When people in the world of publishing, people who knew about the business, rejected my first novel, I saw Mrs Blight's laughing face and heard that little tut/huff of dismissal. No more than a small nasal throaty insignificant sound that was actually anything but. It was in fact a scythe to my ambition and the pulling up of the small tendrils of confidence that had started to take root in my young mind. Quite wicked, really. I can't think it was her intention. My adult brain has analysed the exercise, the moment, the mood, the teacher's demeanour and I can only now assume that she was laughing in the way one might at something so unattainable that it *was* almost funny. And maybe it was unattainable for her. If this was the case, all she had to do was add a sentence after that little noise:

'Well, Amanda, there are plenty of people who want to write books, but be warned, it's very tough to make it happen. Good luck though!'

Or even better:

'Well, Amanda, I can't wait to read your book, but I would suggest you have a plan B!'

What would have been the harm? She could have said something, anything, words of positivity and encouragement that I could mentally lasso in times of self-doubt, words that would not snap the saplings of self-confidence as they bloomed. Words that might help a little girl, who was still very much figuring out who she was and where she was heading, form an identity and picture a future where anything was possible. But now that I have this thought and these words in my head I can say, 'Thank you, Mrs Blight!' because her words have inadvertently spurred me on in ways she could not have imagined – turns out *that* was my plan B, to use her dismissal as fuel and make it happen anyway!

I surround myself with those who champion my journey and who are positive. Anyone whose sentence starts with a big sigh and the word 'but' has lost me before they reach 'the thing is . . .' as I don't want to hear all the reasons why I might fail, as if I don't know them already. Fear of fat and fear of failure are no longer my jailors. I follow my instinct, knowing you never know anyone's story by looking at them, and I can write the next chapter of my life in any way I choose and the one after that and the one after that.

Mindset is fundamental to my success. It has to be on my terms, my agenda and my timescale, otherwise, I know I'm setting myself up for failure. I've learned not to look at my body several times a day with disgust, nor do I spend time in self-reproach. If I look at my body, I make a conscious effort to think something positive, to notice a good thing. 'My skin is soft today.' Or 'this body has just walked for six miles – amazing!' Changing that internal dialogue so I am used to hearing words of encouragement and support in my mind instead of the very opposite. It didn't work at first. I felt like I was joking or lying to myself, I even found it embarrassing, but after doing this every day, I believe it.

I told you earlier in the book how I used to put stars by words in the dictionary if I had to look them up so I would learn them properly – I opened that very precious dictionary randomly and was surprised by how few words were starred, but these were two that stared back at me from the page that fell open, starred by my nine-year-old self:

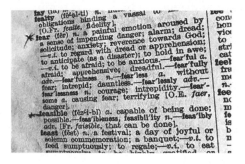

It made me catch my breath. If ever there were two words that summed up my battles they were these two. *Fear: a painful emotion aroused by a sense of impending danger: alarm: dread: anxiety.* And *Feasible: capable of being done: possible.*

It's time I conquered my fears and began to believe that the amazing life that sat on the other side of that wall I'd built was feasible! It's feasible for me, for you, for women like us. Every single one of us at times feels self-conscious, self-doubting, inadequate and awkward for a million different reasons. I am not alone, and *you* are not alone with these sometimes less than helpful or destructive thoughts. And those destructive thoughts were detrimental to me, held me back from achieving success when it came to getting my weight under control. And the more my mental state suffered the more my physical journey stalled. To separate the conjoined twins of mental and physical health is in my mind like going into a restaurant and saying, 'I'll take the omelette, but hold the eggs!' The best advice I give myself every day is this: 'You *can* do it. You *are* doing it. Keep going! I'm proud of you! Remember to breathe . . .' It's amazing how much clearer everything feels when I take a deep, deep breath.

I also focus on what I've achieved in other areas of my life: working hard at my career, being the best mum I can to our boys, trying to make a difference in both the community I live and the writing community I try to support, cooking supper, making my pups happy, letting go of guilt about incidents we have already discussed that made me feel so rotten that I turned to food for comfort. I celebrate my achievements and the great aspects of my life rather than the opposite. It's almost as if I have given myself permission to feel happy and confident about my achievements. It feeds my confidence and happiness, helping me to stay on course. The big shift in my mindset has definitely led to a shift in pounds and inches.

Banning 'weight-loss diets' and the word 'dieting' is something that's freed me mentally. Diets did not work for me. Evidently! In the past when I've been slimmer, I feared gaining the weight I had lost and looked at *all* food as an almost toxic substance. Nervous to eat anything, I would begrudge putting anything into my system, anything at all, scared that it might trigger overeating and that all the hard work of healthy eating and denial could be undone. To give up on a diet, to fail, *again*, meant having to see the tight smile and hear the small sigh of those who have seen you smaller or who at least believed you to be dieting, succeeding, doing what you *said* you were going to do! For them to see you getting bigger, having fallen off the wagon again and to give you that look, was akin to a teacher/parent sitting you down and giving the 'Oh, Mandy, this is such a shame. You've let yourself down . . . You've let your family down . . .' speech. It felt awful. Humiliating.

That feeling, like I had betrayed those who had faith in me to get the job done, meant I of course turned to the one thing I knew was going to bring me comfort: food. Yep, as ever, my answer to being overweight, my solution to feeling sad and uncomfortable in my own skin, was to eat more and gain more weight. I didn't say it was logical. But like the gambler who, about to lose the shirt off his back, puts his last fiver down to try to win back what he has lost, it is very, very hard to ignore the call of addiction that wraps all thoughts and prods you in the ribs. I hated being beholden to food. I hated my weakness. And equally I hated the judgement of others.

The answer for me is to DIET NO MORE! The very thought of restricting myself to one food group or starving myself or all the other weird and wonderful methods that I have employed to give me a short-term fix are consigned to history.

My failure, as you know, wasn't starting diets or being willing to try them, it was sticking to them. And then it occurred to me – *don't* start them, *don't* put yourself under that pressure. Diets are banished! I am not on a diet – the very thought of being on a diet for me had such negative implications of denial and bland, unappealing, counted, measured and restricted food that it felt like a punishment – I am not on a diet, but I have changed much of the food I eat and changed my lifestyle and I believe it is this radical overhaul that has made success possible. Like a smoker giving up smoking, but who keeps one or two ciggies in a drawer just in case – like they can't fully commit or let go and once they've smoked the 'just in case' stash – they buy more and are back to square one – that was always my pattern of dieting. I would give it a timeframe – a week, a month, six months and sometimes I would stick to it, but each and every day of denial that passed was spent with one eye on the date in the calendar when I could get back to 'normal', and for me normal was eating excessively.

I no longer fear the obesity topic . . . in conversations, in books, in podcasts, whatever . . . We need to remove the embarrassment and shame and start having the conversation. I think once you realise that everybody is the same, has the same hopes, dreams, fears, aspirations, wants and needs, then you can really start to break down barriers. People are just people, no matter how they are wrapped. And we really do need to be KIND. So, let's:

Keep

It

Nice

Darling

You can't change the whole world, only your bit of it, and that's a very good place to start. If someone says mean things to me about my weight or appearance, I now think it's like the verbal froth sitting on top of a pint of unhappiness or dissatisfaction and I feel sad for them: who wants to drink that? Everyone is sitting cloistered behind computer screens judging themselves against the perfect. If you stepped away from the screen and met everyone face to face, you'd see that everyone is perfectly imperfect and that's just fine! But the language around weight, weight loss and obesity needs to be addressed. We need to bring it to the fore and be open about our experiences. Only by ridding ourselves of the fear around the topic can we hope to address it and better understand it.

My weight and self-esteem – in fact, it is impossible for me to separate the two – have been the biggest factors influencing my happiness and unhappiness for as long as I can remember and have greatly influenced what I thought was possible for a woman like me. Not that my life is over just yet, and trust me when I say I have a hell of a lot of living left to do. But when seeking advice on how to 'fix' my weight, I never felt able to relate to people without weight problems who announce they have always been 'slim' giving *me* advice on how to be slim. I *knew* they knew how to do it – the evidence was right in front of my eyes! I can only liken it to someone on the outside of a complex maze, while I was stuck in the middle, shouting over the hedge at how great the view is and willing me on with words of motivation like 'you got this!' and 'just find the exit!' and 'wonderful things await!' What I actually wanted was to read something written by someone who knows what it's like to live inside a morbidly obese body and has found the way out of it, leaving markers for others to follow and giving good advice. I hope this in some small part might be it.

'Trusting The Process' is the umbrella under which my new regimen sits. Success has come because I stood at the bottom of a mountain with ropes of self-belief holding me fast, meaning I could not fall, and I told myself that I had all the time in the world. All I had to do was take one step every day or whenever I felt able, just one step, and when I was comfortable, I would take another and, eventually, almost quicker than I dared hope, I would be halfway up the mountain, able to look back at the route I had taken, slowly, surely and steadily, but climbing at my own pace and setting my own agenda. And I look forward to reaching the summit where I'm sure the view from the top will be bloody wonderful!

So, what about my weight? Well, I am not skinny, not even slender, nor lithe and I don't think anyone will ever refer to me as worryingly thin . . . but I have at this point lost a little over 5 stone or 70 lb. Yaaay for me! And it's made a difference to how I feel about myself. I'm still fat, but not drastically so.

For me it was never about striving for skinny, but more about how uncomfortable I was in the body I was in. Throughout my life, whether I've been obese or slim, young or old, teen goddess or knackered post-menopausal mumma, I've only once or twice felt comfortable in my skin. It has taken until I hit my mid-fifties to feel any semblance of confidence – yes, now! When physically I have more saggy bits, stretched bits, bits that don't work, bits that have failed and even dropped off . . . Who knew?

It has taken me years to learn this. I have one body, a vessel in which I present all that really matters about me, my heart, my mind, my thoughts and my behaviours, to the world. Just this one body and we have done some incredible things together. I have noticed that the more love I show it, the more that love is reflected in my skin that is glowy and clear. My eyes, which sparkle. My breath, which is fresh. My teeth, which no longer hurt. My shiny hair. My stronger nails. I no longer suffer with constipation or diarrhoea. My irritability has gone. I have more patience and feel calmer. My joints don't ache as much. My sleep is regulated: I no longer nap during the day and go through the night with ease, waking with a spring in my step. And it all feels brilliant! And to think I arrived at a crossroads where my weight and health were in danger of ending my life.

How ridiculous is it that I'd finally got that swimming pool but was too self-conscious and uncomfortable about my size to get in the bloody thing! What the hell is that all about? There was a huge gulf between being a little overweight, carrying some extra pounds, which I probably always will, and the point I reached where I couldn't put on my own socks, my ankle snapped, I got severe chest pains, couldn't climb the stairs without gasping for breath and would cry for twenty-four hours straight, declaring I couldn't leave the house any more because I didn't want to walk everywhere dressed like a Demis Roussos tribute act.

I've learned, physically and metaphorically, to DIVE INTO THAT BLOODY SWIMMING POOL! A reminder that life is for living and how it's vital we do just that. Keeping my weight and the way I look in perspective, I now know it shouldn't be the thing that defines me or the thing that defines you. Don't let your size, large, small or otherwise, hold you back from living the life you want to live. Be brave, own it, feel confident, go out and let your voice be heard and let your beauty shine!

Embrace your health – reward your healthy body with love!

I lived cloaked in shame and guilt over my size, felt anxious about my weight being raised at nearly every encounter – I mean, why would it be raised by the man at the bus stop, the lady in the shop or by someone interviewing me about a book? But such was my level of heightened awareness. On a low day, I would walk away and exhale as if I'd been holding my breath, having expected someone to say, 'That'll be four pounds fifty, please, and by the way, you have a very big bottom!'

My obesity felt like a dark, dirty topic that I was fearful of broaching. Such fear! It needs to stop. It needs not to be a taboo topic and therefore one we can address. If we are better able to express and support the emotional and psychological reasons behind why someone like me overate, that can only be a good thing, right? When the thing that needs addressing is glaringly obvious, a critical issue for some, but it cannot be mentioned – how is that supposed to make them feel? I shall tell you. It made me feel useless, less than . . . Let's be clear, my medic friend is right; being overweight and becoming overweight are complex issues, far more complex than the act of simply pushing biscuits into your gob, but to acknowledge it surely has to be a good step towards addressing the reasons *why* rather than burying our heads in the sand and talking about it in whispers or behind cupped palms, hoping it might all go away. I want to make conversations around obesity easier to have. At the very least, I hope it might actually help with the feelings of low self-worth that are often associated with it. And encourage those sharp-fingered, slack-jawed keyboard warriors who can't wait to spew judgement to be a little nicer. I can but hope.

Many of the answers of how to let go of obsessions about my body and face came to me from the very source where I had learned many good life lessons: at the knee of my mum, nans, great-nan, aunts and great-aunts. Yes, they indulged in great Sunday feasts but were spare women who worked off that food with movement and physical activity. They concentrated on what really mattered: each other's company, making life the best it could be for those they loved and not letting vanity have a place at the table. Now when I peel off and dive into my pool, I think of those women, I hear their laughter and I sometimes see their faces under the water, cheering me on.

Anne, Doreen, Auntie Elsie, Auntie Kit, Nanny Ivy, Nanny Simpson, Josie.

My life, like all of our lives, has been something of a roller coaster. I've experienced the lowest lows and the highest highs, but the majority of the time my life bumbles along a flat track with the odd bump, and I cling on, waiting to see what's around the bend and tensing for the next dip or rise, hoping I can sit there long enough without needing the loo.

I wake up early to the sound of cow farts, pig grunts and chicken clucks – it is actually bliss. I can't function without caffeine, and before my eyes have properly focused and my hair is still in knots, I put on my coffee machine and smile at the prospect of getting that rich dark nectar into my system. If I could have it intravenously, I would.

I then go for a wander, wellies on over my PJs, mug in hand. I chat to the various cats that congregate on the top of walls and under shrubs and make my way up to the paddock where I sit on a creaky bench and look out over the Severn estuary. I like to sit quietly and have a think, count my blessings, throw out thanks into the universe and see what comes back . . . I then swap wellies for thick socks and go to the snug where on a chilly day I light a fire before curling into a comfy sofa with my laptop primed. These are my very best days. I then get lost, entirely lost to the novel I am writing, and can tip tap for hours and hours, pausing only to nip to the loo, feed the washing machine or to forage for more coffee.

I always stop for supper, and we eat something shoved in the Aga hours earlier, always in the kitchen and as a family. I contribute very little to the conversation, as I know nothing about bloody rugby or cricket and spend most of my time in the snug, writing! Post supper I go straight back to work.

I always have a long, hot bath before bedtime and think there is nothing nicer than climbing into clean sheets, in my cotton nightdress with a long night of sleep ahead. I've just read this back and realise that I am the most boring person on the planet! I am, however, happy and that has to be the goal, right?

Maybe I should take up an exciting or exotic hobby like belly dancing, snake charming or the luge . . . I'll keep you posted. But the point is, I nearly missed out on this lovely, lovely life because I was too entrenched in my food addiction and self-loathing to step outside and appreciate all I had.

Is my life perfect now I have my weight and my eating more under control? Of course not! Far from it. But that's just part of being human. And I continue to trust the process. There are still days when it can feel like I'm living at the end of a bowling lane, standing upright and enjoying the view, when without warning, a bloody great big bowling ball comes hurtling towards me and knocks me onto my arse. But now? Instead of grabbing food and retreating under the covers, I stand up, brush myself down and go outside to look up at the sky, and if I listen very carefully, I can hear my Aunty Kit saying, 'Bloody 'andsome!' and I smile.

My wrinkles increase year on year. My hair is getting greyer and duller. I'm not skinny, never will be. I'm big, but not morbidly obese. Not perfect, but I'm fine with that too, oh, and we're getting the bedroom redecorated. I'm thinking of going for a sturdy chandelier, one that's well anchored to the ceiling . . .

And finally, dear reader . . .

'Women Like Us' #WLU is not just about this book, it's about reclaiming a natural, gentle, slower way of living, of understanding that the face you have is the face that you were born with and the face that you will die with and you should not feel under any pressure to change it/alter it/smooth it/plump it – unless of course you want to. It's all about finding *your* happy. I stress I am not saying to do those things is wrong and I judge no woman on executing the habits/rituals/tasks that bring her joy and confidence, but I *am* saying there is another way! The body we inhabit is a sacred and remarkable thing, in every shape and size. Women who give up their place in the race and hang back where life is a little less pressured, a little greyer, a little plumper, a little more wrinkled – where we are allowed to age – give confidence to those who are unsure of the way ahead.

What are little boys made of?
Snips and snails
And puppy-dogs' tails
That's what little boys are made of
What are little girls made of?

380

Sugar and spice
And all things nice
That's what little girls are made of.

Well, not this little girl. I mean, sugar and spice are great in moderation but give me a break . . .

◆ ◆ ◆

So, we reach the end of this book and again I want to ask the question, what kind of woman am I? Well, you know those women who saunter into a room, immaculately coiffed and primped from head to toe? Those women who seem to have it all together? Raven-haired beauties who can pull off red lipstick? The women who teeter pertly on killer heels and in skinny jeans? The women who flick their hair with a sexy smile, as they stride in confidently to talk to whoever looks to be of most interest, grabbing a glass of bubbles from a passing tray as they go?

Well, if you look behind her, you'll see me.

I'm the woman wearing the same thing she wore to the last event: a floaty top and jeans because she can't be bothered to buy clothes. A woman who is clutching her oversized handbag not only as a prop, but so that her reading book, Fox's Glacier Mints and box of panty liners don't roll out in public. I am quite likely to have a false eyelash stuck to my cheek that has slid off, as I am not used to putting on make-up. The woman who clings to the wall, kind of wanting to join in, smiling a lot, hoping someone talks to her, but not someone too clever so she feels stupid. The woman who asks if she can have Diet Coke instead of champagne, as she prefers the taste, and does it all with one eye on the clock so she can work out how quickly she can go home, ping off that damned bra, shove on her PJs and climb into bed to watch *MasterChef* on catch up.

Yep, that's me.

I am a wife, mum, daughter, sister, auntie, cousin, niece and friend.

I'm a writer.

I'm a Londoner, who now lives on a farm in the middle of bloody nowhere and who owns a wax jacket, proper wellies and two stinky dogs.

I only clean the house when I'm expecting visitors.

I swear in the car. A lot.

I'm a bit boring.

Most often I am to be found with my head in a book or staring into a cupboard wondering what I can rustle up for supper.

I have the sense of humour of a twelve-year-old (apparently) and a good day now is one where I have laughed until tears have rolled or I've needed to pee. My body, it seems, insists on leaking from one end or the other if something is *that* funny.

I make award-worthy Yorkshire puddings. From scratch.

I can't tell the time on a 24-hour clock.

I don't particularly like ice cream (I know!).

I love driving on the motorway (while swearing).

I grow epic spider plants.

I will love Duran Duran until the day I die.

I wake up at a little before 6 a.m. every single day.

And my favourite cheese is any variety with a hole in it.

My blood type is Americano with an extra shot.

Oh, and I've sold millions of books all over the world.

And I like being me!

In fact, I like everything about me, although sadly for most of my life this hasn't always been the case. I have always felt a little uncomfortable in my skin, a little less than . . . but not any more. I took a wrecking ball to the wall I had constructed in my mind, shattering it to let the light in. This is my time. A new age. And I like what I see in the mirror and on some days, I even bloody love it!

Me. Wrinkles and all.

ABOUT THE AUTHOR

Photo © 2012 Paul Smith
www.paulsmithphotography.info

Amanda Prowse is an internationally bestselling author of twenty-eight novels published in dozens of languages. Her chart-topping titles *What Have I Done?*, *Perfect Daughter*, *My Husband's Wife*, *The Coordinates of Loss*, *The Girl in the Corner* and *The Things I Know* have sold millions of copies around the world.

Other novels by Amanda Prowse include *A Mother's Story*, which won the coveted Sainsbury's eBook of the Year Award. *Perfect Daughter* was selected as a World Book Night title in 2016 and *The Boy Between* a World Book Night title in 2022. She has been described by the *Daily Mail* as 'the queen of family drama'.

Amanda is the most prolific writer of bestselling contemporary fiction in the UK today. Her titles consistently score the highest online review approval ratings across several genres.

A popular TV and radio personality, Amanda is well known for her insightful observations and infectious humour.

Amanda's ambition is to create stories that keep people from turning off the bedside lamp at night, that ensure you walk every step with her great characters, and tales that fill your head so you can't possibly read another book until the memory fades . . .

You can follow her @mrsamandaprowse on all social media or sign up for her newsletter at www.amandaprowse.com. Or follow her on Substack: Tangerine by Amanda Prowse.